HISTORICAL
ATLAS
OF
ANCIENT
GREECE

HISTORICAL
ATLAS
OF
ANCIENT
GREECE

ANGUS KONSTAM

Checkmark Books™

An imprint of Facts On File, Inc.

HISTORICAL ATLAS OF ANCIENT GREECE

Checkmark Books
An imprint of Facts On File, Inc.
132 West 31st Street
New York, NY 10001

For Library of Congress Cataloging-in-Publication data, please contact
Checkmark Books. Control Number 12803030.
   ISBN 0-8160-5220-4

Checkmark Books are available at special discounts when purchased in bulk quantities
for businesses, associations, institutions or sales promotions. Please call our Special
Sales Department in New York at:
(212) 967-8800 or (800) 322-8755.

You can find Facts On File on the World Wide Web at:
http://www.factsonfile.com

For Thalamus Publishing
Project editor: Warren Lapworth
Maps and design: Roger Kean
Illustrations: Oliver Frey
Four-color separation: Proskanz, Ludlow, England

Printed and bound in Italy

10 9 8 7 6 5 4 3 2 1
This book is printed on acid-free paper

PICTURE CREDITS

Paul Almasy/CORBIS: 28–29; Archivo Iconografico S.A./CORBIS: 27, 48, 55, 124, 131, 141. 145, 173, 178; Yann Arthus-Bertrand/CORBIS: 104–5, 114, 116–7, 121, 148, 161, 186–7; Dave Bartruff/CORBIS: 120 (both); Bettman/CORBIS: 54 (right), 72, 109, 111, 150; Jonathan Blair/CORBIS: 100, 125 (top); Burstein Collection/CORBIS: 11, 58, 125 (bottom); Christie's Images/CORBIS: 22; Stephanie Colasanti/CORBIS: 79; CORBIS: 2–3, 12, 65, 91 (top); Gianni Dagli Orti/CORBIS: 13 (top), 22, 26, 38, 39 (top), 39 (bottom), 42, 54 (left), 70, 77, 91 (bottom), 118 (bottom), 139, 144 (top), 144 (bottom), 151, 156, 166, 169 (left); Araldo de Luca/CORBIS: 1, 41 (bottom), 46, 82, 118 (top), 171 (left), 180; Kevin Fleming/CORBIS: 29, 34; Franco Frey/Thalamus Publishing: 134, 164–5; Oliver Frey/Thalamus Publishing: 30, 40 (top), 40 (bottom), 41 (top), 50, 52 (left), 96, 135, 142–3, 146 (bottom), 149 (left), 154, 158, 184; Chris Hellier/CORBIS: 53 (top), 155; David Hosking/CORBIS: 85; Hulton-Deutsch Collection/CORBIS: 10; Mimmo Jodice/CORBIS: 25 (left), 49, 52 (right), 59, 61, 66–7, 119 (top), 168, 169 (right); Wolfgang Kaehler/CORBIS: 35, 60, 87, 89, 103, 112 (bottom); David Lees/CORBIS: 73, 97, 160; Charles & Josette Lenars/CORBIS: 23; Francis G. Mayer/CORBIS: 171 (right); Gail Mooney/CORBIS: 19; Michael Nicholson/CORBIS: 110, 127; Diego Lezama Orezzoli/CORBIS: 162; José F. Poblete/CORBIS: 37; Jose Fuste Raga/CORBIS: 170; Vittoriano Rastelli/CORBIS: 182; Roger Ressmeyer/CORBIS: 184–5; Reza/Webistan/CORBIS: 163; Kevin Schafer/CORBIS: 10–11, 16, 78; Thalamus Studios: 31 (top); 31 (bottom); 51, 71, 94, 98, 101, 119 (bottom), 140, 146 (top), 174, 175 (bottom); Gustavo Tomisch/CORBIS: 14–15; Gianni Vanni/CORBIS: 99; Ruggero Vanni/CORBIS: 25 (right), 43, 53 (bottom), 84, 86 (right), 112 (top), 113, 115, 123, 126, 147, 149 (right), 167 (right), 176; Sandro Vannini/CORBIS: 159, 179; Werner Forman Archive: 6 (National Museum, Athens), 47 (British Museum, London), 74, 88 (Museo ostia, Italy); Roger Wood/CORBIS: 13 (bottom), 15, 17 (top), 17 (bottom), 86 (left), 108, 133, 136, 157, 167 (left), 172, 175 (top), 185.

Page 1
The Ram-Bearer, statue fragment by the sculptor Moskophoros, dating from the Classical Age, sixth to fifth centuries BC.

Pages 2–3
The Peloponnese, Corinthian isthmus, Attica, central Greece and Macedon seen in a low-orbit satellite photograph. The fragmented and mountainous nature of Greece goes a long way to explain the development of the numerous ancient Greek city-states, each jealous of the other.

CONTENTS

The Glory of Greece

Left: Look at this bronze head of a Greek youth from the fifth century BC and you are looking at the face of ancient Greece. The far-seeing look in the eyes and the determined set of his features seem to sum up the strengths (and weaknesses—a touch of arrogance?) that make the times of ancient Greece such a fascinating period of history.

Spelling of names used in this book

Greek names can be a minefield, since the romanization of the spelling is more commonly recognized. This book attempts to use the older Greek form, unless to do so would render the name of place or person unrecognizable to modern eyes. For instance, as we do not know how the ancient Greeks called Sicily and southern Italy, you will find *Magna Graecia* (Latin) used, and *Mycenae* rather *Mykenai* because the former spelling is widely accepted; however, *Kleisthenes* and *Kimon* rather than *Cleisthenes* or *Cimon*.

Dates

All dates quoted are before the Christian era (BC) unless otherwise stated.

Visitors to Greece will find a place that is in many ways the same as it was in the time of Homer, a world he described as "many glittering seas and many shadowy islands." It can seem strange to us that this scattering of long peninsulas and sea outcrops could have formed a homogenous whole, let alone a culture of any distinction. Yet between the semi-legedary adventures of wandering Odysseus after the Trojan War—the time of the Bronze Age—and the Roman annexation in 146, Greece rose from prehistoric primitivism to become a civilization unsurpassed by subsequent human endeavor.

Certainly, today we owe much of modern civilization to the ancient Greeks. The Greek concepts of humanity, freedom of thought and expression, and self-government are cornerstones of modern society. Although it could be argued that these notions were developed before the Greeks adopted them, it was the ancient Greeks who embraced these ideals, cultivating them into the cohesive social doctrine that underpins society today. Greeks developed the concepts, vocabulary, and philosophy of modern democratic government, even-handed state administration, and political and fiscal accountability. Our world owes a debt to the Greeks for this immense cultural legacy.

During the Bronze Age, the first Greek societies emerged in the southern Aegean Sea. These early states created the framework for the cultural revolution that would transform Greece into the light of the ancient world. Although the Minoan island culture of Crete is all but forgotten, the Mycenaeans of southern Greece—the *Peloponnesos* (Peloponnese)—are from the heroic age, celebrated in the epics of Homer. This was the era of the Trojan War: Odysseus, Jason and his Argonauts, Achilles, and Hector. Today, knowledge of the Greek Bronze Age is a mix of verbal and written mythology and archaeological discovery.

At about 1100, these societies collapsed. For four centuries Greece entered a cultural dark age. In the early eighth century the Greeks re-emerged as a burgeoning society. A largely sea-faring nation, Greeks established colonies across the face of the known world. This was the period when Greek political structure centered around the *polis* or city-state, and for the next four centuries Greek history was set against a backdrop of rivalry and switched allegiances.

The period encompassing the fifth and fourth centuries has become known as the Classical Age, the era when Athens became a democratic political, cultural, and commercial center. Its major rival, Sparta, retained a monarchy. Organized as a martial state, the Spartans came to possess the finest army in Greece. The growth of the Persian Empire and its covetous invasions of the Greek mainland forced the Greeks to unite in defense of their common culture. The rest of Greece had need of the Spartans, but the true victor of the Persian wars was Athens. Having defeated the Persians on land and sea, Athens emerged as the pre-eminent Greek state.

Growing enmity between Athens and Sparta exploded into the self-destructive Peloponnesian Wars. Weakened, the Greek city-states fell under the political and military sway of Macedon, a country on the northern fringes of the Greek world. Macedon finally united the Greek city-states as Hellas before Alexander the Great led a Greek army across Asia, conquering everything in his path, from Egypt to Afghanistan and India. Following his death in 323, Alexander's empire divided into Hellenistic successor states, ensuring that the Greeks would continue to dominate the Middle East for centuries.

The conquest of the Hellenistic world by the Romans marked the end of Greek political independence, but not of Greek culture, since the "less civilized" Romans eagerly adopted much of the cultural spectrum they encountered. Through the massive romanization of the Mediterranean basin and Europe in subsequent centuries, the survival of Greek ideas was ensured. Thanks to this and the incredible legacy of written work, building, and artworks, we are able to view ancient Greece as a unique phenomenon. Here was a favorable combination of time, space, and human development that sowed the seeds of civilization on a hitherto barren world.

CHAPTER 1

A GREEK DAWN

Since the first traces of Greek civilization were discovered on Minoan Crete over a century ago, new archaeological discoveries have changed our view of this enigmatic culture. The initial discovery of the great Minoan palace of Knossos stunned the archaeological world, and each further find sheds a new and sometimes contradictory light on the Bronze Age people behind it. Recent archaeological breakthroughs have helped further our understanding of how prehistoric Greece was settled, and how the people interacted to produce the foundations of the Greek world.

Even today scholars are divided over several crucial aspects of this formative, early Bronze Age phase. There is no clear agreement on the language spoken in Minoan Crete or even Mycenaean Greece, despite the discovery of tablets bearing inscriptions in a proto-Greek language known to scholars as Linear B. Did the Greek tongue stem from the Bronze Age settlers who reached the Aegean from the north and east, or from the tongue spoken by the Minoans? We are unsure of exactly when Knossos fell, or when the cities of Mycenae and Troy were established to the north.

What can be agreed is the dramatic expansion of trade, social structure, and urban development during this period. Improved methods of agriculture and animal husbandry and the cultivation of olives and vines marked the establishment of a well-organized agrarian society, capable of supporting the creation of powerful cities as centers of political power and religious worship.

The great palace and city of Knossos was evidently the seat of power in Crete, and taken in its entirety it constituted the most impressive population center in the Aegean for over a thousand years. Even today the remains of its walls, palace rooms, temples, and courtyards are impressive. To the early Bronze Age visitor, they must have seemed incredible; as impressive as a Gothic cathedral to a medieval villager, or one of the great pyramids to an Egyptian.

The three Minoan palaces of Knossos, Phaistos, and Mallia indicate that the northern shores of Crete were divided into three social and political units, and while Knossos remained the pre-eminent Minoan center, the other palaces must have acted as the administrative focus for their region. While the political, economic, and religious information supplied by these structures is immense, the clues they provide about the Minoans themselves are more fascinating. Interior palace walls were sometimes covered with a hieroglyphic script, allowing scholars to discover something about religious observance, literacy, and social order. The people who inhabited them were cultured, lived in an ordered, law-abiding society, and were able to attain a high level of wealth and comfort.

The Minoans continue to fascinate us, partly because each discovery only seems to raise more questions. Although we can provide likely explanations for the final collapse of Minoan culture, in truth we might never fully understand the culture of these early Greek people and the reason why their civilization came to a close.

• Mycenae

This pair of boxing boys appear in a fresco from the walls of Akrotiri, the town on Thera preserved under volcanic ash.

P E L O P O N N E S O S

KYTHERA

major Minoan sites
▣ city with palace
• town/village

sites destroyed c.1450 BC
▣ city with palace
• town/village
→ Cretan colonists 2500–1450 BC

inset map
Minoan influence c.1300 BC

Phoenicia
— Minoan trade
— Phoenician trade

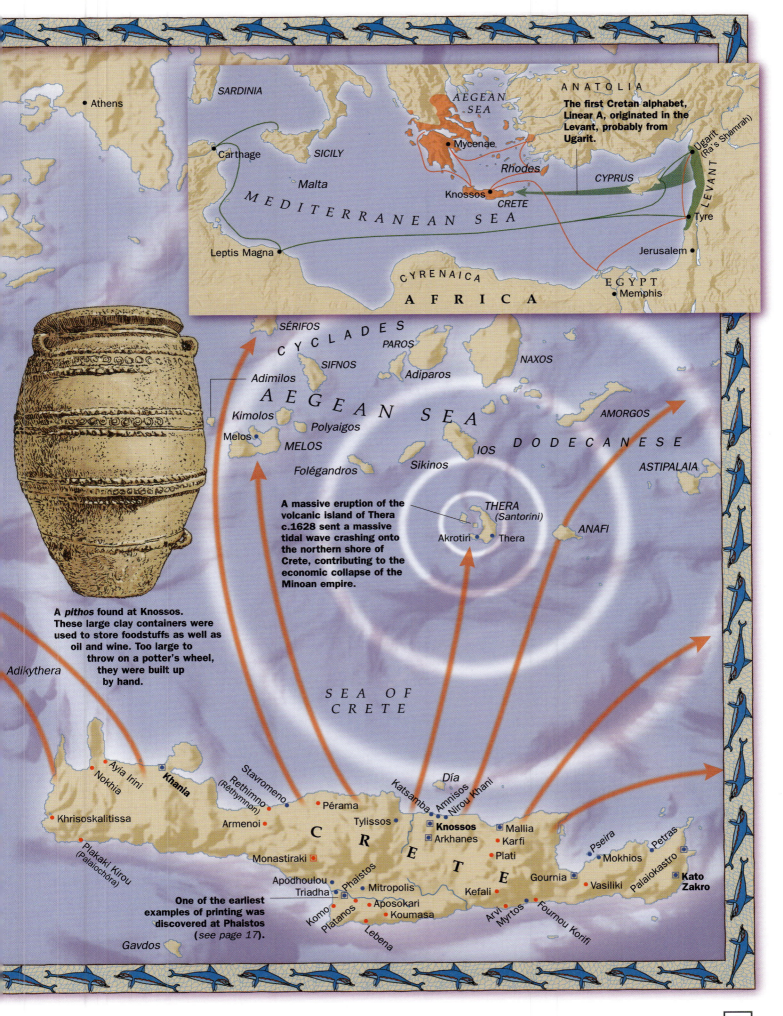

SARDINIA

• Athens

SICILY

ANATOLIA

AEGEAN SEA

• Mycenae

Carthage

Rhodes

Malta

The first Cretan alphabet, Linear A, originated in the Levant, probably from Ugarit.

Ugarit (Ra's Shamrah)

MEDITERRANEAN SEA

Knossos
CRETE

CYPRUS

LEVANT

Tyre

Leptis Magna •

• Jerusalem

CYRENAICA

EGYPT

AFRICA

• Memphis

SÉRIFOS

CYCLADES

PAROS

SIFNOS

NAXOS

Adimilos

Adiparos

AEGEAN SEA

AMORGOS

Kimolos

Polyaigos

Melos

MELOS

DODECANESE

Folégandros

Sikinos

IOS

ASTIPALAIA

A massive eruption of the volcanic island of Thera c.1628 sent a massive tidal wave crashing onto the northern shore of Crete, contributing to the economic collapse of the Minoan empire.

THERA (Santorini)

Akrotiri • • Thera

ANAFI

A *pithos* found at Knossos. These large clay containers were used to store foodstuffs as well as oil and wine. Too large to throw on a potter's wheel, they were built up by hand.

Adikythera

SEA OF CRETE

Ayia Irini

Nokhia

Khania

Stavromeno

Rethimno (Réthymnon)

Dia

Katsamba

Amnisos

Nirou Khani

Khrisoskalitissa

Armenoi

Pérama

Tylissos

C R E T E

Knossos

Mallia

Arkhanes

Karfi

Pseira

Petras

Plati

Mokhios

Monastiraki

Apodhoulou

Phaistos

Mitropolis

Kefali

Gournia

Vasiliki

Palaiokastro

Kato Zakro

Plakaki Kirou (Palaiochóra)

Triadha

Aposokari

Koumasa

Arvi

Fournou Korifi

One of the earliest examples of printing was discovered at Phaistos (*see page 17*).

Komo

Platanos

Lebena

Myrtos

Gavdos

THE FIRST GREEKS

Greece was a rocky, infertile land, and other areas of the Mediterranean were initially more conducive to human settlement. The Aegean Basin remained sparsely populated in the prehistoric era, while great civilizations emerged in the fertile regions of Mesopotamia and Egypt. The one exception was Crete, where a sophisticated indigenous culture emerged.

O n the southern edge of the Aegean Sea, Crete was first inhabited during the Neolithic or Later Stone Age, which began around 6000. It is likely that these islanders reached Crete from the mainland of Asia Minor (now modern Turkey), and although archaeological traces show that they were primitive, they were not simply hunters. They were farmers, cultivating the soil, raising livestock, and producing pottery to hold grain and other foodstuffs; all signs of a society on the road to civilization.

Cretan ceramics recovered from this prehistoric period are of a high quality, burnished, decorated, and skillfully produced. The geometric patterns used by these islanders would be seen on Greek pottery produced centuries later. The same people also built stone dwellings, but signs of cave habitation suggest outsiders threatened them, forcing refuge in secure, well-furnished strongholds. The discovery of crude female figurines suggests that they worshipped deities; the figurines probably represented a fertility goddess.

Above: Pictured in 1936, Sir Arthur Evans, the archaeologist who uncovered Knossos, examines a Cretan bull's head (*see also picture, page 15*).

While metal was not yet available, numerous stone tools such as axes, hammers, and knives have been found. It is highly significant that these include a number made from obsidian, a hard stone only available on the island of Melos, some distance to the north. This confirms that by the early second millennium, trading links had been established within at least part of the Aegean region.

A legendary culture

Trade certainly took place between Asia Minor, Egypt, and Mesopotamia, and by about 2500, trading links had been established between these and the Cretans. About the same time, Greece and the Aegean Basin were settled by migratory peoples, assimilating or destroying the Stone Age tribes that already inhabited the region. Although the origins of these newcomers is

c.6000	c.2600–1100	c.2000	c.2000	c.1700	c.1600	c.1500	c.1250
Crete inhabited in the Neolithic Age	The Minoan era	Sailing vessels trade in the Aegean Sea	Palaces built on Crete	Linear A script in use, evolves into Linear B	Birth of Mycenaean (Bronze Age Greek) culture	Peak of Minoan culture	Minoan culture wiped out by Sea Peoples and earlier Mycenaean raids

Left: The Blue Ladies, one of the fine wall paintings in the palace at Knossos. It should be noted that this fresco and others at Knossos are modern reconstructions taken from fragments (which can be seen in the photograph) and accumulated knowledge of Minoan art from many sites.

Below: This ivory figurine represents a Minoan goddess or a priestess. Other examples, similarly dressed, have been discovered; all wave snakes in their hands.

obscure, we know they reached Greece from Thrace and Asia Minor. It seems most likely that an invasion or other major demographic upheaval further to the east served as the impetus for the migratory invasion.

These new peoples brought bronze-working skills with them, ending the Neolithic period and ushering in the Bronze Age in the Aegean Basin. Fragmentary archaeological evidence suggests they established trading links with the Cretans, and adopted the agrarian culture of the older civilizations. Links between the two cultures were reflected in the mythological story of Theseus and the Minotaur, where the Cretans (under the rule of King Minos) forced their Aegean neighbors to pay human tribute to the Cretans, as fodder for the legendary Minotaur. Certainly Crete assumed a dominant position in this emergent Aegean society by the early Bronze Age, having adopted the metal-working technologies brought to the region.

The reason for this political and economic dominance was partly geographic. Crete lay within the trading sphere of both Phoenicia to the east and Egypt to the south. Trading links helped encourage the flow of ideas, technology, and cultural advances, which stimulated a vibrant, prosperous civilization.

This Bronze Age period of Cretan history lasted roughly 1,500 years, from 2600 to 1100—an era and culture given the appellation "Minoan" by British archaeologist Sir Arthur Evans (1851–1941), the man who first uncovered traces of this once-great civilization. The label was derived from Minos, the mythological Cretan king.

Evans devoted his life to the excavation of Minoan remains, particularly the sumptuous Minoan palace at Knossos, on the north coast of Crete. The discoveries he made established the Minoans as the first true Greeks, and his work helped explain their involvement in the establishment of a Greek culture, incorporating the Cretans, their satellite colonies in the Aegean, and the Bronze Age settlers who now called Greece their home. The Minoans were the forefathers of the Greeks, and their civilization helped to shape the greater culture that followed.

KNOSSOS

The most impressive remnant of Minoan civilization is the palace of Knossos. Along with smaller palace complexes at Phaistos, Mallia, and Zakro, it stands as an example of the vibrancy of Minoan culture and the importance and splendor of its court.

Below: A detail from the Corridor of the Processions frescos shows servants carrying drinking vessels. Knossos was not the only Minoan palace. Four others line the northern shores of Crete, emphasizing the fact that the Minoans dominated the Aegean basin for almost a thousand years.

Heinrich Schliemann, the man who discovered Troy and Mycenae, wanted to excavate a promising site in Crete. Wrangling with the local landowner prevented any work before Schliemann died, and instead the opportunity was presented to British archaeologist Sir Arthur Evans. Work began at this site in Knossos in 1895, and slowly Evans unearthed the remains of a huge palace.

Evans discovered evidence that the palace site of Knossos had been occupied during the third millennium, and buildings constructed before 2600 were elaborate and substantial. This Neolithic settlement was built over during the early Bronze Age, creating a multi-layered site,

which remained in continuous occupation until around 1100, the date associated with the start of the Greek "heroic age" of Troy, Mycenae, and Homer.

The palace occupied the flattened top of Kefala hill and covered an area in excess of 226,000 square feet. The immense size of the site precludes its complete archaeological excavation, therefore attention has focussed on the palace itself. It is likely that its size meant that, while it formed the seat of royal power, the palace was also a center for religious observance and housed administration facilities for the Minoan state. It was therefore a city within a city, like the Kremlin in Moscow, and was thus divided into numerous distinct areas.

In all, the complex contained around 1,400 rooms or chambers, plus countless courtyards and corridors. Although it was surrounded by a stout wall, this was pierced with so many doors that defense would have been virtually impossible. While archaeological debate has raged over the function of the buildings within the complex—with some labeling areas as mausoleums and temples with abandon—continued excavations have established the probable function of most palace areas.

A civilization's snapshots

Excavations at the center of the complex revealed traces of an earlier, smaller palace structure built around 2000. It was destroyed three centuries later, possibly by an earthquake, or even by the eruption of the island of Thera (Santorini, *see pages 18–19*). The later palace was arranged around an immense courtyard, with the principal entrance to the complex lying on its western edge. To the west lay an area for religious ceremonies, complete with altars and sacrificial pits. The outer western end of the palace housed numerous store rooms, while to the south a network of corridors and antechambers gave way to a wing of religious rooms and the central courtyard.

On the northern edge of this central area lay a *propylaion*, a pillared hall now referred to as the Customs Hall, surrounded by smaller store rooms and chambers, while to the east lay the

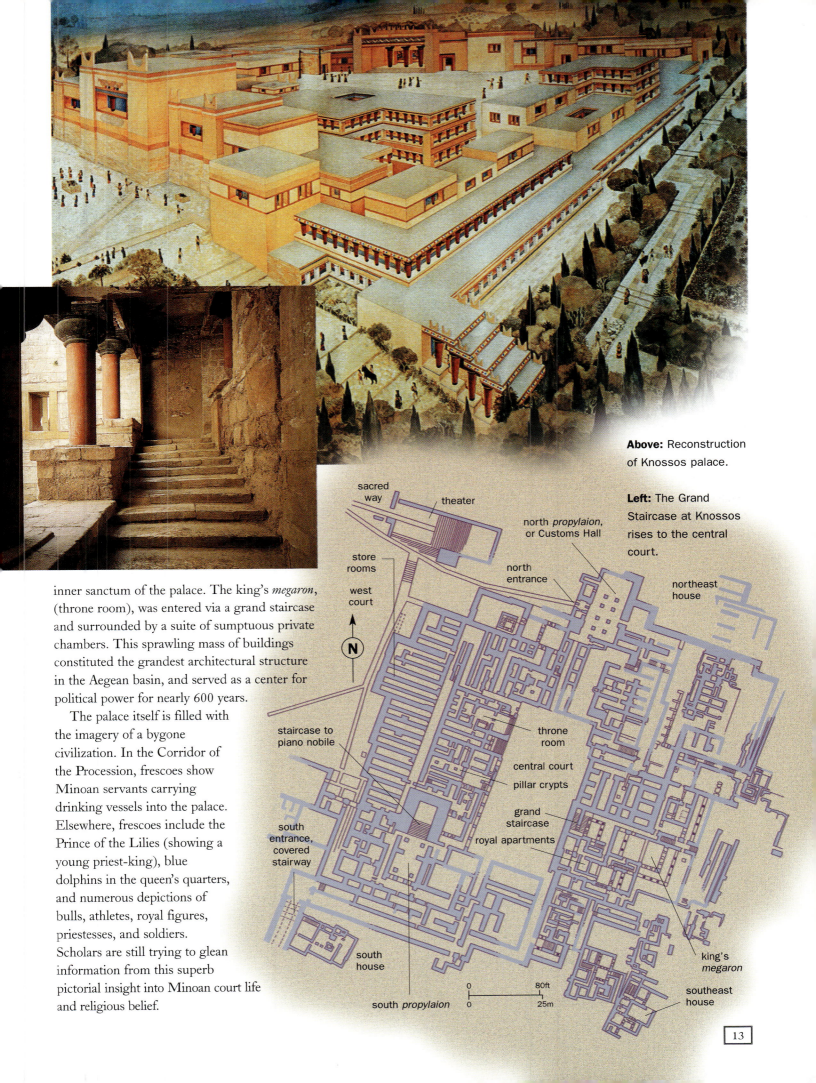

Above: Reconstruction of Knossos palace.

Left: The Grand Staircase at Knossos rises to the central court.

inner sanctum of the palace. The king's *megaron*, (throne room), was entered via a grand staircase and surrounded by a suite of sumptuous private chambers. This sprawling mass of buildings constituted the grandest architectural structure in the Aegean basin, and served as a center for political power for nearly 600 years.

The palace itself is filled with the imagery of a bygone civilization. In the Corridor of the Procession, frescoes show Minoan servants carrying drinking vessels into the palace. Elsewhere, frescoes include the Prince of the Lilies (showing a young priest-king), blue dolphins in the queen's quarters, and numerous depictions of bulls, athletes, royal figures, priestesses, and soldiers. Scholars are still trying to glean information from this superb pictorial insight into Minoan court life and religious belief.

sacred way

theater

north *propylaion*, or Customs Hall

store rooms

west court

north entrance

northeast house

N

staircase to piano nobile

throne room

central court

pillar crypts

grand staircase

royal apartments

south entrance, covered stairway

south house

king's *megaron*

southeast house

south *propylaion*

0   80ft

0   25m

THE LABYRINTH

Minoan civilization's past glories prompted later Greek writers to use Crete as a backdrop for mythological stories, emphasizing the "barbarous" bull culture of the Minoans and the relationship between Minoan kings and the heroes and gods of mainland Greece.

Below: Dating from 1600–1440, this fresco from the east wing shows athletes engaging in what must have been a dangerous sport. Whether this depicts an entertainment or a ritual is not known, although the majority of Knossos paintings feature athletic activity and seem to be decorative rather than religious.

According to Greek mythology, the first ruler of Crete was King Minos, son of Zeus and Europa. In Cretan mythology, Zeus was born in Crete, and was buried under the sacred mountain of Jouchtas overlooking Knossos. Minos ruled Crete from his palace in Knossos, and his wife Pasiphai (the daughter of Perseus) bore him several children. Minos had to fight his brothers Sarpindon and Rhadamanthys for the throne, and exiled them to Lydia (Asia Minor).

The god Poseidon helped him defeat Sarpindon. To celebrate the victory, Poseidon sent Minos a magnificent bull to sacrifice in honor of the sea god. Minos balked at killing such a splendid animal and sacrificed a lesser one in its place. Angered by the sleight, Poseidon sought revenge by making Pasiphai lust for the animal. Queen and beast mated, and she gave birth to a monstrous offspring that was half-bull, half-human.

This creature, the Minotaur, fed on human flesh, and Minos enlisted the help of the famous Athenian artist Daidalos to create a labyrinth to contain it. Minos later discovered that Daidalos had helped Poseidon bewitch Pasiphai, so he was imprisoned in his own labyrinth, along with the Minotaur. Daidalos constructed wings from bird feathers and, with his son Ikarios, he flew out of the labyrinth. Unfortunately, Ikarios flew too close to the sun, which melted the wax holding his wings together, and he fell to his death.

Blood for the Minotaur

Minos launched military expeditions to pacify the tribes of mainland Greece. According to mythology, his son Androgeion was killed on one such campaign against Athens. After defeating the Athenians, Minos imposed a blood tribute by way of retribution, and every year, seven youths and seven maidens were sent to Knossos as food for the Minotaur. Theseus, son of the king of Athens, pleaded to be a blood tribute. He entered the labyrinth with the help of Ariadne, the daughter of Minos. He fought and killed the Minotaur, ending the need for blood tributes, and ushering in a new era of peace between the Cretans and the tribes of mainland Greece.

Legend has it that Minos met his end

through his vendetta with Daidalos, who he pursued to Kamikos in Sicily. There, the local ruler, Kokalos, had given Daidalos refuge. Kokalos welcomed Minos as a guest, but while Minos took a bath, Daidalos poured boling liquid through a pipe in the ceiling onto the king and killed him.

Minos was succeeded by his son Deukalion, who in turn was succeeded by his son Idomeneus. Relations between Cretans and the Greeks must have improved by this stage, since Idomeneus supported Agamemnon of Mycenae in his attack on Troy. This was the mythology of Minoan Crete.

Arthur Evans considered Minos a bona fide historical character, however, and used his name to label the entire Cretan Bronze Age culture. Archaeologists uncovered depictions of bulls, including sculptures, frescoes, and figurines, so there was some ritual link between bulls and the Minoans. Later Greek poets and writers who used elements of this bull cult in their mythological tales clearly remembered this. The

labyrinth may be another example of half-remembered fact. The palace site contained almost 1400 rooms, in addition to numerous galleries, corridors, and courtyards. To many, this would appear to be a maze, and after the collapse of the Minoan civilization the memory of this labyrinthine palace became the maze referred to in the story. The term "labyrinth" stems from the Greek *lavyrinthos*, a reference to a two-bladed ax. Recent archaeological evidence suggests that the Minoans practiced human sacrifice and even cannibalism. The link between the executioner's ax, the maze-like palace, and the bull culture may have combined to form the myth of Theseus and the Minotaur. As for Minos, no hard evidence of his historical presence has been uncovered, and it is probable that he represents a part-remembered tyrant of the Minoan age who subjugated the Greeks of the Peloponnese and Attica.

Left: A glance at the plan of the palace of Knossos on the previous page shows its labyrinthine quality. This combined with the Minoan bull culture may have given rise to the myth of the minotaur— a half-bull, half-man monster. Many bull represenations have been discovered, of which this sculpture is one of the finest and most realistic.

Below: The victory of Theseus over the Minotaur was a popular theme on later ceramic ware, such as this red-figured painting on the side of a Greek vase.

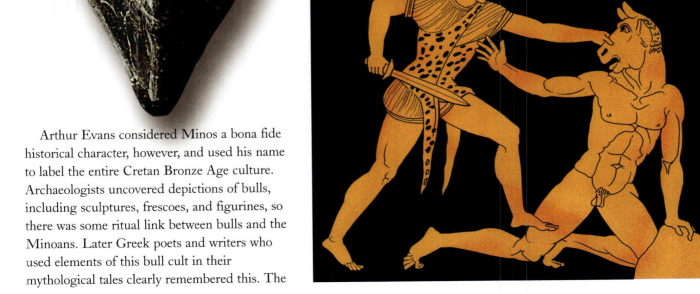

THE MINOAN EMPIRE

The Minoan civilization of Crete is a historical enigma. A great culture appeared, flourished, and died within the middle Bronze Age. It left behind an unparalleled archaeological legacy, including exquisite works of art.

Above: Wearing typical dress, proud parents reward their son for his boxing skills.

Archaeology has shown that during the high point of the Minoan period, towns and villages were built all along the coast of Crete and in its mountainous hinterland. Homer mentioned the island's "hundred towns" and these discoveries have confirmed his estimate.

The Minoans also colonized many of the closer islands of the southern Aegean, and its political control almost certainly extended into the mainland of Greece itself (as suggested by the story of Theseus). Both trade and political power were therefore based on control of the seas, and decorations on ceramic artifacts and seals show the types of ship they used.

Herodotus claimed that King Minos of Crete built a fleet to conquer the Cyclades (the islands of the southern Aegean), cleared the seas of pirates, and imposed taxation on his new-found

hegemony—the *Pax Minoica* referred to by some Greek scholars.

This era of prosperity and cultural advancement reached its peak around 1500, the time most of the palaces, frescoes, and Minoan art were produced. Goldsmiths, sculptors, painters, and seal-makers thrived under the patronage of the Minoan court, creating an artistic legacy that rivaled and even exceeded the contemporary output of Egypt. Trade flourished, as reflected by the presence of Cretan artifacts in Egypt and Phoenicia and the written legacy of the Minoans.

A mysterious language

The excavation of the Cretan palaces uncovered numerous examples of a courtly hieroglyphic script, often inscribed in conjunction with a linear script, which archaeologists labeled Linear A. Although progress has been made in deciphering the hieroglyphics, Linear A has still to reveal its secrets. This language was used in the centuries leading up to 1700, when a series of earthquakes damaged Knossos and other palaces, prompting the rebuilding of Minoan cities. From the 17th century onward, a new form of writing was developed. Arthur Evans discovered numerous clay tablets covered in this Linear B script. The tablets showed signs of having been baked by a fire, possibly the conflagration that finally engulfed the Minoan center of power.

In 1952 amateur linguist Michael Ventris deciphered Linear B, proving that the language was syllabic and an early form of Greek. It also helped explain the nature of the hieroglyphic pictograms found on several tablets, giving scholars a far greater understanding of the final period of Minoan civilization. Inscriptions refer to the use of the palaces as vast storehouses, but do little to explain the final disaster that overtook the Minoan world.

A simple comparison between archaeological remains of the Minoans and those of mainland Greece during the late Bronze Age shows that the Minonans' cultural superiority was not passed directly to the rest of the emergent Greek world. Despite the proven linguistic similarities

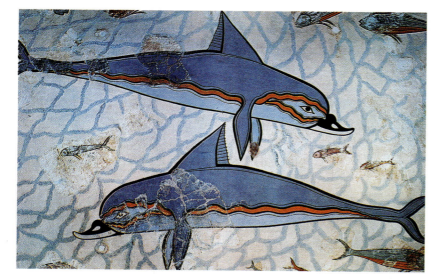

Above: The most widely know fresco from Knossos depicts blue dolphins.

colonies. It is significant that Knossos and Phaistos palaces were built without stout walls, suggesting that the Minoan state was reasonably secure from attack. Since its civilization was based on the relatively prosperous island of Crete, its fleet was sufficient to protect the state from invasion, and the same security was extended throughout the islands of the Minoan

and the suspected political and mercantile links between the Minoan maritime empire and the small city-states of mainland Greece, few aspects of Minoan culture seem to have been adopted by the Greeks. This indicates that when the end came for the Minoans, it was not through assimilation or gradual conquest, but through a more dramatic stimulus, which prevented the culture being exported.

By the late 13th century, some cataclysmic disaster brought the Minoan civilization to its knees. Whether this was a single event or a culmination of a series of natural or manmade disasters has yet to be determined, and the arguments surrounding the collapse of the Minoan world continue to be debated.

The Phoenician form of the alphabet was adapted by the Greeks after the Dark Age

Phoenician		Greek		Modern
ALEPH	⊿	ALPHA	A	A
BETH	9	BETA	B	B
GIMEL	∧	GAMMA	Γ	C
DALETH	⊲	DELTA	Δ	D
HE	⅄	EPSILON	E	E
VAV	⅄			F
HETH	H	ETA	H	H
TETH	⊕	THETA	θ	
YOD	⅄	IOTA	I	I
KAPH	⅄	KAPPA	K	K
LAMED	∟	LAMBDA	∧	L
MEM	⅍	MU	M	M
NUN	⅂	NU	N	N
SAMEK	⧻	XI	Ξ	
AYIN	O	OMICRON	O	O
PE	⅂	PI	Π	P
SADE	⅄			
KOPH	ⱷ			Q
RESH	⅁	RHO	P	R
SHIN	W	SIGMA	Σ	S
TAW	T	TAU	T	T
		UPSILON	V	V
		PHI	Φ	
		CHI	X	X
		PSI	Ψ	
ZAYIN	I	ZETA	Z	Z
		OMEGA	Ω	

THE ORIGINAL ATLANTIS?

The beautiful volcanic island of Santorini appears to hold the key to the Minoan's fate. In the mid-second millennium it was the site of the greatest volcanic eruption ever known. While half the island disappeared, a giant tidal wave swept through the southern Aegean and smashed into the Cretan cities.

The events that caused the decline and destruction of the Minoan culture are largely unknown, but scholars agree that traces of decline can be traced back as far as 1500. A century later, most of the Minoan cities were destroyed by fire and the Minoan civilization collapsed. We know from the rebuilding of Knossos that a natural disaster such as an earthquake destroyed Knossos about 1700, but the culture remained prosperous enough to rebuild the Minoan palace on an even grander scale.

The Cretans dominated the less developed cultures of mainland Greece and the Cycladic islands for a further two centuries, until another disaster struck. The volcano on the Island of Thera (now Santorini, in the Cyclades) erupted around 1628 and half of the Minoan-held island disappeared into the sea. A vast tidal wave estimated at over 650 feet high swept south, where it crashed into the northern shore of Crete. Some scholars still believe the catastrophe happened almost two centuries later, but growing scientific evidence supports the earlier date.

The effect of the eruption was devastating, filling the air with ash and poisonous gas, but the volcano alone was not the reason for the collapse of the Minoan empire. The tidal wave must have caused immense damage to the Minoan urban centers, causing economic chaos. Despite this, given the earlier date for the disaster, it coincided very approximately with the date given for the destruction of the first palace at Knossos and the construction of a new and even more sumptuous one.

Sea Peoples' raids

The acknowledged date for the highest degree of artistic output from the Minoans dates from over a century after the eruption. While earlier scholars believe the disaster brought about the collapse of the civilization, it is now considered more likely that it weakened it but that civilization survived and even prospered in the following centuries. The only real long-term effects were damage to agricultural land in the region and the destruction or submergence of most of the Minoan city on Thera, a loss that possibly gave birth to the Atlantis myth.

The Minoans survived for a few more centuries, but increasingly the balance of power was changing in the Aegean. By the start of the 15th century, warlike people from mainland Greece began to encroach on the weakened Minoan empire. Initial raids were followed by campaigns of conquest. First the Minoan island possessions fell to raiders from the Greek mainland, and then raids were launched against Crete itself. By 1450 the newcomers—most probably Mycenaean Greeks—had conquered Minoan Crete and destroyed all of its palaces and cities, with the exception of

AEGEAN SEA

Oia
Finikia
Pori

The central island of Nea Kaimena is actually a lava plug in the volcano's throat.

VOLCANIC CRATER

Nea Kaimena

Therasia

Skala

THERA (SANTORINI)

Thira (Fira)

Karterados

Messaria

Palaea Kaimena

Athinios
Pyrgos
Episkopi

Aspronisi

VOLCANIC CRATER

Megalochori

Kamari

Excavations at Akrotiri have uncovered frescos as well preserved by ash as those at Pompeii.

Akrotiri

Thera

Emporio
Perissa

SEA OF CRETE

area of Thera destroyed by the eruption of 1628

Thera was founded in the ninth century by Dorian colonists from mainland Greece.

Knossos, which was probably retained as a capital for the island's new rulers. For some unknown reason, the Greek conquerors withdrew from Crete around the start of the 14th century, which allowed the Minoans to attempt to rebuild their shattered country.

Following the reduction of their cities, the loss of their mercantile fleet, and the devastation of their agrarian economy, the Minoans found it difficult to survive. No attempt was made to rebuild on the ashes of the old cities, and gradually the distinctively Minoan culture of the island ebbed away, leaving Crete as little more than an autonomous Greek island, now located on the southern fringe of a newer, dynamic Aegean power.

During the later 13th century an influx of invaders from Europe or Asia, generally known as the Sea Peoples, raided Crete and, after destroying any settlements they found, used the island as a base for further excursions against the eastern Mediterranean and Egypt. A great civilization had been destroyed, and the remains of its once-grand cities would lie buried for 3,200 years.

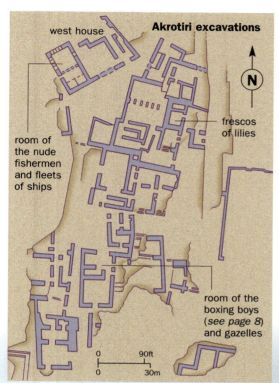

Akrotiri excavations

west house

room of the nude fishermen and fleets of ships

frescos of lilies

room of the boxing boys (*see page 8*) and gazelles

N

| 0 | 90ft |
| 0 | 30m |

Below: Black sand on the beaches of Santorini (Thera) is a testament to the catastrophic volcanic eruption that blew out the island's center and covered it in ash. The view south from above Oia looks down on the volcano's flooded crater toward the central plug of Nea Kaimena. The eruption caused a giant tidal wave to wreak havoc on the shores of Crete, 75 miles away.

CHAPTER 2

GREEK MYTHOLOGY AND RELIGION

When the earliest Greek poets of the Mycenaean era recorded the deeds of their gods and heroes over 3,000 years ago, they were writing in an age that itself would become the stuff of legend. The flowering of the Mycenaean period was followed by what became known as the Dark Age. What came before gained the aura of a gilded age, when gods and heroes walked the earth.

The two great epics of Homer, the *Iliad* and the *Odyssey*, entwined the semi-historical account of the war between the Mycenaean Greeks and the Trojans and its aftermath with a tale of malicious gods, golden heroes, and feats of magic. As a result, the age of Agamemnon, Menelaos, Paris, Ajax, and Achilles became mythological, providing a superb account of the Greek view of their divinities, as well as the actions of warriors who became heroes.

The collection of Greek myths—the stories of the labors of Herakles, the opening of Pandora's box, Orpheus the musician, Ikarios, Pygmalion, Phaiton, Io, Kephalos, and numerous others—

has become enmeshed in modern culture. This is partly because the tales encapsulate timeless literary conflicts between good and evil, right and wrong, loyalty and betrayal. Pandora's curiosity led to the release of all of the evils that prey on humans. Ikarios flew like a bird, but his pride led to his fall. Odysseus the traveler embodied wily cunning as he fought the Cyclopes (Cyclops in the singular) and numerous other evil monsters in battles of wits.

Many myths had a regional element, being associated with a particular place and time. This meant that the nature of the myths altered between regions. It was only when the individual stories were collated into larger mythologies that a semblance of a coherent framework appeared.

Above the mortal and semi-mortal heroes and heroines the gods looked down. Mighty Zeus,

Below: Detail from the Great Melos Amphora, which is decorated in the red-figure style with scenes showing a battle between the gods and giants. The mounted figure thrusting with a *kamax* spear is probably intended to be one of the brothers Kastor or Polydeukes (the Roman Castor and Pollux).

father of all the gods, reigned over the Immortals (or lesser gods) on Mount Olympos. From this height he interfered with his creation as he saw fit. To the Greeks, their gods were neither benign nor even terrible. More often they were capricious, capable of using humanity as a weapon in power struggles among their own kind. Greek religious observance was unlike many others of the ancient world, and the dysfunctional nature of the gods on Olympos was taken into account during religious observances.

To the ancient Greeks, the gods were constantly around them. Religion became an integral part of everyday life. With such a strong bond between society and religion, it was inevitable that beliefs changed to suit new social mores, and that religious observance took on a regional slant—it was widey believed that certain gods favored individual cities or states. Above all, theirs was a practical religion, a part of life to be celebrated and, if possible, to be harnessed for the good of the individual, the family, or the state. The gods walked the earth beside them and could affect their lives at any moment, for better or worse. This immediacy remained a powerful element in Greek belief throughout the era.

ORIGINS OF GREEK RELIGION

The roots of Greek religious observance are buried in the mists of time. Although traces can be found in the earlier Bronze Age cultures of the Aegean, it was in the Classical Age that the Greek religion we know emerged as an amalgam of old and new beliefs.

Below: The realism of classical Greek sculpture developed over centuries from the more primitive Boeotian culture represented by these female Chthonian idols. They date from perhaps the eighth century, a period of geometric decoration, but similar Mycenean finds date from as early as 1300.

Greek religion has no clearly defined origin. If we assume that the first Greeks were migrants from an Indo-European environment, they brought elements of their own beliefs, which intermingled with Aegean religious ideas. The emergent civilizations of Egypt and the Middle East had contact with Bronze Age Greece through trade and probably contributed elements of their own thought. While the pre-Doric inhabitants of Greece and the Aegean had their own religion, the extent to which this was adopted by the invaders is difficult to determine. The exception is the effect of the Minoan religion, whose influence on Mycenaean Greek religious beliefs can be traced through archaeology.

The notion of the supreme god followed a pattern associated with Indo-European notions of a God who ruled in Heaven. Similar supreme deities were found in proto-Celtic, Egyptian, and Mesopotamian religions in the ancient world. Most of the inner circle of Greek gods had counterparts in other religions, although the Greek emphasis on interplay between the gods appears to have been a largely local phenomenon.

From clay tablets written in Linear B deciphered in the late 20th century, we can show that the majority of the Greek pantheon already existed, since they were worshipped by the Mycenaean Greeks during the late second millennium. Evidence also suggests that at least some of these gods were worshipped by the Minoans. Zeus, Hera, and Poseidon were certainly worshipped by the Minoans and Mycenaeans, while lesser members of the inner circle of gods such as Artemis, Ares, Athene, and Hermes could be loosely identified with earlier deities, although names differed. From the Minoan period onward, the discovery of figurines representing female priestesses or goddesses suggests that the Chthonian gods (gods of the earth) were widely worshipped, but in a different form, representing earth, fertility, and nature.

Ubiquity of god cults

Following the collapse of the Minoan and Mycenaean cultures by the 12th century, four centuries of the Dark Age meant that little evidence of religious continuity survived. When written records re-emerged in the eighth century, it appeared that older forms of religion had survived, amalgamated with newer forms from the east.

The result was the body of religious belief that Homer and Hesiod laid down and which formed the basis for the later myths and legends we associate with ancient Greece. These eastern elements included the notion of a war god, adopted from the Hittite system of belief, and a greater emphasis on a supreme deity, ruling the other gods from a heavenly perch. The lesser deities Hecate and Adonis were both directly transplanted into Greece from eastern sources.

This openness to eastern influence never died out completely: during the Classical and Hellenistic periods, fresh minor gods from the east were accepted into the Greek pantheon. The whole notion of the "cult" was primarily eastern and became an important element in Greek religious observation.

Each god had a cult, which dictated the manner of observing the deity, as well as the conduct of the observers. Respect to the gods was all-important, whether expressed directly through religious devotion, or through the pursuit of life in a way that would please the gods. Although they were far from perfect examples of morality, it was believed that the gods were ready to punish those who spurned them, or who

The family tree on page 25 gives a visual impression of the Greek pantheon as outlined by Homer and Hesiod. In the beginning, before the creation of the world, there was Chaos. From Chaos emerged Gaia, first of the Titans, gods and giants who ruled the earth before their overthrow by Zeus. Without mating, Gaia produced a son called Uranos, who represented the heavens. She then mated with Uranos and they had many Titan children. These included Kronos, who came to rule after defeating Uranos. He married his sister Rhea, but fearing his own position, he ate all his offspring as they were born, until Rhea tricked him into eating a rock instead of the newborn Zeus. Later, Zeus rebelled against Kronos and the other Titans, and banished them to the underworld. Meanwhile, Oceanos (oceans) and his sister Tethys produced the rivers and the 3,000 ocean nymphs. Hyperion, an early sun god (*not shown in the family tree, next page*) married his sister Theia, who gave birth to Helios (sun), Selene (moon), and Eos (dawn).

Iapetos married a nymph and fathered Prometheus (forethought, wisdom), Epimetheus (afterthought, stupidity), and Atlas. Unlike his brothers, Atlas supported Kronos against Zeus. After the fall of Kronos, Zeus punished Atlas by making him support the world on his back. Zeus then directed Prometheus and Epimetheus to create humankind.

The overthrow of the Titans (the Chthonian earth gods) by the Olympians (sky gods) evidently represents some major shift in the social structure of prehistoric Greece. Later Greek writers reorganized the way the pantheon worked to take account of this upheaval. Zeus drew lots with his brothers Hades and Poseidon to become supreme ruler. Zeus won, and became ruler of the sky, Poseidon received the seas, and Hades the underworld, to rule over the dead. The Olympians, therefore, comprised the brothers and sisters of Zeus, as well as his children born of numerous liaisons, including with his sister and jealous wife Hera.

The addition of the lesser gods was probably determined by social needs of changing times: adoption of Middle Eastern divinities through early trading, and simple acceptance of the gods of neighboring Greek tribes on the "more the merrier" principle. Dionysos, for instance, was a lowly Olympian, but grew to be a principal deity by the Classical Age (*see also pages 124–5*). As the god of wine, his festival is in the spring, when leaves appear on the vines and, when under the influence of wine, a man might become greater than he is.

committed serious breaches of accepted conduct, such as breaking oaths or dishonoring the gods. This notion appears to have been a home-grown Greek concept, first outlined by Homer and later clarified by Hesiod.

By the time the two writers laid down the basic concepts of Greek religious thought, the pattern of belief in ancient Greece had already been firmly established and the role of the gods clearly defined. So too had the risks of offending Zeus or his fellow Olympians.

Left: The Greeks adopted a number of deities from the Hittites of the Middle East, such as Jarri, the god of war, also known as the "lord of the bow." In the Greek pantheon, he is associated with Ares, god of war.

THE GODS OF OLYMPOS

The sheer number of Greek divinities is staggering. From Zeus, through his immediate family and inner circle, down through the ranks of lesser Immortals, the pantheon of Greek deities had defined roles, although these sometimes conflicted or overlapped.

Facing: Reconstructed Archaic representation of Artemis (right), from the west pediment of her temple in Kerkyra on the island of Corfu, c.800–700. Associated with the hunt, she is every inch the Chthonian earth goddess, and her snake girdle recalls that of the Minoan snake goddess on page 11. The small sculpture of Zeus and Hera enthroned (left), shows the two deities in—for the bickering pair—an unusually cozy domestic pose.

Above: Writing at some point near the end of the eighth century and beginning of the seventh, Hesiod's *Theogeny* was a genealogy of the Greek gods.

As early as the Mycenaean era the names of some of the Greek gods appeared on clay votive tablets, suggesting a longevity of belief that spanned the Dark Age. The Bronze Age Greeks predominantly worshipped earth gods (Chthonians), while the Dorian invaders worshipped sky gods. It has been suggested that the gods of the Classical Age represent an amalgamation of the Olympian sky gods and the older group of goddesses associated with fertility, the earth, fire, and water (represented by the Chthonians). This also indicates a switch from a matriarchal society to a more male dominated one with the Dorian invasions. However, we know little of the origins of these deities. It was as late as the eighth century that they were first chronicled by Homer. A century later, Hesiod's *Theogony* provides a detailed genealogy and characterization for the Olympians.

So the Greek gods were an evolving group of deities, incorporating old gods with new, and their roles also changed with time. To the Greeks, their divine exchanges and their enforcement of order on Earth explained the natural cycles and disasters such as volcanic eruptions, storms, drought, and earthquake.

The gods take centerplace in Greek mythology, a unique group compared with other deities of the ancient world, although the Greeks shared elements of their beliefs with other religions. For example, their version of the creation of the world and the adoption of supremacy of Zeus match similar accounts in other beliefs, and can even be traced as late as the Scandinavian mythological accounts of Odin and the creation of the Viking world.

What set the Greek deities apart was their relationship with the mortals below and their supposed constant interference in Greek life. This polytheist religion invited the worship of all the gods individually, since to omit one was to incur his or her wrath.

Zeus was the father of the gods, ruling from the cloud-capped summit of Mount Olympos like a patriarch supervising his extended family. He was assisted by an inner circle of nine other Olympians, including his wife Hera, his brother Poseidon (god of the sea) and his daughter Athene, patroness of arts, crafts, and later the city of Athens. Other members of this coterie were Apollo (god of light, music, beauty, and medicine), Artemis (goddess of virginity, hunting, and the moon), Aphrodite (goddess of love), Hermes (messenger god of journeying), Hephaistos (god of fire and metalwork), and Ares (god of war).

Beneath these supreme immortals were lesser gods (or demi-gods), such as Dionysos (god of wine) and Prometheus, who Zeus condemned to eternal punishment after he stole fire from the gods to give to man. Pan, the Nymphs, and other lesser figures played an important part in Greek belief and cult, as did the Chthonian gods. Hades, brother of Zeus and god of the underworld, headed this group, accompanied by his wife Kore (or Persephone). Such gods and accompanying spirits were often associated with particular streams or glades and the nourishment of crops, since plants sprout from the earth.

Unruly immortals

The Olympian gods were constantly feuding with each other and used mortals to aid them. Examples include Homer's account of Zeus's allegiance with his Greek favorites during the Trojan War and the subsequent interference of the gods in the adventures of Odysseus.

These were not necessarily benign gods, and accounts of their treachery, sexual intrigues, and duplicity reflected the commonly perceived sins of mankind. They were not moralistic deities— Greek religion largely centered around appeasing the gods, rather than following their example. Later still, Greek writers apologized for their gods, and criticized Homer and Hesiod for helping to portray them as capricious beings. This created a dilemma for philosophers such as Xenophanes and Aristotle, who advocated that mankind was ruled less by indulgent gods than by the nature of man himself. This inevitably led to a religious crisis, from which the Greek system of belief never fully recovered.

In the later Greek world of civic duty, order, and moral conscience, the Gods of Olympos proved something of an embarrassment. While their worship continued, it became increasingly incorporated into a philosophical and social framework that better served the Greek world of Plato, Aristotle, and Sophokles. Goddesses such as Athene survived the transition as mascots of an emergent superpower. The older, more capricious gods were not so fortunate.

Origins of the Greek deities and first men

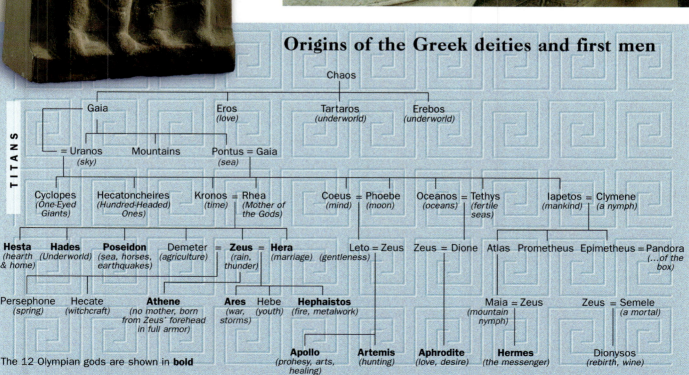

Chaos

TITANS

Gaia — Eros *(love)* — Tartaros *(underworld)* — Erebos *(underworld)*

= Uranos *(sky)* — Mountains — Pontus = Gaia *(sea)*

Cyclopes *(One-Eyed Giants)* — Hecatoncheires *(Hundred-Headed Ones)* — Kronos *(time)* = Rhea *(Mother of the Gods)* — Coeus *(mind)* = Phoebe *(moon)* — Oceanos *(oceans)* = Tethys *(fertile seas)* — Iapetos *(mankind)* = Clymene *(a nymph)*

Hesta *(hearth & home)* — **Hades** *(Underworld)* — **Poseidon** *(sea, horses, earthquakes)* — Demeter *(agriculture)* = **Zeus** *(rain, thunder)* = **Hera** *(marriage)* *(gentleness)* — Leto = Zeus — Zeus = Dione — Atlas — Prometheus — Epimetheus = Pandora *(...of the box)*

Persephone *(spring)* — Hecate *(witchcraft)* — **Athene** *(no mother, born from Zeus' forehead in full armor)* — **Ares** *(war, storms)* — Hebe *(youth)* — **Hephaistos** *(fire, metalwork)* — Maia = Zeus *(mountain nymph)* — Zeus = Semele *(a mortal)*

The 12 Olympian gods are shown in **bold**

Apollo *(prophesy, arts, healing)* — **Artemis** *(hunting)* — **Aphrodite** *(love, desire)* — **Hermes** *(the messenger)* — Dionysos *(rebirth, wine)*

GREEK MYTHOLOGY

The word "myth" means story, and a collection of linked myths became a mythology. Today it reflects the framework of stories that surrounded the Greek gods and their relationship with mortals. Homer's epic poems in the same vein added structure, forming a body of tales that helped to establish a Greek identity.

The myths of ancient Greece are familiar to most modern readers. Part folklore, part poetry, elements of morality tale, action adventure, and ghost story are thrown into the melting pot. The tight definition of a myth as a type of traditional story hardly does justice to the mythology of ancient Greece or its effect on the Greeks. Other cultures produced myths, including the Egyptians, Norse, Celts, and Native Americans, but Greek mythology has long been regarded as something different. It relies less on talking animals and magic and more on the interplay between heroes set apart from other mortals, and the gods who take an interest in their adventures.

These traditional tales were first written down by poets, drawing on an earlier tradition of storytelling devised to help explain the natural world. In mythology, the onset of winter was not a strictly natural phenomenon but related to Kore, wife of Hades, who lived on Mount Olympos but had to return to her

husband in the underworld for a third of the year. Other natural phenomena were attributed to gods through myths, and eventually these became closely intertwined with Greek belief and culture.

Religious cults arose around certain mythological tales, such as the Eleusinian disciples (centered in Eleusis), whose annual devotional rituals recreated the mythological winter activities of Demeter, the mother of Kore, searching Greece for her daughter (*see aso page 61*). Demeter fasted during her journey, and her disciples did the same during their period of observance. Similar ceremonies were enacted throughout Greece, involving ritual separation, pilgrimage, chastity, and isolation, designed to recreate conditions experienced by mythological characters as a symbol of religious respect to the gods. Some myths reflect ethical themes such as fidelity, theft, and incest, and these in turn had a direct impact on moral codes.

Matching society

Some of the earliest myths were cosmological, involving the creation of Heaven and Earth, but unlike other mythologies, the Greeks paid scant attention to the origins of humanity as a whole, and the origin of the Greek people in particular. Rather, the myths as recorded by the poets and writers of the Classical Age looked on the Greece of the Mycenaean era as a golden age, when gods visited the earth.

It was a view of history in which heroes like Odysseus, Theseus, Perseus, Jason, Ajax, and Achilles reflected the spirit of the past. History and myth were united, particularly when the place names mentioned by Homer were real and could be visited by the classical Greek traveler.

Mythology was not completely static, and the relationship between mythology and history led to the portrayal of historic figures in mythological contexts, even though the rulers and heroes of the recent past were real people.

In this respect history found its roots in mythology, as did poetry and drama. It was only when the adoption of a more scientific approach to the natural world and the recording of events was introduced by writers such as Thucydides and Herodotos that this changed.

From the fifth century onward, Greek religion and mythology found itself under pressure from these revisionist writers. Rather than explain the flooding of rivers in springtime by the movement of river gods, or attribute the growth of crops to earth goddesses, natural cycles became linked to tangible phenomena, such as the melting of winter snows or the movement of the sun. The old beliefs did not die, but divine influence on the world was rethought to reflect the increasing sophistication of Greek culture.

There was no orthodox version of a myth, partly because there was no firm religious organization to enforce a definitive form of worship. It was inevitable that the Greek myths would evolve, with slightly different emphases keeping the traditional tales relevant in a changing world. This focus on relevance has sustained Greek mythology long after the collapse of the culture that created it.

Left: A small panel of the fifth century, depicts Demeter, seated with Hades, holding symbols of fertility. However, this *might* also be Kore, Demeter's daughter, who is associated with the spring.

Facing: Detail from a fascinating panel on a late fourth-century cistern shows the companions of Odysseus suffering lethargy in the Land of the Lotus Eaters. Greek myths are a mix of history, morality tale, and high adventure. Theseus is known for his dispatch of the Minotaur, but the story of this almost certainly real king of Athens was embellished by many mythic adventures that hint at a real history, similar to those of Odysseus. Perhaps Jason and the Argonauts is the most famous myth. Jason, who went in search of the fabulous golden fleece of Colchis in order to prove his right to the throne of Iolkos, was probably not real. His story illustrates an early expedition to the Black Sea, land of the Amazons. The women-warriors later attacked the Athens of Theseus, who had stolen an Amazon to be his wife.

THE HOMERIC GREEK HEROES

Between gods and mortals were the heroes, celebrated in Greek mythology and in the works of many Greek writers such as Homer. Cult figures, they included real warriors as well as ones of legend, and were an inspiration to ordinary people.

The origins of the hero cult lie in the tenth century, but it was only firmly established two centuries later, when the first epic and heroic poems were written. These masterpieces intertwined the tradition of the hero with a version of history that helped define what it was to be a Greek. They created role models for a later age.

The earliest heroes were associated with the development of a particular part of Greece, such as Heraios, founder of the city of Heraia (from which the word "hero" derives) and Apoikos "the Colonist" who settled Teos. In part, these are simply a mythological explanation for the creation of a particular state. The names were taken from prominent rivers, settlements, or other natural features. Historical origins were therefore linked to a heroic past. Genealogical and regional roots were important to the Greeks, as reflected in comments by writers such as

Below: Achilles is depicted dragging the body of Hector, who he has just slain in open combat, while his father Priam begs for his dead son's return. Bas-relief on a Roman sarcophagus.

Herodotos, who recorded that certain local rulers claimed an ancestry stretching back some 16 generations to the original, mythical heroes.

Greek mythology might have contained accounts of the actions of gods, goddesses, nymphs, and satyrs, but the central characters were usually heroes, many of whom were the offspring of the gods, or at least of illustrious royal parents who were particularly blessed by the gods. These heroes were raised above common mortals, yet shared their human lifespan.

The majority of heroic tales recounted interlinked adventures of a particular hero, or of the heroic activities of a ruling dynasty from the distant past. Through the writings of Homer (in his *Iliad* and *Odyssey*), most of these heroes became associated with the Mycenaean era, which ended in about 1184. This was the period of the Trojan War, when King Agamemnon of Mycenae led a fleet and army to besiege the Lydian city of Troy (Ilium to the Greeks), on the far side of the Aegean Sea.

Tales of fate and irony

Those who accompanied Agamemnon became the ultimate Greek heroes. Warriors such as Achilles, Ajax, Menelaos, Nestor, Diomedes,

Left: Detail from an early fifth-century red-figured vase depicts Odysseus lashed to the mast of his ship. One of the stories of the hero's wandering return journey from Troy tells of how he became the first human to hear the song of the Sirens and survive. These huge birds with women's heads used their sweet singing to lure sailors to their deaths on dangerous rocks. Odysseus had his men block their ears with beeswax so they would not hear the Sirens' song and himself lashed to the mast, with orders not to free him no matter how much he begged them to do so. To ancient Greek sailors, who hugged coastlines, this myth helped explain why so many ships were wrecked on rocks—by supernatural forces, not their own lack of skill or abundance of misfortune.

Philoktetes, and Odysseus were almost matched by the heroism shown by their Trojan rivals, Priam, Hector, and Paris. Achilles was dipped in a pool whose waters made him invincible, save for the ankle by which his mother held him. Helen, Spartan wife of Menlaos, was reputedly the lovechild of Zeus, as was her brother Pollux. The goddess Athene protected Odysseus on his post-war travels.

This blend of hero and divinity was a heady

concoction for the Greeks, since these Homeric characters were historic to the classical Greeks. They had lived only a few centuries earlier, and in the same part of the world. The burial sites of the Mycenean era were frequently used for classical Greek cult worship ceremonies, invoking the memory and spirit of Homer's heroes.

A common theme in these tales is the fate of the superheroes, who returned from the Trojan Wars as heroes but were unable to escape their mortal fate. On his return to his capital, Agamemnon was murdered by his wife in a palace coup. Odysseus spent ten years wandering the seas trying to return home, only to have to kill his wife's suitors, after his spouse had given him up for dead. This notion of irony and fate was a continual theme, from the tale of King Oedipus of Thebes or Ikarios, the son of Daidalos, to Theseus, who slew the Minotaur, to Pygmalion, king of Cyprus.

This blend of moral statement, heroic deed, and revenge over enemies and unfaithful partners bound the Greeks to their heroes, ensuring their durability as icons. The Greek heroes were humans, albeit ones with superhuman power or special links to the gods. As such, the same fate could be bestowed on anyone. It is little wonder that the Greek heroes served as an inspiration throughout the era of classical Greece.

A PRACTICAL RELIGION

For the ancient Greeks, religion was rarely a solemn affair—feasting, gatherings, and celebration were accepted forms of worship. Religion addressed the essential elements of life, and involved the entire community in celebrating the gods.

Below: Reconstruction of the great ivory statue of Athene in the temple of the Parthenon in Athens. Her appearance is based on small copies, since the original vanished long ago.

Greek religious belief was practical, worship given to gain the good grace of the gods, or at least not to lose it. It helped ensure good harvests, safe journeys, skilled building work, and healthy families. The Greeks were rarely concerned with less practical aspects, such as the afterlife or individual redemption, although later sects tried to introduce these themes.

Religion was a serious matter and formed a constant element in the Greeks' daily lives. Every gathering had its religious element, and both large panhellenic meetings, such as took place at Delphi and the Olympic Games, served as opportunities for religious observance as much as sport or political debate.

The Greek calendar was punctuated with religious ceremonies and observations. Formal ceremonies, such as sacrifices of animals or the offering of produce, were rigidly adhered to, each designed to celebrate (or placate) a particular deity. Festivity and banquets were a means of communicating with the gods, and celebrating was a means of ensuring the pleasure of the appropriate deity. Herodotos mentions religious supplicants "sacrificing, and having a good time."

Although some religious occasions could be full of pomp or solemnity and involve acts of brutality or bestial sacrifice, the majority appear to have been spirited occasions, appealing to the people as much as to the gods. Some celebrations could even be ribald, involving excessive drinking, coupling, and "ritual obscenity." If it entertained the god concerned, it was deemed a viable form of expressing devotion and respect. The worshippers were offering their joy, sacrifice, or bounty as part of a pact with the gods, and in return they laid claim to a fitting response or return gift from the gods, such as a bountiful harvest or healthy offspring.

Doubts from the east

Religion was practiced in homes—small figurines representing the gods were usually set outside them. Temples and shrines were presented with similar votive offerings, designed to curry favor with the appropriate gods. With these exceptions, religion to the Greeks was a communal affair, usually involving the collective efforts of a city's population, not just a spiritual elite or devout minority. For centuries, cult worship of particular gods had been the prerogative of an elite minority, but following the advent of the notion of the *polis* (or city-state), worship became a collective enterprise.

The rewards gained from the celebrations were usually worldly, although they also marked rites of passage, like the transformation of

youths into warriors, or a birth, marriage, or death within the community. Death was particularly important, since there was no tradition of suggested immortality—any reference to an afterlife tended to involve the underworld realm of Hades, where if souls existed, they did so as ghostly wraiths.

Religious movements that questioned traditional religious tenets were imported into Greece from the East. These theological theories were the result of a general change in emphasis from the mythical to the practical, as espoused by a new generation of classical Greek writers, philosophers, and scholars. Xenophanes questioned the notion of the Greek gods, while the sophist Protagoras took this a stage further in the late fifth century. He argued that there was no proof that the gods existed at all.

Atheistic notions were the exception, and the majority of Greeks appear to have continued to have faith in their gods and celebrate them into the Hellenistic Age. By then, the personal hero

cult encouraged by Alexander the Great and his successors blurred the boundaries of accepted religion. Traditional Greek religion encompassed these changes and survived into the second century AD. The spread of Christianity brought the age of Zeus, Hera, and the Olympians to a close, partly through adaptation of older religious concepts for use by the new unifying religion of the ancient world.

Left: Detail from a red-figured cup of c.530 by Epiktetos showing two athletes wrestling. Sporting events served as opportunities for religious observance as much as sport or political debate.

Below: Some festival celebrations were ribald and involved excessive drinking, but if the god concerned was entertained, it was deemed a viable form of devotion. In the case of Dionysos, drinking and licentiousness was common among his adherents. This red-figured vase shows Dionysos drinking with two satyrs and a woman.

CHAPTER 3

THE AGE OF HEROES: MYCENAEAN GREECE

The map includes the following labels:

Mt. Olympos

Dorian Greeks

EPIRUS

THESSALY

Iolkos became a late Mycenaean refuge.

Iolkos

The Dorians went on to overrun the Peloponnese, Crete, the Cyclades, and Rhodes.

Leukas

AETOLIA

Thermon

PHOKIS

Astakos

Orchomeno

Ithaca

Delphi

BOE

Kalydon

Gla

KEPHALONIA

Gulf of Corinth

ACHAEA

ZANTE

ARCADIA

ARGOLI

Corinth

ELIS

Olympia

Mycenae

Argos

Tiryns

IONIAN SEA

PELOPONNESE

Asine

MESSENIA

Thouria

Sparta

Pylos

LAKEDAIMON

KYTHERA

The importance of the Peloponnesian city of Mycenae was recorded by Homer, who described it as the seat of King Agamemnon, the high king of all Greece. Excavations by German archaeologist Heinrich Schliemann confirmed Homer's statement that the city was an important political center, hence late Bronze Age Greek culture from around 1600 to 1100 has been labeled Mycenaean. This was the heroic golden age recorded by Homer, when the gods supposedly influenced the struggles between kings, heroes, and states. Although similar Mycenaean cities existed in other parts of Greece, a combination of Homer and Schliemann ensured that the Peloponnese fortress city came to represent the power and culture of the age.

The excavation of Mycenae and other cities of the period revealed that these were prosperous centers, maintaining trading links with the eastern Mediterranean and the Aegean, including the Minoan empire on Crete. This growing prosperity was reflected in the size of civic buildings, the girth of city walls, and even more evidently, in the rich funerary items buried alongside the bodies of their kings.

While many aspects of Mycenaean society, such as religion or social structure, are still unclear, elements of Minoan influence can be found. Traces of Mycenaean religious belief recorded in clay tablets show that many of their notions transcended the subsequent Greek Dark Age to re-emerge in the religion practiced during the Archaic period that followed. By this time, the historic Bronze Age of Greece had become the Homeric "heroic age." Even today, the era is known more for its association with the Trojan War, Ajax, Agamemnon, and Odysseus than with any archaeological fact.

Archaeological finds from this period have both confirmed some of the Mycenaean associations with Homer's epics and suggested that late Bronze Age Greek society was highly advanced, prosperous, and well-organized. There seems to have been a political and cultural dynamism unmatched in Greece until the emergence of the Classical Age in the fifth century.

To later Greeks, the incredibly thick walls of Mycenae seemed to be the work of cyclopes or giants rather than of men. It seems that the Greeks had forgotten the achievements of the Mycenaean period a few centuries after the collapse of Bronze Age Greece, so there is little wonder Homer's semi-mythical interpretation of its history was readily accepted.

Certainly by 1100 Mycenaean culture was in decline, subjected to invasion from the north and possible internal strife and economic stagnation. The collapse of this civilization ushered in a centuries-long Dark Age.

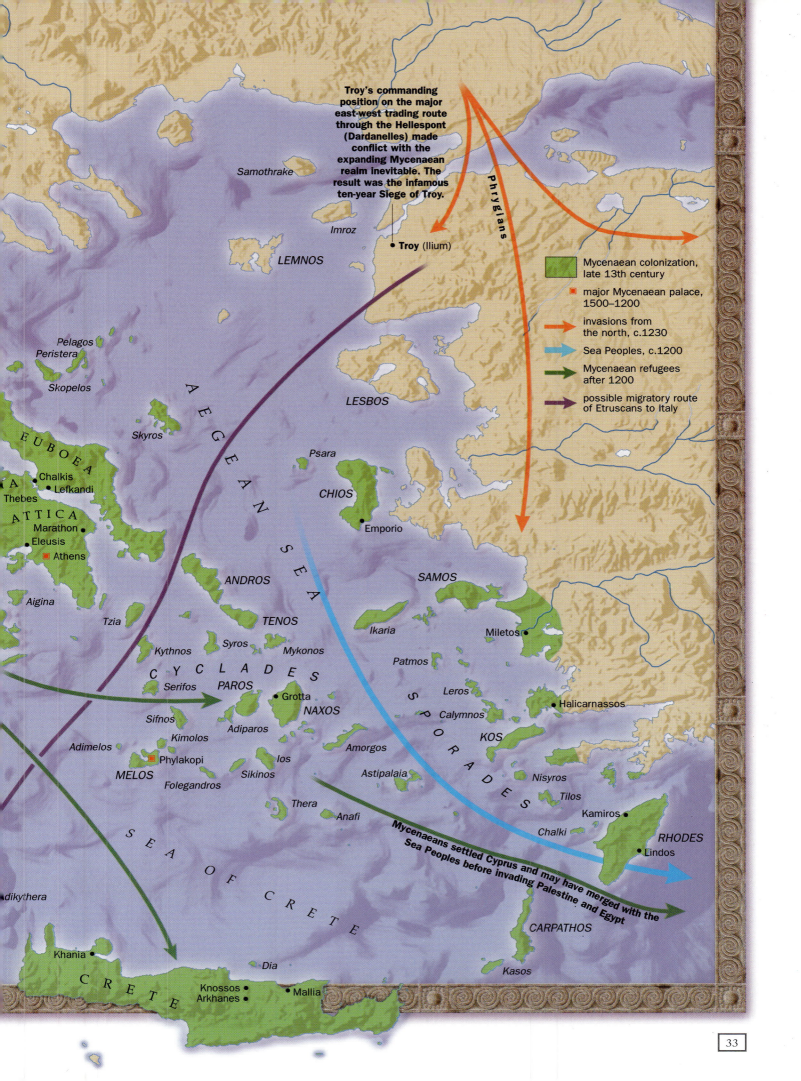

Troy's commanding position on the major east-west trading route through the Hellespont (Dardanelles) made conflict with the expanding Mycenaean realm inevitable. The result was the infamous ten-year Siege of Troy.

Phrygians

Samothrake

Imroz

LEMNOS

Troy (Ilium)

Pelagos
Peristera

Skopelos

Skyros

LESBOS

Psara

CHIOS

Emporio

EUBOEA

Chalkis
Lefkandi

Thebes

ATTICA

Marathon
Eleusis

Athens

SAMOS

Aigina

ANDROS

Tzia

TENOS

Ikaria

Miletos

Kythnos

Syros

Mykonos

Patmos

Serifos

PAROS

Leros

Grotta

NAXOS

Calymnos

Halicarnassos

Sifnos

Adiparos

KOS

Kimolos

Adimelos

Amorgos

SPORADES

Phylakopi

Ios

Nisyros

MELOS

Sikinos

Astipalaia

Tilos

Folegandros

Thera

Kamiros

Anafi

Chalki

RHODES

Lindos

adikythera

Mycenaeans settled Cyprus and may have merged with the
Sea Peoples before invading Palestine and Egypt

SEA OF CRETE

CARPATHOS

Kasos

Khania

Dia

CRETE

Knossos
Arkhanes

Mallia

AEGEAN SEA

CYCLADES

■ Mycenaean colonization, late 13th century

▫ major Mycenaean palace, 1500–1200

→ invasions from the north, c.1230

→ Sea Peoples, c.1200

→ Mycenaean refugees after 1200

→ possible migratory route of Etruscans to Italy

THE RISE OF MYCENAEAN GREEKS

Indo-European people built settlements across central and southern Greece, displacing or assimilating the indigenous people they encountered. Their settlements grew into prosperous cities. By the late 12th century they were the dominant power in the Greek world.

Below: The view of Mycenae looking south at the imposing Lion Gate. To the right of the gate can be seen Grave Circle A, the burial site of Mycenaean kings.

We know little about the migratory people who entered the Greek mainland and the Aegean Basin during the late third millennium. They settled in suitable coastal regions and fertile low-lying areas, apparently concentrated in the Peloponnese peninsula of southern Greece. These settlements grew into powerful

fortified cities such as Mycenae, Tiryns, and Pylos, political and military centers that exerted control over their hinterland. Each was the seat of power of a king or regional ruler. Mycenae was sited in a strategically important location, dominating the isthmus of Corinth, the land route linking the Peloponnese with the rest of the Greek peninsula.

While our knowledge of Mycenaean development is limited, archaeological clues hint that the cities shared a common heritage but that they also lacked unity for much of the period. The exception to this disunity was provided by Homer in the *Iliad*, where he refers to King Agamemnon of Mycenae as a high king, with King Menelaos of Sparta his brother, suggesting the presence of a ruling dynasty, as well as a supreme ruler.

A type of grave circle that has been exclusively associated with the Mycenaeans first appeared in the Peloponnese around the late 17th century, indicating that a settled Mycenaean culture existed by that period. Within three centuries these simple graveyards had given way to a grander variant, typified by Mycenae's Grave Circle A, or royal burial circle, located immediately inside the city's Lion Gate entrance. This and other similar grave circles produced evidence of spectacular wealth. This suggests that even before the collapse of the Minoan culture, the Mycenaeans had achieved a comparable if not a greater level of wealth.

City or grand palace

Finds also betray evidence of the trade links, which the Mycenaeans had developed by the 14th century. Artifacts from Crete, the Cyclades, and even further afield suggest that raw materials and finished goods produced in Greece were exported throughout the region, and in return precious objects were imported to the city kingdoms.

However, this evidence of wealth is illusory.

c.2000	c.1600	c.1500
Achaeans/ Mycenaeans migrate south into Greece	Birth of Mycenaean (Bronze Age Greek) culture	Mycenaean colonies established

While grave finds suggest a booming economy, the archaeological remains of Mycenaean settlements reveal that the cities remained small, a fraction of the size of the sprawling centers found on Crete. While Cretan palaces were surrounded by a town, the heavily fortified Mycenaean cities could only have held small populations and can be more readily identified as fortified palaces.

They housed artisans and craftsmen, but the real producer of Mycenaean wealth was the rural farmer, shepherd, or miner, while the greatest display of conspicuous wealth was associated with the monarch himself. This suggests a subservient society, and recent excavations in minor Mycenaean settlements reflect this. Between 1700 and 1200 evidence of wealth increased, and although a greater degree of social responsibility on the part of Mycenaean rulers is apparent, the disparity between ruler and subjects continued throughout the period.

Ceramic finds suggest the Mycenaeans established colonies in the Cyclades and in Crete by the late 15th century, but it also appears that Cretan occupation had ended around 1400. Trade increased during the 15th and 14th centuries— Mycenaean artifacts have been found as far afield as Upper Egypt, suggesting links with the eastern Mediterranean. How much this prosperity benefited the ordinary people is unknown, but the vast increase in military expenditure evident from the 13th century suggests that the majority of profits went into the royal war chest.

The first foreign reference to the Mycenaeans was made about 1300, when a Hittite king referred to the "King of the Ayyiwah," a term loosely translated as King of the Achaeans, a term also used by Homer in referring to the Mycenaeans. While they might have been called the Achaeans—a region further to the northwest—it is clear that Mycenae was by far the most important city in late Bronze Age Greece, and the Hittite must have been referring to the ruler of the "Lion City."

Above: On its discovery, Schliemann said of this death mask of thin beaten gold that "he had looked upon the face of Agamemnon." Whether or not he existed, Homer ensured the mythic king's immortality.

c.1500	c.1400	c.1350	c.1300	c.1200	c.1150	c.1150	c.1100
Crete conquered then abandoned by invaders, probably from Mycenae	Mycenaean cities are protected with walls	Mycenaeans trade around the Aegean and east Mediterranean	Mycenae is destroyed, later rebuilt	Troy is razed to the ground; Trojan War ends	Mycenaean resources devoted to the military and city defenses	Mycenae is destroyed once more	End of Mycenaean culture; beginning of the Dark Age

MYCENAE

Following his success at Troy, Heinrich Schliemann traveled to the Peloponnese to excavate the supposed location of King Agamemnon's city. Although he was unable to prove that the city he uncovered was the one mentioned in Homer's _Iliad_, he had discovered one of the wonders of the Bronze Age.

Below: Reconstruction of Mycenae in the 13th century. The great court and _megaron_ are at the left to center; the house of columns is at the far right.

Schliemann had listened to accounts of the imposing ruins of an ancient hilltop fortress some distance inland from the Aegean Sea, in the northeastern corner of the Peloponnese. After revealing enough at the site in Hisarlik in northwestern Turkey to convince skeptics that he had found Homer's Troy (_see pages 40–41_), he decided to find where the Greek army gathered before sailing against the Trojans. The German archaeologist arrived at Mycenae in the late 1870s and within weeks he found proof that this was no ordinary fortress.

Excavations revealed that what appeared to be a ruin on a dusty hilltop was once the center of a sumptuously wealthy court. Homer described Mycenae as being "rich in gold," and some of this civic wealth was indeed recovered by Schliemann. In a circular burial ground near the main entrance to the city, Schliemann found golden funerary masks, together with grave goods—weapons, golden ornaments, jewelry, and jewel-inlaid domestic items.

Later, when finds were uncovered at Knossos (_see pages 12–13_), similarities were noted between the art found in Mycenae and the contemporary Minoan palace. Evidently cultural and economic links were maintained between the waning Greek civilization in Crete and the burgeoning one in the Peloponnese.

Perhaps the most impressive of Schliemann's finds were the death masks, created to be placed over the face of a dead ruler or nobleman and shaped to resemble the deceased. Schliemann was driven by his desire to link the site with the Mycenae of the _Iliad_, and after finding the most impressive of the bearded funerary masks the amateur archaeologist wrote, "I have looked upon the face of Agamemnon."

While the individual rulers cannot be identified, and probably predate the period described by Homer, the emotive connection made by Schliemann is still a popular one. Unfortunately, the masks he found have been scientifically dated to the 16th century, some

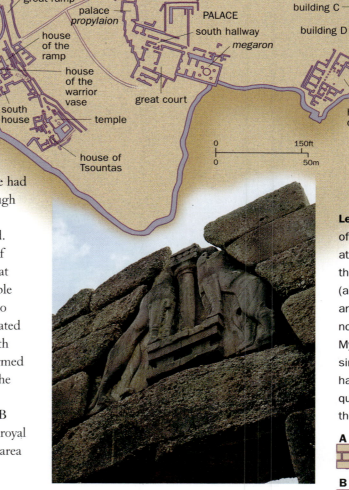

three centuries before the fall of Troy. Another site, which the archaeologist identified as the tomb of Agamemnon's unfaithful wife Clytemnestra, cannot be accurately associated with an individual, although the large circular tomb was certainly the last resting place of a prestigious Mycenaean woman.

Expanding the evidence

Schliemann died with the conviction that he had unearthed Agamemnon's palace, and although his finds captivated the imagination of the world, his claims could not be substantiated. Science triumphed over romance. By way of compensation, further archaeological work at Mycenae has revealed much about the people who built the fortress city and the kings who ruled it. The tombs and grave circles excavated by Schliemann dated from the 16th and 15th centuries and the imposing entranceway formed by the Lion Gate was constructed around the same period.

The discovery of tablets bearing Linear B script indicated that the site was a center for royal power and a repository for provisions. The area identified as the royal palace stands on the

highest point, emphasizing the monarch's superiority. The incredibly thick walls surrounding the site suggest that Mycenae was more of a bastion than a city, and while it lacked the houses to support a large population, it had all the facilities it needed to act as a seat of political, military, and administrative power.

Work still continues at the site. Archaeologists are trying to discover who ruled from the city, what Mycenaean civilization was like, and why the culture came to an abrupt end in about 1100. Evidence of destruction, rebuilding, and further destruction during the 12th century suggests that the city was sacked at least twice in less than 50 years. As more artifacts are uncovered, we are able to learn a little more about the Mycenaeans, and although scholars will probably never be able to unreservedly identify the fortress city with Homer's epic, archaeology confirms that Homer's prose was built on a foundation of perceived fact.

Left: The magnificence of Mycenae is hinted at in structures like the Lion Gate (although the beasts are heraldic and may not have been lions). Mycenae is unique, since nowhere else have buildings of such quality survived from the late Bronze Age.

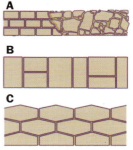

Above: Built over 125 years, Mycenae's walls show three distinct styles. Earlier work used ashlar and rubble—thin-cut dressing stones over irregular stones held by mortar (A). In later additions, massive, precisely cut, squared stone blocks were used (B) and even polygonal walls, with each stone shaped to fit its neighbor (C).

MYCENAEAN SOCIETY

Mycenae was only one of a number of Greek cities that thrived during the era. Recent evidence allows us to glimpse how early Greek society functioned and trace how this culture developed its unique identity.

While Mycenae was one of the most important cities in late Bronze Age Greece, other cities also grew and flourished. Thebes, linked with the myth of King Oedipus who unwittingly married his mother, had become a prosperous regional center by 1500. The smaller Mycenaean cities of Athens and Orchomenos were also growing, as were the Peloponnesian cities of Tiryns and Pylos.

At Pylos, a series of Linear B clay tablets provided archaeologists with evidence of a well-organized society. The tablets, which have been dated to the early 13th century, were clearly intended as jottings—temporary notes that would subsequently be transferred onto more permanent papyrus-reed scrolls. In this period soft clay tablets were used, then smoothed over, allowing fresh inscriptions to be made. For some reason these markings were never erased and a fire caused the tablets to harden. Archaeologists have suggested that the same fire destroyed part of the city, including the palace area where the tablets were found. They reveal a well-oiled bureaucracy, since the tablets formed a small part of a large system of annual records.

The palace at Pylos lay at the center of an administrative network that divided the city's hinterland into 16 districts. Each was further divided in two, then divided again into 16 smaller

Above: The east gallery at Tiryns (1350–1250) shows the massive style of Mycenaean building known as *cyclopean* (because later Greeks could not believe that men could have raised such huge stones, only the giant cyclopes). Tiryns—one of the first citadels with stone walls—eventually became a tributary to Mycenae, only 12 miles away.

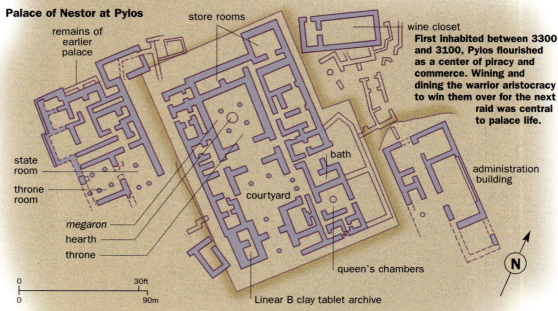

Palace of Nestor at Pylos

remains of earlier palace

store rooms

wine closet

state room

throne room

megaron

hearth

throne

courtyard

bath

queen's chambers

administration building

Linear B clay tablet archive

First inhabited between 3300 and 3100, Pylos flourished as a center of piracy and commerce. Wining and dining the warrior aristocracy to win them over for the next raid was central to palace life.

0   30ft

0   90m

N

administrative units, most probably centering on individual villages, hamlets, or farms. The tablets recorded what flowed into the central warehouse.

The detail of these records provides us with a unique insight into Mycenaean life. Craftsmen were listed—bronze workers, goldsmiths, silversmiths, jewelers, ivory carvers—suggesting Pylos was a major center for luxury items and military hardware. The military aspects are reflected by the mention that some of the bronze workers specialized in chariots and chariot wheels and others were swordsmiths. Stockpiles of weapons were listed in the records, and further evidence of military activity comes from slave numbers, since these usually represented prisoners captured in battle.

Agricultural foundation

This was a time when military tensions were rising in Mycenaean Greece. Cities that had previously co-existed peaceably were now apparently engaged in war with each other. The burning of parts of Pylos may have been caused during one such inter-Mycenaean conflict. The coastal city also maintained a fleet: 600 rowers were listed in a payment ledger, as were 200 garrison troops (or coastal guards).

Further accounts describe rural Mycenaeans who came into the city to sell or buy agricultural produce or livestock. Cowherds, goatherds, fishermen, hunters, farmers, and wood-cutters were mentioned, suggesting a thriving agrarian economy, capable of supporting the urban artisans who created the city's mercantile wealth, and the soldiers and sailors who protected it.

This evidence is supported by further but less dramatic archaeological finds in other Mycenaean sites, and a picture emerges of a well-run and centralized city administration, controlled by clerics through the temple on behalf of the monarch. This society was becoming increasingly militaristic, hence the rigid administrative structure was designed to support that military enterprise. The wealth of these states necessitated the creation of a strong treasure-house, and the remains of suitable strong-rooms in Mycenae add further weight to the evidence of a centralized economy.

In general, the Mycenaean settlements give the appearance of fortresses more than towns, with their thick cyclopean walls and strategically chosen locations. While it appears that the

earliest phases of the Mycenaean period were devoted to the production of cultural items of extremely high quality (thus supporting the notion that patronage of the arts was commonplace), in the last centuries of the era the emphasis shifted to defensive architecture and military accoutrements. In Mycenae, Pylos, Tiryns, Athens, Thebes, Iolkos, and other Mycenaean cities, this military activity peaked in the 12th century, shortly before the complete collapse of Mycenaean society.

Above: Detail of clay Linear B tablet found in the palace at Pylos.

Below: In a palace fresco from Tiryns, two women travel in a typical Mycenean chariot: light-bodied with bent wooden frames and tires.

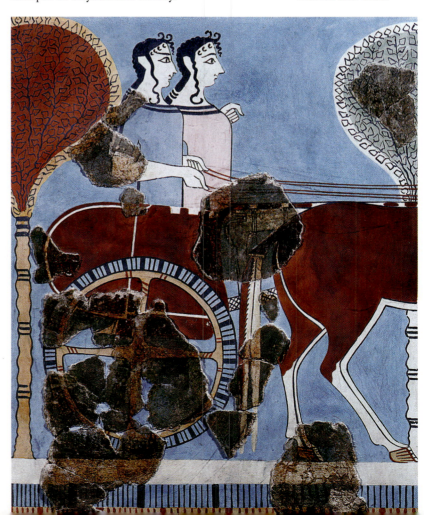

THE TROJAN WAR

During the 13th century the Mycenaean kingdoms came under attack, probably through inter-Greek rivalry over a dwindling economy. Greek eyes turned eastward—the ultimate result was the siege of Troy.

Above: Archaeologist Heinrich Schliemann's passionate belief in the truth of Homer's *Iliad* led him to discover the remains of ancient Troy.

Right: The famous Trojan horse never appeared in the *Iliad*, but attributed to the cunning of Odysseus, it gained currency in the years after the end of the war. This relief from the neck of a large pot from Mykonos, c.675—about 50 years after Homer's lifetime—shows the Trojans wheeling in the gift of the departing Greeks. It is a fantasy based on post-Homeric epic poetry.

There is strong evidence that trade was in decline throughout the eastern Mediterranean of the 13th century. Rivalry between Aegean powers led to increased use of military force and a rise in piracy. Military preparations were reflected in the construction or expansion of city walls—those at Tiryns in Argolis were 26 feet thick.

The Trojan War described in Homer's *Iliad* (Ilium was the Greek name for the city) was set against this backdrop of instability and shrinking economy. It has been assumed that the *Iliad* was written during the early eighth century, the *Odyssey* some half-century later. Written in the Greek script newly adopted from the Phoenicians (*see page 17*), it deals with events at least four centuries before Homer was born, blending history with mythology.

The *Iliad* is the world's first war story, recounting a Mycenaean campaign against the Lydian city of Troy, in the northwest corner of what is now Turkey. Helen, Queen of Sparta, eloped with Paris, one of the sons of King Priam of Troy. King Menelaos of Sparta sought revenge and solicited the help of his brother Agamemnon, King of Mycenae. As high king of Greece, Agamemnon turned the punitive expedition into a panhellenic enterprise.

The flower of the Mycenaean kingdoms accompanied Agamemnon, Menelaos, and their fleet of "black ships" across the Aegean. A ten-year siege ensued,

and Homer's epic details the final climactic year of the siege. In a series of attacks, sallies, and duels, most of the Greek heroes who accompanied Agamemnon were killed, as were their Trojan counterparts. The battle between Achilles and Trojan champion Hector, and the account of Agamemnon's men fighting with their backs to their ships during a spirited Trojan attack are some of the most vivid accounts of battle ever written.

Beware Greeks bearing gifts

According to the *Odyssey*, in the end the Greeks resorted to trickery, feigning an abandonment of the siege and sailing away from Troy, leaving a large wooden horse as an offering on the beach. The Trojans wheeled the prize into the city and celebrated their victory. That night, the Greek fleet crept back, and when Greek soldiers hidden inside the horse emerged and opened the city gates, Troy fell to Agamemnon. The few Trojans who survived were enslaved and the city was razed to the ground.

When Homer wrote the *Iliad* he probably believed the events he described really happened. The question of their accuracy has

been debated by archaeologists and classicists ever since, but for the Greeks, there was no reason for debate. For them, Homer provided a stirring account of Greek prowess, ancestral histories that helped assert the importance of heroic myth and religious belief in Greek culture. In subsequent centuries these epics were retold and even altered, but they remained an important part of Greek cultural imagination.

Heinrich Schliemann believed passionately in the accuracy of Homer's narrative. In 1870, following geographical clues in the *Iliad*, he began to excavate a mound at Hisarlik, on the northwest coast of Turkey. He was convinced he had located Troy, confirmed by the discovery of massive city walls, rich personal finds, and evidence of a major city destroyed by fire.

Subsequent excavations at Hisarlik have also proved that several cities were built on the same site, from the early Bronze Age to the late Hellenistic period. Although several of these cities were destroyed, archaeologists have tentatively identified the ruins labeled Troy VIIa as Homer's city, which was apparently razed by fire around 1200, close to

the end of the Mycenaean period. Damaged city walls, hasty repairs, large storage jars (for massed grain storage), and signs of conflict all suggest that this particular version of Troy was besieged, assaulted, and burnt. Archaeology has shown that Homer's epic was, to some extent, based on factual events, and that Schliemann was right to follow his convictions.

Left: Two Mycenaean warriors of the 12th century, wearing studded leather helmets adorned with goats' horns. The circumference of the rounded shield was broken by concave hollows, presumably to fit comfortably over hip or thigh. This reconstruction—based on the pottery fragment shown on the following page—shows how the Greek warriors who sailed to Troy would have appeared. Later Hellenic Greek art portrayed the heroes in a way we are more familiar with today (**below**), as shown in the scene of the destruction of Troy on a krater of c.490.

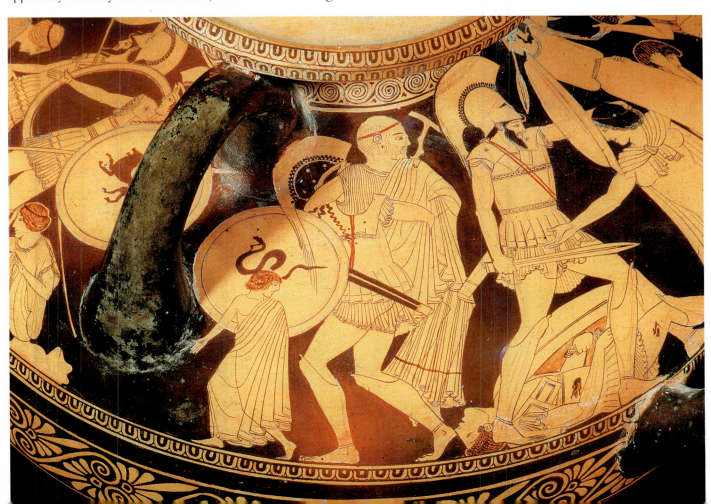

THE COMING OF THE DARK AGE

If we assume that the Trojan War ended about 1200, Mycenaean Greek supremacy was short-lived. Within a century the great cities of central Greece and the Peloponnese lay in ruins, and the Mycenaean age had come to an abrupt end.

While the exact reason for the end of the Mycenaean culture cannot be definitively asserted, archaeological evidence does suggest causes for its rapid decline. All the large Mycenaean cities encountered some form of catastrophe during this period, and most showed damage by fire. Scholars are still debating the sequence of events and whether the disasters that befell Mycenae were in any way linked to those that devastated the last traces of Minoan culture.

The principal evidence for a series of cumulative disasters is the extensive rebuilding on top of earlier levels within the walls of Mycenae and Tiryns. Circumstantial evidence also exists in Hittite documents and Homer's narratives, and isolated Linear B inscriptions (including the Pylos tablets) suggest that the 12th century was a period of intense rivalry between the various small city-based kingdoms in Mycenaean Greece. In fact a state of near-perpetual war may have existed. City walls and palaces were rebuilt and new armies were raised and equipped, but over time the economy supporting these kingdoms faltered.

Mycenae was devastated during the early 13th century and rebuilt, only to be destroyed again c.1150. During the last years of the Bronze Age, Greek culture was destroying itself through warfare. Even Homer alludes to these struggles: on his return to Mycenae Agamemnon was murdered by his wife Clytemnestra, but his death was avenged by his son Orestes, who killed his own mother to avenge his father's death. In the *Odyssey*, Odysseus returned home to find that rivals coveted his throne and his wife. It is possible that Homer drew his inspiration from tales of unrest within the Mycenaean world.

Other proposals for the decline of Bronze Age Greece have been proposed. Warfare would have led to a mass movement of refugees, causing a depopulation of the city kingdoms in favor of less volatile parts of Greece or the Aegean. Some scholars cite over-population, leading to a struggle between kingdoms, vying for a share of the decreasing agrarian production base needed to feed their subjects. Others cite a decline in eastern Medierranean trade, linked to increasing instability due to the invasion of the Sea Peoples.

The Dark Age descends

Of all the theories surrounding the collapse of the Bronze Age Greek culture, the most popular concerns external invasion. Later Greek writers claimed that the heroic age had been brought to an end by waves of migrating "Greek-speaking" peoples from the north. While archaeological evidence supports this—it includes the construction of a defensive line across the Isthmus of Corinth to protect the Peloponnese—other finds suggest that traces of Mycenaean culture survived the collapse of the city kingdoms.

The Egyptians coined the term Sea Peoples but the Greeks referred to these invaders as Dorians and claimed they hailed from the mountains of northern Greece. The collapse of Mycenaean culture was mirrored by similar decline elsewhere in the eastern Mediterranean: the Egyptians were subject to attack by the Sea Peoples and the once-mighty Hittite Empire was destroyed by the same raiders.

While the Sea Peoples and Dorians may not be the same people, it has been proven that some Greek-speaking raiders took part in attacks in the eastern Mediterranean basin. It is also unclear whether the Dorians entered Mycenaean Greece as invaders or simply migrated into a land torn apart by internal war.

Whatever the cause, the end of the Mycenaean cities ushered in the Dark Age, a period from which no written evidence survives and precious little archaeological clues remain. For four centuries, Greece remained a mysterious and barbaric land, ignored by the rest of the Mediterranean. Artistry, industry, and government ceased, and the depopulation of Greece and the settlement of the western shore of Asia Minor suggest a demographic change, where the remnants of post-Mycenaean culture fled to the relative safety of the distant Aegean.

Facing: Detail of warriors from a Mycenaean vase of the 13th century. Their horned helmets and concave-base shields are clearly visible. As the Mycenaean realm fell further into civil war, the cities' warriors were less able to defend against invasions from outside. When the Dark Age fell, the culture of Mycenae survived in small enclaves, especially at Iolkos in Thessaly where even the old-style domed tombs (**below**) continued to be built.

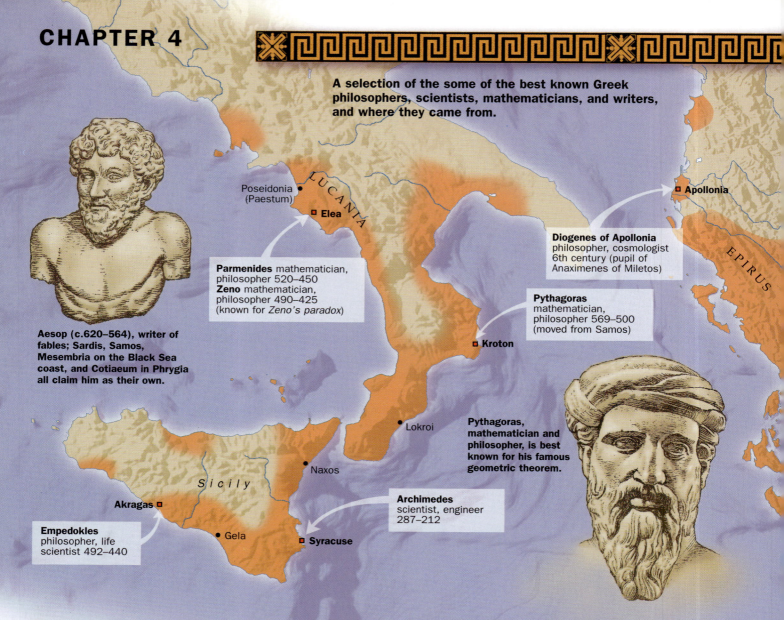

CHAPTER 4

A selection of the some of the best known Greek philosophers, scientists, mathematicians, and writers, and where they came from.

Diogenes of Apollonia philosopher, cosmologist 6th century (pupil of Anaximenes of Miletos)

Parmenides mathematician, philosopher 520–450
Zeno mathematician, philosopher 490–425 (known for *Zeno's paradox*)

Pythagoras mathematician, philosopher 569–500 (moved from Samos)

Poseidonia (Paestum)

Elea

Apollonia

LUCANIA

EPIRUS

Kroton

Lokroi

Aesop (c.620–564), writer of fables; Sardis, Samos, Mesembria on the Black Sea coast, and Cotiaeum in Phrygia all claim him as their own.

Pythagoras, mathematician and philosopher, is best known for his famous geometric theorem.

Sicily

Naxos

Akragas

Empedokles philosopher, life scientist 492–440

Gela

Archimedes scientist, engineer 287–212

Syracuse

THE THINKING PROCESS

Unlike the peoples of ancient Egypt or the Middle East, the Greeks do not appear a distant civilization, with little to connect them to the modern world. Instead, through their incredible legacy of literature and literary science, we have come to understand their society and what influenced their everyday lives. This outpouring of literature was a direct result of a new form of writing.

Before the eighth century, or rather until the onset of the Dark Age at the start of the 11th century, the Greeks used hieroglyphics. As with the Egyptian glyphs, the mass population did not use these complex pictographic symbols. Hieroglyphics were the exclusive preserve of royal scribes and administrators, who used them

as a bureaucratic tool to help their efficient ordering of early Greek society. Even when the script known as Linear B replaced hieroglyphics, it remained a restrictive writing form practiced by a minority, used as a tool of government rather than as a means of expression.

In the eighth century the Greeks adopted a new alphabet copied, then adapted, from the Phoenician writing system (*see page 17*). The concept that any known word could be recorded through the juxtaposition of individual letters was revolutionary. Compared to earlier systems of writing, the Greek alphabet was easy to learn, and fast and simple to write. Writing became the preserve of an educated minority rather than a closed administrative sect, while reading was an

Aristotle life scientist 390–330 (tutor to Alexander the Great, worked mostly in vicinity of Pella, later in Athens)

Protagoras philosopher 480–420
Demokritos philosopher 460–370

Greek territories and colonies, seventh to fifth centuries

BLACK SEA

MACEDON

Pella •

THRACE

Abdera •

Thasos •

Thasos

Byzantion •

SEA OF MARMARA

Methone •

Stageiros ▫

CHALKIDIKE

Poteidaia •

Samothrace

Imbros

Lampsakos ▫

Kyzikos ▫

Lemnos

THESSALY

AEGEAN SEA

Strato physicist 340–290

Kallipos astronomer 370–300

Sappho may have been born in either Eresos or Mytilene

Plutarch (Metrius Plutarchus) historian AD 45–125

Pindar poet active 550–446 Kynoskephelai, near Thebes

Eresos ▫

Mytilene ▪

Lesbos

Sappho poet 613–570
Alkaios poet contemporary of Sappho

Anaxagoras scientist, philosopher 480–430

Aesop? writer, poet 7th century
Pythagoras mathematician, philosopher 569–500 (moved to Kroton)
Epicurus philosopher 341–270

Delphi •

Chaironeia •

Thebes ▫

Chalkis •

Aischylos playwright 525–456

Chios

Klazomenai ▫

Thales astronomer 624–560
Anaximenes scientist 570–500
Hekataios philosopher 560–490
Leukippos scientist 5th century (introduced concept of atoms)

Ephesos ▫

Megara •

Eleusis ▫

Athens ▫

Samos ▫

Heraklitos philosopher 535–475

Corinth ▫

Miletos ▫

Herodotos historian 484–425

Olympia •

PELOPONNESE

Archilochos poet 7th century (creator of iambic meter, moved to Thasos)

Paros ▫

Naxos •

Halikarnassos ▫

Sparta •

Kos ▪

Pylos •

Kos

Epidauros •

Sophokles playwright 496–406
Euripides playwright 480–406
Thucydides historian 471–396
Sokrates philosopher 470–399
Aristophanes playwright 448–380
Antisthenes philosopher, cynic 440–370
Plato philosopher 430–350
Xenophon historian 430–335
Menander playwright 342–291
Chrysippos philosopher 280–207 (originally from Soli in Cilicia)

Hippocrates medicine 460–377

Rhodes

Rhodes ▫

Diogenes philosopher, cynic 390–323 (originally from Sinope on the Black Sea)

Eudemos mathematician 4th century

ability most educated Greeks came to possess.

It permitted the first philosophers to convey their reasoning and allowed the first historians to record the events that shaped their lives. Above all, it provided a wonderful vehicle for expression, and gave poets the tool they needed to enthrall listeners with their literary efforts. It gave Homer the chance to, as he put it, "always be best, and distinguished above the rest." Homer and his successors gave us the ability to understand the society of ancient Greece in a way that gives it immediacy. As

Homer wrote in the *Odyssey*, "He saw the cities of many men, and knew their mind."

This literary record of a long-lost civilization includes the first examples of poetry, prose, historical record, philosophical discussion, and drama—unparalleled access to the hopes, thoughts, memories, beliefs, and fears of the ancient Greeks. It can be argued that civilization as we understand it first appeared in Greece, and that the Homeric epic was the first expression of this cultural phenomenon.

HOMER AND THE GREEK LANGUAGE

As Greece emerged from its Dark Age, its adopted new alphabet created a versatile, rich language. The first real examples of its use were Homer's poetic epic masterpieces, the *Iliad* and the *Odyssey*. For the first time, Greek mythology was recorded.

Right: A Roman copy of a bust of Homer conveys the tragic face Greek sculptures liked to use to portray the visionary author.

According to mythology, the Greeks received their alphabet as a gift from the founder of Thebes, a Phoenician called Cadmus. Certainly the Greek alphabet has Phoenician roots, but it is more probable that traders introduced it to Greece as a substitute for

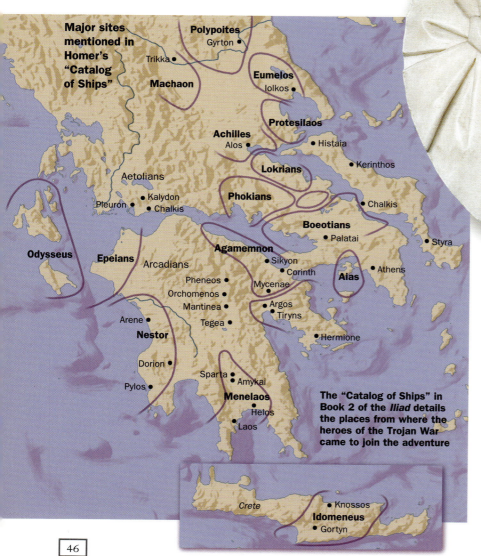

Major sites mentioned in Homer's "Catalog of Ships"

Polypoites
Gyrton

Trikka

Eumelos
Iolkos

Machaon

Protesilaos

Achilles
Alos
Histaia

Aetolians

Lokrians
Kerinthos

Kalydon
Pleuron
Chalkis

Phokians
Chalkis

Boeotians
Palatai
Styra

Agamemnon
Sikyon
Corinth
Athens

Odysseus
Epeians
Arcadians

Pheneos
Mycenae
Aias

Orchomenos
Argos
Tiryns

Mantinea

Arene
Tegea

Nestor
Hermione

Dorion

Sparta
Amykai

Pylos

Menelaos
Helos
Laos

Crete
Knossos
Idomeneus
Gortyn

The "Catalog of Ships" in Book 2 of the *Iliad* details the places from where the heroes of the Trojan War came to join the adventure

Linear B. Although elements of the older Linear B can still be identified in the new Greek script, all traces of the earlier Minoan hieroglyphic script had vanished. The Greeks made the new writing their own—the word *alphabet* derives from the first two letters of the Greek alphabet, *alpha* and *beta*. By the mid-eighth century, the new 20-letter Greek script seems to have been in use—albeit eight centuries after Cadmus died, which squashes the Theban myth. And at this time, the first of the great Greek authors began work.

The identity of Homer has long been questioned. Did he exist, or was he an amalgam of several writers? Did he write both of his epics, or was the *Odyssey*, written some 50 years after the *Iliad*, the work of a different author? A 19th-century writer even claimed Homer was a woman, but scholars have dismissed that theory.

Long before Homer began writing his epics in the eighth century, Greek bards must have told tales of the past, of the gods and of myth. Scholars have debated whether Homer (if he *did* write both the *Iliad* and the *Odyssey*) originated both works or if he only recorded the oral traditions of unknown storytellers. Aspects of his works have been criticized for their lack of accuracy, their intertwining of fact and fiction, and their implausible relationship between men, heroes, and the gods and monsters who walked the mythological earth. Despite all this, his were the first and possibly greatest works of poetry ever written.

Father of Greek religion

It is fairly certain that Homer was an Ionian, raised on the western shores of his "wine-dark sea," as he described the Aegean. His use of stock phrases and stylized passages, such as the way he described the Greeks donning their armor before the battle, hints at an oral source for the work. If that is the case, Homer collated the mass of myths and stories recited by Greek bards during the end of the Dark Age into poetic epics. Storytellers used traditional passages or stock phrases as an *aide memoire*, to help them remember long passages. This has been used to explain many of the historical inaccuracies in Homer's work.

Homer produced the first written account of the Greek gods, a fact that prompted Aristotle to describe him as the theological father of Greece. His gods displayed human fallibility and their activities were linked to the main plot as a constant thread, observing and influencing the course of history.

Homer's accounts of Greek warriors fighting outside Troy and Odysseus combating all manner of perils on his voyage home gave the Greeks heroes to emulate. The warrior spirit of the Greeks that allowed them to defeat the

Persians and gave Alexander the Great impetus to conquer half the known world was strongly influenced by the Homeric epics.

Homer's true genius was to set down the oral traditions of the early Greek world, allowing later Greeks to regard his work as a true account of a heroic past and an accurate portrayal of the pantheon of gods. His oeuvre had an incredible impact on the cultural development of the Greek world, ensuring that the new Greek language and literary works defined the nature of what it was to be Greek. His recording of the language, religion, and shared history of Greece was a unifying factor, binding the politically and culturally diverse elements of Greece into one recognizable civilization.

Above: The second- or third-century "Apotheosis of Homer" by the sculptor of Prienne—a small Greek town in Asia Minor—was found near to the Via Appia in Rome. Many such items were made to commemorate Homer as if the writer had become a god.

POETRY AND PROSE

The flowering of the Greek language created a surge of human development mirrored nowhere else at the time. At first Homeric epics dominated Greek poetry, but developments took it far beyond these confines.

Below: Detail from a fourth-century red-figured vase, by the potter Nikias, shows a group of musicians playing their instruments. It was common for public recitals of poetry to be accompanied by music, which in turn encouraged the development of complex choral works.

From its first inception until the end of the Classical Age, literature was not usually written for private consumption. Instead, it was designed for public performance, in front of small select groups or at large public gatherings. Homer's works drew from a long tradition of public storytelling, in the same way later Icelandic saga writers committed centuries of Scandinavian folklore, historical development, and mythology to paper.

The adoption of the Greek alphabet and the development of writing made literary composition possible. However, setting them down in written words created a definitive record of the previously ever-evolving tales and so curtailed both the bardic tradition and the stories' mutability. So the first written Greek poems—designed for public performance—became scripts read by performers without alteration or embellishment. And it can be assumed that early Greek poets adapted their oratory to suit their abilities and to match the needs of their audiences.

During the Classical Age, poetry and prose were written on papyrus sheets imported from Egypt and stored in a roll. It was not until the Hellenistic Age that papyrus gave way to the use of parchment, when early books (or codexes) were created by binding parchment leaves together. Private ownership of literary works was unusual, although it did happen—Athenian dramatist Euripides reputedly had a substantial collection, on which he drew for inspiration.

Early lyrical poets such as Archilochos, Alkaios, and Sappho recorded the trials of mankind through war, love, travel, emotion, and

Left: This Roman fresco painted in about the 1st century AD of a young woman with tablet and stylus is probably an idealized portrait of the Greek poet Sappho, who was born at some point between 630 and 612. An aristocrat with a wealthy husband, Sappho could choose to live how she pleased. She spent much time on the island of Lesbos, which was a cultural center at the time, but traveled widely. The Greeks of Syracuse were so honored by her visit to Sicily, they erected a statue to her. Poetry was customarily declaimed to the accompaniment of a lyre, so the poets were referred to as *lyrists*, and their verse as *lyrical*. Sappho was an innovator of lyric poetry, and one of the first poets to write from the first person, describing situations from the individual's point of view rather than that of the gods, muses, or fabled heroes.

temptation with a hitherto unknown level of emotion and realism. Poetic recitations involved one or more performers. Poems were sometimes recited with dramatic flourish, and sometimes sung. A musical accompaniment of flute or lyre appears to have been common. This encouraged the creation of choral narrative works. Religious odes, public epitaphs, and works of communal celebration were frequently designed for presentation by a choral group.

Particular examples include the public memorial by Simonides for King Leonidas of Sparta and the later works of the poet Pindar (active c.550–446), who specialized in formal, powerful pieces designed for female choruses. The tradition of poetry written in elegiac meter stemmed from these roots, producing somber and moving works for public mourning, or for the celebration of past heroes.

The romance of early prose

Prose developed later than poetry. It was first the preserve of philosophers, natural scientists, and historians, who strove to clarify their search for truth through reasoned argument and precise observation. It was not until the Hellenistic era, probably during the first century, that prose became a vehicle for dramatic expression. Although some scholars have dismissed the earliest examples of fictional prose as romantic works, their literary merit should not be ignored. Certainly many of the surviving examples (both complete and fragmentary) concern romantic assignations and their plotlines are similar to each other, but they also served as expressions of emotion, social comment, and often sharpened observation of the morals of a bygone age.

These were the world's first novels, and although designed for the private consumption of the Hellenistic middle and upper classes, they also show a sophistication of emotion and description that makes them ageless in their relevance. The Greeks were the first to record their hopes, fears, and emotions in writing, and through the surviving works we can understand this incredible people like no other society of the ancient world.

THE HISTORICAL NARRATIVE

Since the Bronze Age Greeks never produced written records of their deeds, scholars of the era rely on Homer's epics to supply a narrative. This changed in the fifth century, when a series of Greek writers produced the world's first historical narratives, free from mythology, religion, and poetic license.

Facing: Detail from a black-figured vase (c.540–530, Athenian, by the potter Exekias) shows Achilles vanquishing the Amazon champion Penthesilea at Troy. Vase painters invariably showed their heroes as naked, but this is artistic license—it seems unlikely that ancient Greek warriors really went to war as unprotected in front as this shows.

Right: Clockwise from the top—Herodotos, Thucydides, Plutarch, and Xenophon—pioneers who defined the shape of written history.

It has been said that the Greeks invented history. Certainly their tradition of producing historical narrative set the standards for all later historians, and although much of it has been lost over the centuries, the body of historical writing that survives forms a vital part of our understanding of the Greek world.

Unlike other ancient histories (such as those produced by the Hebrews or the early Romans), Greek historical writing attempts to distinguish between fact and fiction, avoiding circumstantial accounts in favor of maintaining a running narrative. This also means that unlike some contemporary historical works, it fails to catalog the writers' sources (unlike the later works of the Hebrew Josephus, for example). Reference to religion or mythology is avoided, in favor of straightforward accounts of mankind's endeavors. Like the contemporary Greek philosophers—and the newly emerging lyrist poets—by keeping religion separate from their work, Greek historians created a new intellectual discipline.

Poetry may have been the first recorded form of Greek writing, but as early as 500 the philosopher Hekataios of Miletos wrote his *Description of the Earth*, a narrative-style geographical study, supported by maps. Prose later became the accepted medium for philosophers and geographers, who employed reasoned argument and clear narrative to seek the truth. It was inevitable that history would be dealt with in the same way.

The man accredited as the father of modern history is Herodotos, born in the Ionian city of Halikarnassos in the early to mid-fifth century. He moved to the Greek mainland in about 440, where he wrote his *History*. It dealt with the recent war between Greece and Persia and included first-hand accounts and personal reminiscences. He was more a recorder of oral history than an archivist, but the result was one of the best military narratives ever written.

A warrior's life

Herodotus's work is not only the earliest example of pure Greek prose to survive, but also the world's first true history book. He described the Persian invasion of King Xerxes in 480, then expanded the work to cover the state of the world at the time, based on his travels, interviews, and research. A generation later, the Athenian general Thucydides wrote a history of the Peloponnesian War between Athens and Sparta (*see pages 128–139*). He commanded an Athenian force during the early campaigns of the war but his failure to relieve a besieged Athenian-held city during the Delion campaign of 424 (*see page 132*) led to his dismissal and exile from Athens.

He might have been a convenient scapegoat to cover other Athenian military disasters.

Like many later old soldiers, he decided to write his memoirs. By the time he was allowed to return to Athens in 404, Thucydides had started to produce his own *History*, the contemporary narrative of a soldier. He set out to write an impartial account of events, drawing on archival records, written statements, and first-hand accounts. Like the later prose-writing general Julius Caesar, his style was simple, direct, and succinct.

Thucydides died before the work was completed, having covered events from the outbreak of war in 431 until 411, when the war was nearing its weary conclusion. The narrative was continued by Athenian nobleman Xenophon, who traced the collapse of Athens in 404 and the establishment of a fragile peace. Xenophon went on to write his own masterly *Anabasis*, covering the campaigns of a Greek mercenary force against the Persians, culminating in the Battle of Cunaxa (401) and the retreat of the Greeks from Mesopotamia to the coast of the Black Sea.

The tradition established by these first Greek historians was continued by later writers such as Plutarch, and their work has provided modern historians with a scholarly and literary benchmark ever since.

THE INVENTION OF DRAMA

In drama, the Greeks invented a new art form. Cult followers of the god Dionysos produced the first plays during the sixth century. Following their lead, dramatists created the comedies, tragedies, and high dramas we have associated with theater ever since.

Right: Two Greek theatrical masks. The one on the left dates from the fifth century, while that of the comical slave on the right is from the second century.

Dionysos was originally one of the lesser Greek gods, a relatively late addition to the Olympian pantheon who came to be regarded as a fertility god. His adherents were reputedly prone to sacrificial dismemberment, but the sixth-century followers of Dionysos used dramatic speeches and actions to underpin their devotions. When the Athenian tyrant Peisistratos introduced a Dionysian festival during the late sixth-century, an artist named Thespis devised a sequence of dramatic exchanges between an orator and a Dionysian chorus on stage. His name provided the basis for the word "thespian," meaning actor.

Less than 50 years later the dramatist Aischylos (525–456) introduced the first written plays, involving troupes of no more than three masked actors. Actors and choruses were all-male and, because masks hid their faces and flowing gowns their bodies, the emphasis was on speech, not action.

The chorus (*orchestra*) provided off-stage commentaries, impersonating a supporting cast of animals in comedic pieces and acting as a counterpoint to acts of exceptional heroism or villainy acted out on the stage in tragedies and high dramas. The tenor of these dramas remained religious, since early productions were a unique combination of Dionysian worship and dramatic presentation.

Athens boasted the world's first theater, constructed next to the temple of Dionysos on the southern slope of the Acropolis. A later theater at Epidauros (*see picture, page 133*) is still regularly used. The shape of the theater evolved to become a semi-circular stage, surrounded by a tiered amphitheater of benches, while space for an *orchestra* was provided around the fringes of

Above: Men for all reasons—Euripides (top) and Sophokles covered the dramatic gamut of emotion and human frailty in their writing for the Greek stage.

the stage. In Epidauros, modern actors marvel at the acoustics, where a word whispered on stage can be heard at the back of the auditotorium.

Dramatic festivals lasted several days, with tragedies and a satyr play (a style which produced the term "satirical"), followed by a final day of comedic pieces. During the fifth century the Athenian theater was dominated by Sophokles (496–406), recognized as the greatest of the Greek dramatists, and Euripides (484–406), one of the greatest tragic dramatists of all time.

Birth of comedy and tragedy

Sophokles employed a directness to his works such as *Antigone* and *Oedipus Rex*, and the superb characterization he employed caught the imagination of theatergoers. He was a master of dramatic tension, bringing his plays to explosive conclusions that still excite audiences today. His works emphasized moral conflict, encouraging the audience to consider their own actions in the light of the fate of his characters.

By contrast, Euripides focused on the common emotions and weaknesses of mankind, and his characters remained accessible to the audience. The tragic finale often involved the

Above: Dating from 297–272, the theater of Dodona in Epirus is is set in an enclosed valley, with the auditorium—which originally seated over 14,000 spectators— partially cut into the acropolis hillside.

after the death of Euripides; in an age when Athens was losing its status as a dominant Greek power, people turned to comedy for relief.

The final day of most festivals was devoted to bawdy comedies, combining contemporary satire with slapstick sketches. The great master of this was Aristophanes (448–c.380).

His works were the talk of Athens, despite their frequent attacks on "the establishment" and the pompous nature of Athenian bureaucracy. Through Roman adaptations by Plautus, these works dominated theater until the time of Shakespeare. Greek comedy represented entertainment at its best: movement, catchy music and lyrics, witty recitations, and amusing, even ludicrously farcical plots. Comedy provided insight into accepted social, moral, and political conventions. Above all it remained irreverent, democratic, and hugely popular.

Greek theater survived the conquest of Greece by the Macedonians and remained popular in the Hellenistic period, but lacked enlightenment or social comment. Less than 50 plays survive from the Classical Age, serving as the invaluable inspiration for the great dramatists of the modern era.

actors subjecting their fate to the judgment of the gods, re-emphasizing the religious nature of Dionysian plays and creating dramatic interplay between reality, religion, and mythology. The production of tragedies appears to have ceased

DEVELOPMENT OF PHILOSOPHY

Philosophy has been defined as the quest for truth through the means of rational thought, without interference from the preconceptions and dogmas of external influences. An entirely new discipline, philosophy was a Greek intellectual development that radically altered man's view of himself and the world.

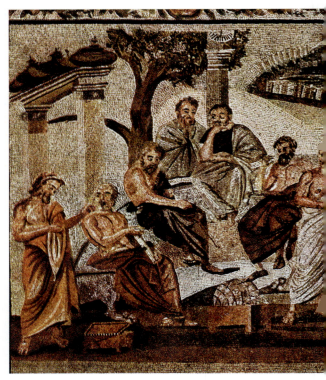

Below: The utterances of Sokrates placed him at odds with Athenian authorities, and he was sentenced to death. Famously, he chose to take poison.

The first known philosophers emerged during the sixth century, on the Ionian coast of the eastern Aegean. Fragments of their writings survived. They posed some of the fundamental questions, such as, "What caused the universe to be created?" and "How did it develop into the world we know today?"

Thales of Miletos was probably the first named Greek philosopher. He argued that the primal substance of the universe was water, since the liquid was fundamental to life. Anaximines, his philosophical sparring partner, disagreed, arguing that air was the most vital. In response, Empedokles the Sicilian claimed that earth, fire, air, and water were all critical elements, and were influenced by the two contradictory human states of love and discord. Heraklitos of Ephesos claimed the entire world was in a state of flux, without any discernible order.

What is astonishing about this first recorded example of philosophical debate on the basis of life is that there was no reference to the gods, thereby setting the standard of impartial thinking that all later philosophers strove to emulate. We know little about these first thinkers, but their debates encouraged later philosophers to use the same impartial principles.

Pythagoras, a native of the island of Samos off the Ionian coast, came to dominate the next generation of Greek philosophers. In about 531 he moved to the Greek colony of Kroton in southern Italy, where he established a religious academy and assisted in the town's government. He was the first philosopher to argue that, as an intellectual, he was an ideal person to govern a city, but today he is better remembered for his mathematical theories.

Apart from his famous mathematical theorem, Pythagoras advocated the portrayal of music as a mathematical exercise. More of a theologian and mathematician than a philosopher, he supported the theory of reincarnation, previously an alien notion to the Greeks. Above all, he tried to equate philosophy and mathematics, suggesting that the problems of both could be solved with the application of logic.

The nucleus of philosophy

The next school of philosophers sprang up in Athens, when Anaxagoras befriended Perikles, the Athenian statesman, and settled in the city around the start of the fifth century. Adherents such as Demokritos and Leukippos took the debate over the composition of life a stage further, when they argued that matter consisted of tiny atoms, two millennia before the concept was taken seriously. The Athenian tradition of philosophical discussion paved the way for the most celebrated thinkers of the ancient world.

Sokrates (469–399) questioned the accepted order of society, morals, and religion to such an extent that he was considered a menace. His rigorous dismemberment of other's arguments through reasoned discourse earned him the enmity of his peers, and despite his service to the state, he was accused of corrupting the youth of Athens. Sentenced to death, he elected to drink poison, freeing the Athenians of rigorous moral and intellectual scrutiny, but ensuring his style of analytical thinking would form the basis of future philosophical debates.

Sokrates transformed the study of philosophy by concentrating on matters of ethics. He was also modest enough to acknowledge his failings. When the Oracle of Delphi pronounced him the wisest man in Greece, Sokrates retorted that his wisdom stemmed from his acceptance that he knew nothing.

His greatest disciple, Plato (c.427–348), continued to espouse Sokrates' methods, but exceeded his mentor's achievements by promulgating his thoughts through extensive writing. Plato was probably the greatest of the Greek philosophers, capable of turning complex intellectual arguments into dialogs that almost any reader could follow. His most radical theme

of idealism argued that every object or thought is a shadow of an original idea or form. These original forms could be revealed through thought and reasoning. The Academy set up by Plato attracted some of the most prominent Athenians of the age and helped to shape the political and cultural outlook of Athens throughout the Classical Age.

Left: A Roman mosaic from Pompeii depicts Sokrates' greatest disciple, Plato, in a symposium with some of his students.

Right: A red-figure cup by Kleophon shows a symposium scene. A symposium was a relaxed drinking party—generally of Athens—at which ostensibly verse was quoted and philosophical matters discussed. However, for the all-male guest list, entertainment was frequently offered in the form of music and courtesans.

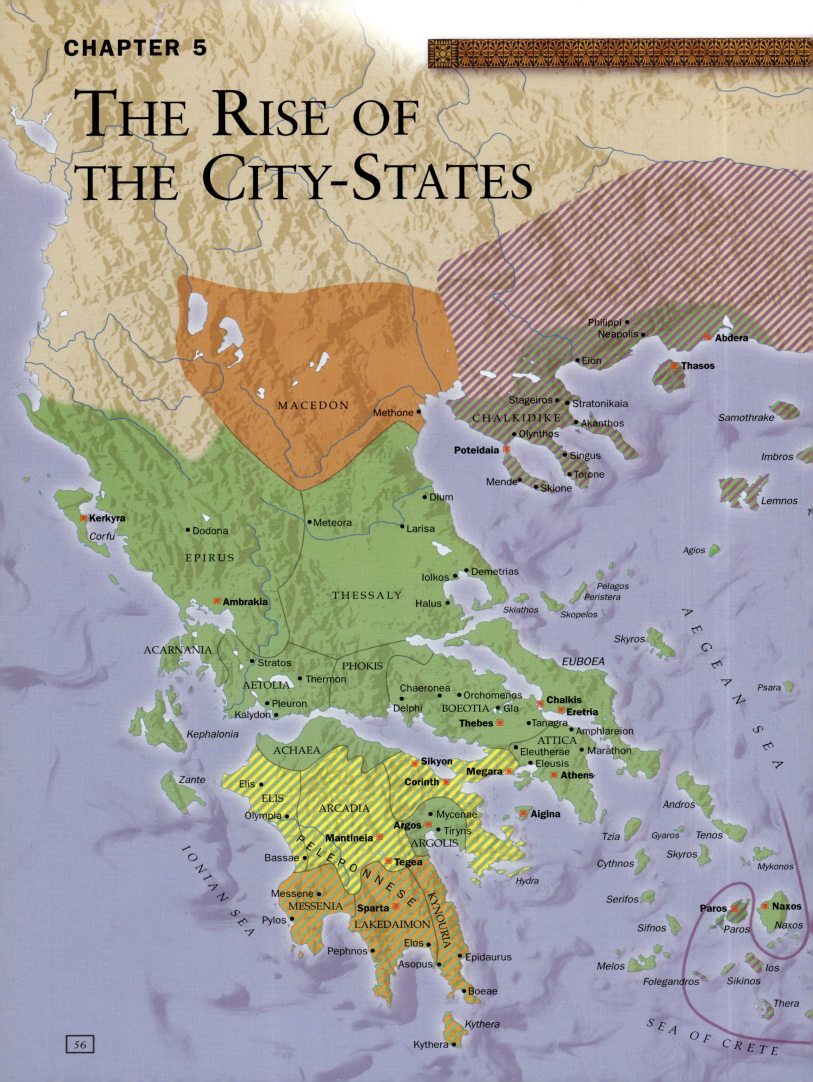

MACEDON

Philippi
Neapolis
Abdera
Eion
Thasos
Stageiros
Stratonikaia
CHALKIDIKE
Akanthos
Olynthos
Samothrake
Poteidaia
Singus
Torone
Mende
Skione
Imbros

Lemnos

Methone

Dium

Kerkyra
Corfu
Dodona
Meteora
Larisa

EPIRUS

Agios

Iolkos
Demetrias

Pelagos
Peristera

Ambrakia
THESSALY
Halus
Skiathos
Skopelos

Skyros

A E G E A N   S E A

ACARNANIA
Stratos
PHOKIS
EUBOEA
Psara
AETOLIA
Thermon
Chaeronea
Orchomenos
Delphi
Chalkis
Pleuron
BOEOTIA
Gla
Eretria
Kalydon
Thebes
Tanagra
Amphlareion

Kephalonia
ATTICA
Andros
ACHAEA
Sikyon
Eleutherae
Marathon
Zante
Elis
Corinth
Megara
Eleusis
Athens
ELIS
ARCADIA
Mycenae
Aigina
Tzia
Gyaros
Tenos
Olympia
Argos
Tiryns
Skyros
Mantineia
ARGOLIS
Cythnos
PELOPONNESE
Bassae
Tegea
Hydra
Serifos
I O N I A N   S E A
Mykonos
Messene
KYNOURIA
MESSENIA
Sparta
Sifnos
Paros
Naxos
Pylos
LAKEDAIMON
Paros
Naxos
Pephnos
Elos
Epidaurus
Asopus
Melos
Ios
Boeae
Folegandros
Sikinos
Kythera
Thera
Kythera

S E A   O F   C R E T E

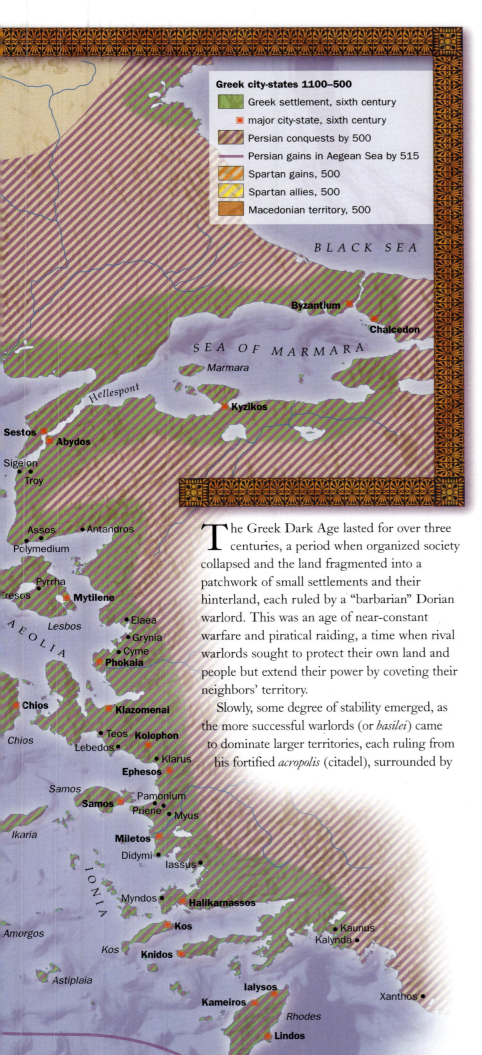

BLACK SEA

Byzantium

Chalcedon

SEA OF MARMARA

Marmara

Hellespont

Kyzikos

Sestos

Abydos

Sigeion

Troy

Assos

Antandros

Polymedium

Pyrrha

resos

Mytilene

Elaea

Lesbos

Grynia

AEOLIA

Cyme

Phokaia

Chios

Klazomenai

Chios

Teos Kolophon

Lebedos

Klarus

Ephesos

Samos

Pamonium

Samos

Priene

Myus

Ikaria

Miletos

Didymi

Iassus

IONIA

Myndos

Halikarnassos

Amorgos

Kos

Kaunus

Kalynda

Kos

Knidos

Astiplaia

Ialysos

Xanthos

Kameiros

Rhodes

Lindos

the peasants who worked his land and sustained his troops. A gradual re-emergence of overseas trade arose through increasing demand for imported luxury goods, feeding the warlords' desires to improve their living conditions. This in turn created a demand for skilled artisans—metalworkers, armorers, potters, and builders—who formed a new middle-class community in expanding urban centers.

The Dorian invasion of the 12th century led to a Greek diaspora, as many communities fled to the islands of the Aegean, or settled as far away as Ionia, on the western shore of Asia Minor, or in Cyprus. This led to a notion that there were two types of Greeks: the Dorians and the original (and in their eyes), more civilized inhabitants. While the former are exemplified by the Spartans, the latter included the Athenians, who claim that their city was founded by Ionian settlers who returned to the mainland during the latter part of the Dark Age.

In time, this increase in trade and the need for maritime communication encouraged the establishment of Greek trading colonies even further afield, from the Iberian peninsula (modern Spain) to Egypt. Trade also led to the flow of ideas and, as the settlements became cities and their hinterlands became small states, a re-awakening of cultural values that lead them out of the Dark Age. Encouraged by the newly adopted alphabet, literature flourished alongside craftsmanship and the foundations of Greek culture were laid.

Like their counterparts on the mainland of Greece or in the Aegean basin, these colonies became city-states in their own right. Although their political structure at home and abroad was still varied, there was a growing tendency for power to be dispersed. Increasingly, *basilei* and the tyrants who succeeded them were forced to share the administration of the city-states with oligarchies, and later still the roots of democratic government were established for the first time.

Although warfare between city-states continued and larger political alliances came and went, the trend was toward co-operation in trade and diplomacy. While each city-state remained fiercely independent, it was tempered by a growing awareness of Greek unity, an ideal that would come into being just in time to meet the threat posed by the Persians.

The Greek Dark Age lasted for over three centuries, a period when organized society collapsed and the land fragmented into a patchwork of small settlements and their hinterland, each ruled by a "barbarian" Dorian warlord. This was an age of near-constant warfare and piratical raiding, a time when rival warlords sought to protect their own land and people but extend their power by coveting their neighbors' territory.

Slowly, some degree of stability emerged, as the more successful warlords (or *basilei*) came to dominate larger territories, each ruling from his fortified *acropolis* (citadel), surrounded by

THE DARK AGE

Between c.1100 and 800, the Bronze Age civilization was swept away and Doric invaders seized power and land. Although cultural development was all but extinguished, life continued for most Greeks, and the structure of a new society slowly emerged.

When the Bronze Age Mycenaean culture was destroyed by a combination of internal strife and external attack, all centralized power in Greece was lost. The nomadic Dorian invaders from the north conquered then settled on the Greek mainland and the Aegean islands. While the Ionian cities on the eastern shore of the Aegean Sea claimed that they were founded by Greeks fleeing the Dorian invaders, the majority of Greeks appear to have accepted their new barbarian overlords.

Little is known of the development of Greece during these three centuries, but it is clear that its inhabitants lived in small scattered settlements—all traces of a larger state structure had been eradicated. Each settlement was ruled by a local *basileios* (warlord; *lit.* kingly) and, in a protection system akin to the feudalism of medieval Europe, he protected the local peasants from harm in return for their labor in his fields.

For these common Greeks, life would probably have changed little from the Mycenaean era, since a similar form of feudalism had existed under the Bronze Age kings of Mycenae and other fortress cities. They still lived in brick or mud hovels, clustered around the fortified dwelling of the *basileios* and his warrior companions. Life was as hard as it had always been. What was different was the lack of an artistic class; artisans capable of producing decorative ceramics, metalwork, or fine ornaments. It would be the reappearance of this middle class that encouraged Greece to emerge from its Dark Age.

Significantly, the one exception was in metalwork, because the later Dorians brought the secrets of a new technology with them. By the start of the first millennium, Greece had entered the Iron Age, where the secrets of iron smelting and forging led to the replacement of bronze weapons with stronger iron ones. In Greece, the production of weaponry and armor remained the prime task for Dark Age smiths.

Ironware for all

Cheaper to produce and work than bronze, iron became more commonplace. Bronze had been the preserve of the elite in the form of arms, armor, and luxury items; iron was used to produce a range of items, from weapons to tools. It was essentially a more egalitarian metal.

This was an age of instability, raiding, and near-constant warfare, when the scattered communities were only safe when their *basileios* was strong enough to resist attack. The warlords of Dark Age Greece frequently raided the territories of their rivals by land or sea, seizing cattle and people from weaker neighbors. In a society lacking structured economy, wealth was measured in livestock and slaves, and the easiest way to enrich yourself was to take from others at the point of a sword.

The major achievement of the Dark Age period was the spread of the Greek population over a wider area, as communities attempted to flee from invaders. New communities were established throughout the Aegean, on the western coast of Asia Minor (a coastal strip known as Ionia), and in Cyprus. Although they

Right: During the Dark Age, local warlords raised their own warrior forces, the basis of the more professional armies that would flower in the Archaic and Classical Ages. This warrior figure dates from the end of the Dark Age.

c.1100 Dorians invade Greece and establish settlements	c.1100 Beginning of the Greek Dark Age	c.1000 Greece enters the Iron Age	c.800 End of the Greek Dark Age	c.750 Communities established by warlords have expanded into cities	c.750 A second wave of Greek colonies is established overseas	c.700 City-states are ruled by oligarchies or tyrants	c.660 Tyrants begin to be replaced by democracies

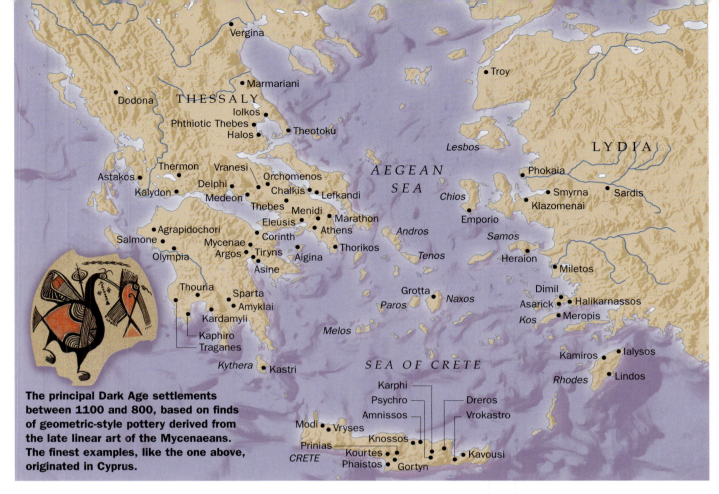

The principal Dark Age settlements between 1100 and 800, based on finds of geometric-style pottery derived from the late linear art of the Mycenaeans. The finest examples, like the one above, originated in Cyprus.

developed along the same lines as those left behind in Greece, they maintained a degree of independence. Their perceived link with a cultural past led these people to consider themselves civilized Greeks—as opposed to their "barbaric" neighbors, who had been assimilated by the Dorians.

Inevitably, when certain *basilei* proved more successful than others in raiding and hoarding wealth (or at least livestock and slaves), their status increased, as did the size of the communities they ruled. By the ninth century some of these warlords had established themselves as heads of sizeable communities, and within another century these

emerged as the first city-states, the political unit that would dominate Greece for the remainder of the ancient period.

Left: Representations of archers in Greek art are rare, since the preferred weaponry was the spear and sword. The most widely used archers toward the end of the Dark Age were Cretan mercenaries, who mostly served with the Spartans of Lakedaimon. For hunting—both as recreation and a necessity—the bow and arrow were more useful. This relief shows two archers, who probably represent the divine hunters Apollo and Artemis.

c.650	c.600	c.590	c.550	511	510	508	c.500
Greek colonies established throughout the Mediterranean	Sparta is the dominant city-state in Greece	Athenian society is reformed under new leader Solon	At Corsica, Etruscans and Carthaginians defeat a Greek fleet	Peloponnesian League captures Athens, after ousting tyrant Peisistratos	Kleisthenes and Spartan King Kleomenes oust the tyrant Hippias from Athens	Struggle between Kleisthenes and oligarchic Isagoras results in Athenian democracy	Athens enlarges army and creates a navy against the Peloponnesian threat

EARLY DEVELOPMENT

Improved agriculture and increased trade of the Iron Age led to the establishment of small city-states. Beginning in the eighth century, these expanded in power and size during the 400 years of the Archaic period, to create the political landscape that would continue to dominate the Greek world for centuries.

Below: At the heart of Greek cities, the *agora* was an open market space that became the center for political debate. The Agora of ancient Athens is now a ruin, topped by the Theseion temple (Temple of Hephaistos, or the Hephaisteion).

The advent of the Iron Age during the Dark Age created an agricultural revolution, since increased access to cheaply produced metal farming implements encouraged an increase in agrarian production. The need for greater agricultural output was there because the increasingly powerful city-states run by the most successful *basilei* had expanded by the eighth century, and large, non-agricultural communities needed to be supported. In return, these communities produced the iron and bronze objects Greeks of the new Archaic society demanded, and which formed the basis for a growing mercantile economy.

As the more powerful *basilei* prospered, they demanded better standards of living. In turn, this created a market for metalwork, wine, weapons, ceramics, furnishings, and all the trappings of wealth. Since much of this had to be imported, it meant that Greece had to manufacture high-quality goods for exchange on the new market. A new middle class of freemen—merchants, craftsmen, large-scale farmers—arose to serve this new demand, a group that would come to rival the aristocracy in economic power.

Around the opulent strongholds of the wealthiest *basilei*, small cities took form, in which the warlord's wants increasingly had to be balanced with those of his citizens. In their physical form, these settlements resembled large-scale versions of the hamlets of old: the lord up on his fortified *acropolis*, the houses of the people huddled below. Beyond lay the fields and olive groves, still the community's economic engine and very much part of the city, for the ancient Greeks never saw town and country as separate places.

The heart of politics

The *agora* at the city's heart was a new development, however: an open space specially designed for citizens to shop, walk, talk, and

debate. That men's opinions, freely expressed, might matter in the scheme of things was a new concept to Greece and, as far as we know, without precedent in any other civilization. The *polis*, or city-state, is the great political invention of ancient Greece—and is the origin of the modern word "politics." For the moment, the aristocracy still exercised unquestioned power, but the very existence of the *agora* hinted at the way things were changing.

The *polis* soon became the defining element of Greek culture. To Aristotle it was the principal distinguishing feature that raised mankind above the animals, and he saw the city-state as the ideal political unit, regardless of its form of government. It was large enough to defend its perimeter and to maintain its cultural integrity, but small enough to ensure it could be governed efficiently. Aristotle wrote that the government of city-states conformed to one of three types: tyrannies, oligarchies, or democracies, and he outlined the merits and limitations of each.

The nature of the Greek political landscape is discussed in chapter six, but apart from Sparta, which retained a king, the city-states at home and overseas were ruled by governments of the types outlined by Aristotle. These small, independent city-states lacked unity, apart from a series of changing alliances with neighboring powers, but they could band together in extreme circumstances, such as during the Persian invasions, or for cultural events, such as the Olympic games. While this lack of unity prevented the creation of an all-embracing state, it ensured that each city developed into a balanced economic model, with an agricultural base able to provide for its citizens.

By the seventh century, the small city-states had established themselves as the political and cultural building blocks of ancient Greece, and they would continue to dominate the Greek political landscape for the next four centuries.

Eleusis and the cult of Demeter

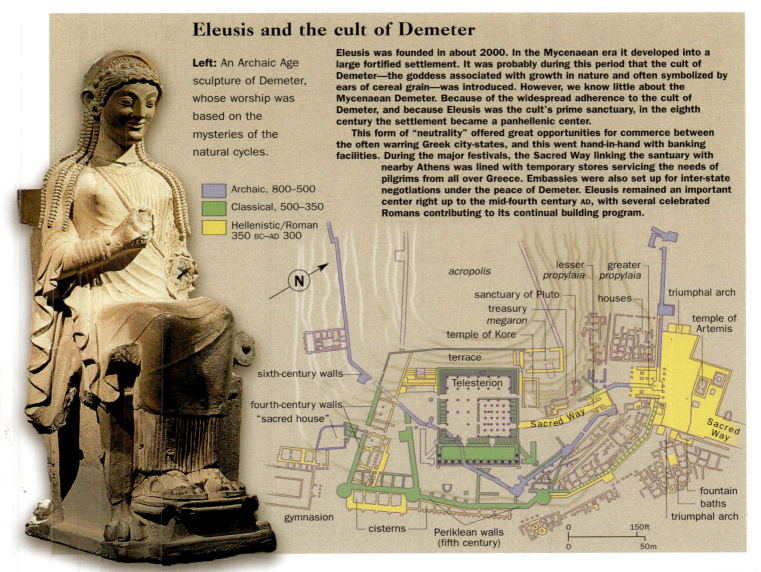

Left: An Archaic Age sculpture of Demeter, whose worship was based on the mysteries of the natural cycles.

Eleusis was founded in about 2000. In the Mycenaean era it developed into a large fortified settlement. It was probably during this period that the cult of Demeter—the goddess associated with growth in nature and often symbolized by ears of cereal grain—was introduced. However, we know little about the Mycenaean Demeter. Because of the widespread adherence to the cult of Demeter, and because Eleusis was the cult's prime sanctuary, in the eighth century the settlement became a panhellenic center.

This form of "neutrality" offered great opportunities for commerce between the often warring Greek city-states, and this went hand-in-hand with banking facilities. During the major festivals, the Sacred Way linking the sanctuary with nearby Athens was lined with temporary stores servicing the needs of pilgrims from all over Greece. Embassies were also set up for inter-state negotiations under the peace of Demeter. Eleusis remained an important center right up to the mid-fourth century AD, with several celebrated Romans contributing to its continual building program.

Archaic, 800–500

Classical, 500–350

Hellenistic/Roman 350 BC–AD 300

N

acropolis

lesser propylaia

greater propylaia

sanctuary of Pluto

houses

triumphal arch

treasury megaron

temple of Kore

temple of Artemis

terrace

sixth-century walls

Telesterion

fourth-century walls "sacred house"

Sacred Way

Sacred Way

fountain

baths

triumphal arch

gymnasion

cisterns

Periklean walls (fifth century)

0   150ft

0   50m

COLONIZATION

As trade blossomed in the eighth century, Greek communities were established overseas, creating trading enclaves and colonies. While many retained links with their *metropolis*, or mother city, others expanded into thriving city-states in their own right.

Agathe
Massilia
Emporion
CORSICA
Ala
SARDINIA
BALEARIC ISLANDS
Hemeroskopeion
Malaca
Mainake
Sexi
Tharros
Sulcis
Caralis
Nora
Lixus
M E D I T E R R A N E A N S E A
Utica
Carthage

Legend	
■	Greek homeland, 11th–10th centuries
■	Etruscan city-states, c.500
■	Phoenicia, c.500
■	coast under Greek influence
■	coast under Phoenician influence by 6th century

Greek settlements
- ● 11th–10th centuries
- ● 9th century
- ● 8th century
- ● 7th century settlement or trading post
- ● 6th century settlement or trading post

During the Dark Age, Greek colonies were established in the Aegean islands and on the eastern shores of the Aegean Sea. The majority thrived, particularly on the Ionian coast, some even rivaling the political power and cultural influence of the emergent city-states on the Greek mainland. The early colonies were created as a result of the Dorian invasion of the Greek mainland, which precipitated the Dark Age.

The second wave of colonial expansion, which began in the mid-eighth century, marked the Greek world's emergence from this phase of history and the renaissance of political and economic organization—the Archaic period. The colonies were not part of an imperialist drive, but represented a desire to expand beyond the country's limiting geographical confines. Although the precise rationale behind the creation of overseas settlements is unknown, the theory that there were simply too many mouths to feed in the city-states is the most plausible.

The creation of new colonies was a highly organized process—a new settlement was set up as a mirror image of its *metropolis*, with the same political structure, laws, and even religious temples or cults as the parent city. These colonies tended to be established on the coast and in areas where trading links were already established.

By the mid-seventh century Greek colonies had been created around the shores of the Black Sea, in Libya (Kyrene), southern Italy, Sicily, and even the coast of what is now southern France. All these regions produced goods that could be imported to Greece: wool from North Africa,

Italy, and Asia Minor, grain from the Black Sea coast, grain, dye, and hides from Sicily, and papyrus from Egypt, where a small Greek colony was established around 650. In effect, a handful of Greek cities spawned hundreds of colonies clustered around the Mediterranean—as Sokrates put it, "like frogs around a pond."

War saps expansion

The first wave of colonization in the eighth century established settlements in southern Italy and Sicily. Most Greek cities were involved in developing colonies, although Athens and Sparta proved the most prolific in these regions. Sicily was so successful as a Greek colonial region that the Romans called the island *Magna Graecia* (Greater Greece). The prosperity of the Sicilian colonies stemmed from the production of wheat, becoming the principal sources of wheat imports to the cities of mainland Greece. The Corinthian colony of Syracuse was by far

Spina

ADRIATIC SEA

Gravisca

Kymai
Pithekoussai — Neapolis
Poseidonia — Pixous
Elea — Siris — Taras
Skidros — Laos — Satyrion
Metapontum
Soloeis — Hipponion — Sybaris
Himera — Medma — Terina
anormos — Zankle — Mataos
Motya — Mylai — Kaulonia
elinus — Minoa — Lokroi
Akragas — Rhegion
Gela
Kamarina
MAGNA
GRAECIA

Naxos
Katana
Megara
Leontinoi
Syracuse
Akrai

Epidamnos

Apollonia

Corfu

Sava   *Danube*

THRACE

Torone   Neapolis
Sane   Thasos
Akanthos   Abdera
Stageiros   Maroneia
Poteidaia
Mende   Ainos
Methone   Kardia
              Madytos
              Sigeion   Limnai
Skioni   Methymna Lampsakos
              Eresos   Abydos
                        Elaious
Chalkis
Eretria   Ilium
Corinth   Phokaia   Erythrai
                        Klazomenai
Athens   Chios   Kolophon
Megara   Teos   Lebedos
Sparta   Samos   Ephesos
              Priene   Myus
              Miletos
Kydonia   Kos   Halikarnassos
              Knidos
Knossus   Kameiros Ialysos
Gortyn   RHODES   Lindos
CRETE

Olbia
Berezean Island
Tyras

Istros

Kallatis
Odessos   Mesembria
              Apollonia
              Byzantium Chalkedon

BLACK SEA

Kytoros   Sinope
           Sesamos
Herakleia Tios
Keiros

Pantikapaion
Mirmekion
Phanagoria
Hermonassa
Theodosia
Nymphaion
Kimmerikon

Dioskurias
Phasis

Trapezous
Kersous

PHRYGIA

Soloi
Side
Phaselis   Kelenderis
Nagidos   Al Mina

CYPRUS   Tell Sukas

**In 531, the
philosopher and
mathematician
Pythagoras moved
from Samos to Kroton**

**Cyprus was largely settled
by Mycenaeans in the the
late 13th century**

Byblos
Sidon
Tyre

MEDITERRANEAN SEA

Leptis Magna
Kinyps

Ptolemais   Apollonia
Taucheira   Kyrene Aziris Platea Island
             Barca
Eusperides
KYRENAIA

Mesad Hashaviahu

Naukratis
Memphis

Daphnai

EGYPT

Nile

the most prosperous Sicilian settlement,
although Akragas (Roman Agrigentum) ran it a
close second.

During the early seventh century, Greek
colonies were founded around the Black Sea
and the Dardanelles, most established by the
Ionian city-state of Miletos. The Libyan colony
of Kyrene spawned subsidiary colonies on the
North African coast, although Carthage, a
Phoenician settlement in what is now Tunisia,
increasingly opposed expansion in this region and
in Sicily. The Ionian Greek settlement established
at Massilia (now Marseilles) in about 600
rapidly expanded into a thriving economic port
that dominated trade between Greece and the
Gallic hinterland. Subsidiary Massilian colonies
were later established in three other locations on
the Mediterranean coast of Gaul.

The Peloponnesian War in the late fifth
century ended this colonial drive, as the city-
states became embroiled in a battle for
supremacy between Athens and Sparta. While
many colonies supported the political and
military actions of their *metropolis*, others elected
to emphasize their independence and tried to
avoid being sucked into the war. Many had
their own military problems, as the increasing
power of the local states of Rome, Macedon,
and Carthage led to conflict and eventually loss
of political independence.

Although Alexander the Great and his
successors created new Greek cities in Asia, these
were founded in a different manner, political
and military factors outweighing economic
motives. Today, the ruins of Greek temples and
cities around the Mediterranean basin serve as
reminders of the economic and political
influence once wielded by the Greek city-states.

THE RISE OF SPARTA

Unlike most emergent city-states, Sparta was ruled by a monarch, backed by a powerful military force. The Spartans considered themselves direct descendants of the Dorians, and they retained their ancestors' warlike nature. By the seventh century, Sparta was the dominant power in southern Greece.

The Dorians and their Spartan successors conquered Lakedaimon, in the southern Peloponnese, enslaved part of the population, and ruled the remainder. The slaves (*helots*) were forced to work on farms run by the state, which provided provisions for the Spartan monarchy, oligarchy, administration, and army. The remainder of the Lakedaimonian population were *perioeci*, akin to medieval feudal serfs but with the added imposition of having to provide troop contingents for the Spartan army.

By the end of the seventh century, Sparta had extended its boundaries by conquering neighboring Messenia, which ensured Spartan control over the entire southern Peloponnese.

In the sixth century Spartan power extended through the Peloponnese when, through a combination of force and diplomacy, a Spartan-led confederation of all Peloponnesian city-states was created. The Peloponnesian League (or more accurately "the Lakedaimonians and their allies," as the Spartans styled the confederation) was the largest political unit in the Greek world and caused concern among neighboring states, who naturally felt threatened.

The first serious offensive action by the Peloponnesian League came in 511. The tyrant Peisistratos and his son had ruled Athens for almost half a century when a confrontation with Sparta led to war. King Kleomenes led a Spartan army into Attica, ousting the tyrant family from power and temporarily seizing power in Athens. The Athenians rebelled and besieged Kleomenes and his small Spartan army in the Acropolis.

Kleomenes was forced into a humiliating capitulation, and when the king returned home he mobilized the entire Peloponnesian League against Athens. At that time, Sparta had two

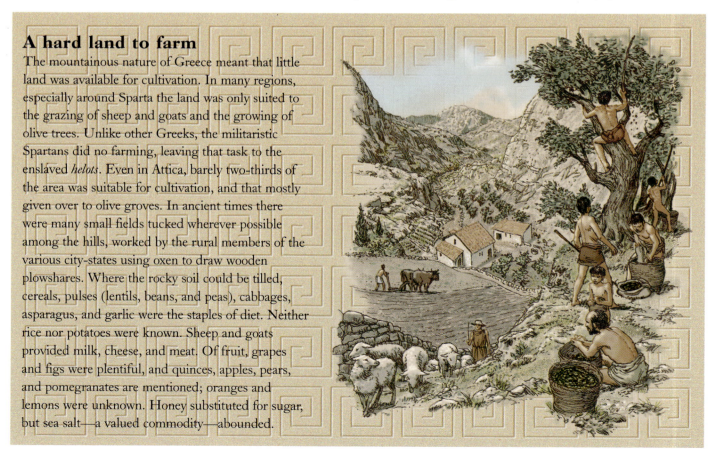

A hard land to farm

The mountainous nature of Greece meant that little land was available for cultivation. In many regions, especially around Sparta the land was only suited to the grazing of sheep and goats and the growing of olive trees. Unlike other Greeks, the militaristic Spartans did no farming, leaving that task to the enslaved *helots*. Even in Attica, barely two-thirds of the area was suitable for cultivation, and that mostly given over to olive groves. In ancient times there were many small fields tucked wherever possible among the hills, worked by the rural members of the various city-states using oxen to draw wooden plowshares. Where the rocky soil could be tilled, cereals, pulses (lentils, beans, and peas), cabbages, asparagus, and garlic were the staples of diet. Neither rice nor potatoes were known. Sheep and goats provided milk, cheese, and meat. Of fruit, grapes and figs were plentiful, and quinces, apples, pears, and pomegranates are mentioned; oranges and lemons were unknown. Honey substituted for sugar, but sea salt—a valued commodity—abounded.

hereditary kings, who ruled concurrently. Accompanied by his co-ruler Demaratos, Kleomenes returned to Attica at the head of a powerful army. The Attican neighbors Thebes and Chalkis promptly declared an alliance with the Spartans.

Slave threat

At that point, with Athens threatened by imminent destruction, an argument flared up between the two kings, which spread to the minor states of the league. The majority decided the war had become an instrument for personal revenge by Kleomenes, and the troops returned home. The Spartan war machine had been stopped by dissent, and probably by Athenian bribes. Taking advantage of the situation, the Athenian army marched north, defeated the Thebans and Chalkidians, and turned Chalkis into a colonial puppet-state.

While the war dragged on into the early fifth century, Athens had weathered the storm, and set about enlarging her army. In response to an existing alliance between Thebes and the island power of Aigina, the Athenians also took the first steps toward creating a navy. The seeds

were sown for the eventual clash between a militaristic Spartan empire and a maritime Athenian one; the Peleponnese War would bring the Greek world to its knees. Although the city-states continued to war with each other and to form alliances, these conflicts would increasingly be dominated by the two leading city-states of the ancient Greek world.

The rapid expansion of Sparta from a small city-state to the dominant power in the Peloponnese brought the seeds of Sparta's eventual destruction. Following the capture of Helos in Lakedaimon, parts of the population of captured cities were made *helots*, altering the social balance in the region. This was the only way the growing Spartan economy could survive; using slave labor to support military endeavors.

Helots greatly outnumbered Spartan citizens and the prospect of an uprising was always present, despite inevitably harsh retribution for any revolt. The Spartans were surrounded by a combination of resentful slaves and equally resentful allies. Spartan power was maintained through her army, and when the power of the army crumbled after its costly victory in the Peloponnesian War, Sparta's decline was assured.

Above: View of the archaeological site of ancient Sparta. Never a large city, it lost importance when Roman occupation began and was abandoned in AD 396, after invading Goths destroyed it.

OLIGARCHS AND TYRANTS

The Greek *polities* shared a common language, culture, and religion, but their political structure varied during the Archaic period. Despite their independence, the majority underwent a similar transition, steadily moving toward democracy.

The Archaic Age, from the end of the Dark Age in the seventh century until the Persian Wars in the first decade of the fifth century, was a time of political and economic development. The rise of the *polis* became the unitary framework on which a variety of political systems was placed.

A *polis* was a community of citizens, whether they were the urban inhabitants of the city or rural farmers in its hinterland who supplied the city with produce. The majority were created following the emergence of a single city, but in a handful of cases several smaller settlements joined forces through *synoikismos* (coming to live together) to form a more powerful political unit.

The *basilei* of the late Dark Age were effectively minor kings, ruling in a similar style to the earlier kings of Mycenaean Greece or Minoan Crete. Power gradually devolved from single powerful warlords to small oligarchic groups. These were often formed from a council of elders, ruling as city magistrates, all members of a tightly knit group known as the *aristoi* (the "best people," those with land and wealth). The exception to this growth of aristocracy was Sparta, where the state was ruled by two kings, supported by annually appointed *ephors* (magistrates) and a council of *gerousia* (elders).

The rise of democracy

For short periods rule by a single person returned in the form of the *tyrannos* (tyrants). They were usually members of the aristocracy appointed to rule by popular acclaim. For the Greeks the term lacked its modern connotations of despotism. According to Thucydides in his *History*: "Indeed, generally their government was not grievous to the multitude, or in any way odious in practice."

It was the oligarchs who first encouraged Greek colonial expansion, since they feared the presence of disaffected elements among a growing population. In turn, the expansion of colonialism and trade created a new mercantile and land-owning middle class. Although they owned land and property, they had no say in power. This lack of political determination became increasingly resented, and Archaic oligarchs found it difficult to retain control.

When established, tyrants tended to pander to the mass of the population, which undermined oligarchic power through the curbing of their influence in the city. Even Athens, the shining example of democracy in the Classical Age, had its share of oligarchs and tyrants during the seventh and sixth centuries.

Tyrants had become a political rarity by the end of the sixth century, and politics in Greece had become a power struggle between the oligarchs on one hand and representatives of the rest of the populace on the other. In this climate of political confusion, members of the new land-owning middle class were often admitted into the ranks of the oligarchy

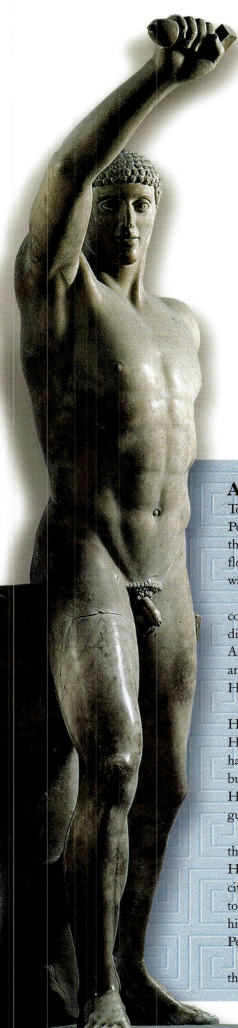

Left: *The Tyrannicides,* sculpted by Antenor at the end of the sixth century, depict Aristogeiton (left) and Harmodios, the two Anthenians who attempted to overthrow the joint tyrants Hippias and Hipparchos. The statues, which were seized by Xerxes in 480 and carried away, were discovered in the Persian city of Susa by Alexander and sent back to Athens.

to strengthen political control. The majority of the lower social strata favored the notion that all citizens of a *polis* should have a say in government. By the start of the fifth century the seeds of democracy had been sown.

This was a period of near-constant warfare between the city-states, when a well-equipped infantry type, the *hoplite*, emerged. Drawn from the ranks of the midde classes, *hoplites* fought for their city, and in return expected a say in its development.

Several unpopular oligarchies were replaced by military tyrants, placed in power by cities' soldiers to encourage the sharing of power. Even tyrants needed to remain popular with the citizens if they were to retain their authority, and this meant demolishing the structure of oligarchic rule. The emergence of true democratic government represented the final effects of this gradual erosion of oligarchy and the changing needs of the Greek people.

Athens' martyrs of freedom

Toward the end of the sixth century Athens was under the oppressive rule of the tyrant Peisistratos. Unrest was widespread among the rising middle class and revolution was in the air. However, it was the act of Harmodios (described by Thucydides as being "in the flower of youthful beauty") and Aristogeiton ("a citizen in the middle rank of life"), who was said to be the youth's lover, that set a match to the fire of Athenian democracy.

When Peisistratos died, his lawful sons Hippias and Hipparchos took control and continued the tyranny along the same lines. In his *Constitution of the Athenians* Aristotle diverges from Thucydides' *History* in that he states Peisistratos had two other sons by his Argive consort, Iophon and Thettalos. Both historians agree that it was Hippias, the elder and wiser, that controlled the government, but Thucydides says Hipparchos fell in love with Harmodios, while Aristotle claims it was Thettalos. Both were said to be "fun-loving."

Whoever, Harmodios rejected the amorous suit which resulted in the tyrant insulting Harmodios's sister by publicly rejecting her from a civic ceremony. Aristogeiton feared that Harmodios might be taken forcibly by Hipparchos (or Thettalos), and so in 514 the two hatched a plot to overthrow the tyranny. The plotters were in league with other Athenians, but Harmodios and Aristogeiton did not wait on concensus of action and rashly slew Hipparchos during a procession. From the procession's rear, Hippias coolly ordered his guards forward and Harmodios was killed on the spot.

Aristogeiton escaped but was soon arrested. During torture, he revealed the names of the accomplices, many of whom were associates of Hippias. Now grown more fearful, Hippias tightened security, had many men put to death, and increased repression of the citizens. Four years later, in 510, Athenian fury boiled over. Hippias fled across the Aegean to Lampaskos—he had married his daughter to the Lampascene tyrant's son to provide him a refuge in case of another revolution—and from there to the court of King Darius of Persia. He would return in 490 as a Greek traitor to guide the Persians at Marathon.

Harmodios and Aristogeiton became heroes, the champions of Athenian democracy, thus underlining that personal grievances are often the catalyst for general political action.

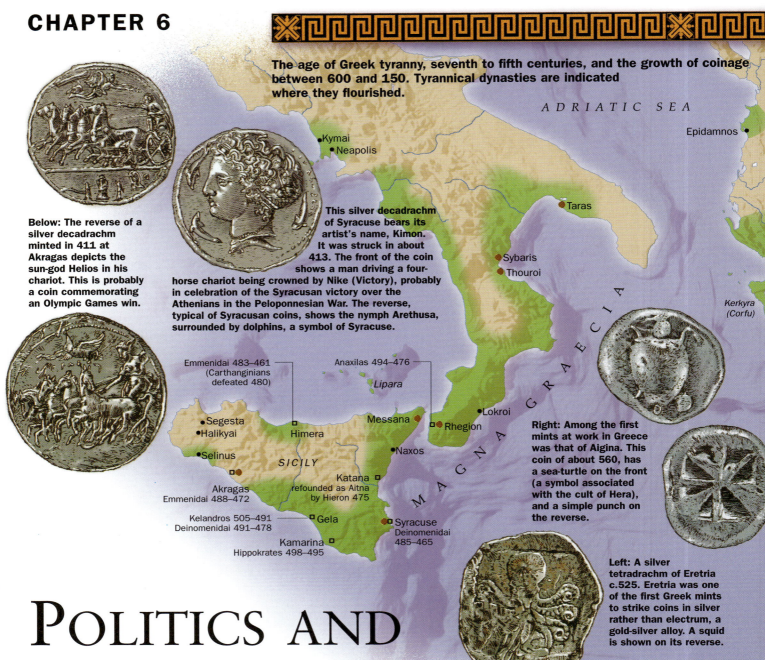

CHAPTER 6

The age of Greek tyranny, seventh to fifth centuries, and the growth of coinage between 600 and 150. Tyrannical dynasties are indicated where they flourished.

ADRIATIC SEA

Epidamnos •

• Kymai
• Neapolis

Below: The reverse of a silver decadrachm minted in 411 at Akragas depicts the sun-god Helios in his chariot. This is probably a coin commemorating an Olympic Games win.

This silver decadrachm of Syracuse bears its artist's name, Kimon. It was struck in about 413. The front of the coin shows a man driving a four-horse chariot being crowned by Nike (Victory), probably in celebration of the Syracusan victory over the Athenians in the Peloponnesian War. The reverse, typical of Syracusan coins, shows the nymph Arethusa, surrounded by dolphins, a symbol of Syracuse.

• Taras

Sybaris •
Thouroi •

Kerkyra (Corfu)

Emmenidai 483–461
(Carthanginians defeated 480)

Anaxilas 494–476

Lipara

• Lokroi

MAGNA GRAECIA

Right: Among the first mints at work in Greece was that of Aigina. This coin of about 560, has a sea-turtle on the front (a symbol associated with the cult of Hera), and a simple punch on the reverse.

• Segesta
• Halikyai
Himera

Messana

Rhegion

• Selinus

SICILY

• Naxos

Akragas
Emmenidai 488–472

Katana
refounded as Aitna by Hieron 475

Kelandros 505–491
Deinomenidai 491–478

Gela

Syracuse
Deinomenidai 485–465

Kamarina
Hippokrates 498–495

Left: A silver tetradrachm of Eretria c.525. Eretria was one of the first Greek mints to strike coins in silver rather than electrum, a gold-silver alloy. A squid is shown on its reverse.

POLITICS AND THE PEOPLE

The emergence from the Dark Age in the eighth century was marked by an increase in population, growth in trade, and the establishment of city-states. Of all the changes wrought during the ensuing Archaic Age, which lasted until the Persian Wars during the first decades of the fourth century, the most profound were political.

By the eighth century most of the warlords who had run Dark Age Greece had been forced to share power with other aristocrats, creating ruling oligarchies. Within a century, this oligarchic system came under threat from growing dissatisfaction among the emergent

mercantile classes. This was exacerbated by a military revolution in which the emphasis on equestrian noblemen changed to well-armed foot soldiers—the *hoplites*. Economic regression due to restrictive policies led to coups by citizens and aristocratic adventurers or officers.

During the seventh and sixth centuries many Greek city-states appointed tyrants, and supported their actions through popular acclaim. The aim—to erode oligarchic power—was achieved, but there was an important side effect: the citizens who had hitherto been denied a say in affairs of state started to flex their political muscles. The result was a democratic movement.

Greek territories and colonies, seventh to fifth centuries
□ location of tyrannies, seventh to fifth centuries
● principal mints, 600–150

Coins first appeared in Asia Minor during the seventh century. The Persians adopted coinage from the Lydians after defeating them in 547. Early coins were replaced by the gold daric, named after King Darius I. An archer, representing the king, appeared on the front. Over the next century, the minting of coinage spread all over Greece. Every major city-state had its own mint, since coinage was a proud mark of independence.

Gold stater of Philip II of Macedon, 359–336. The chariot commemorates an Olympic victory.

This silver stater showing the head of Herakles was actually minted in Cyprus but used by Evagoras of Salamis (411–374).

BLACK SEA
SEA OF MARMARA
AEGEAN SEA
IONIA

Byzantium ●
Dikaia
Abdera ● ● Maroneia
Thasos ● Ainos ●
Thasos
Stageiros ●
Methone ● ● Akanthos
Pella ● Olynthos
Poteidaia ●
Mende ● CHALKIDIKE
Imbros
Lemnos
Cyzicus ●
Lampsakos ●
Larisa ●
EPIRUS
THESSALY
Northern Sporades
Ambrakia ●
AETOLIA
ARCANANIA
PHOKIS
LOKRIS
Delphi ●
Orthagoridai c.650–550
BOEOTIA
Thebes ●
Plataea ●
Chalkis ●
● Eretria
Deceleia ●
Theagenes c.630
Sikyon ● Megara □
ELIS ● Corinth
ARCADIA
ATTICA
● Athens Peisistratidai 560–510
Pantaleon Damophon Pyrrhos early 6th century
● Elis ● Heraia
Argos □
Pheidon c.660
Epidauros □
Temenos
Kypselidai c.657–585
remained a joint monarchy throughout the period
Pylos ●
● Sparta
SPARTA
Aigina ●
Skyros
Lesbos
Methymna ●
Mytilene □
Myrsilos Melanchros 612–608
Phokaia ●
Chios
Andros
Tenos
Ikaria
Delos
Mykonos
Paros
Naxos
Naxos □
Lygdamis to 525
Melos
Thera
Samos
Samos ● □ Polykrates 530–522
● Priene
● □ Miletos Thrasybulos c.610
Ephesos Pindos Melas □ □ c.580
Pergamon ●
Myrina ●
Sardis ●
Halikarnassos ●
Kos
Rhodes

Just as the Greeks created the notions of dictatorship and tyranny, so ancient Greece was the birthplace of the democratic process. Democracy emerged from the political maelstrom in the sixth century, and despite several false starts and setbacks, Athenians created the first example of democratic government. This was some 2,250 years before the notion was revived during the Scottish Enlightenment, and saw a renaissance in America in 1775.

Unlike later democracies, the Greek version was based around the city-state, and the Greeks lacked any finite sense of national identity. They maintained a cultural notion of "Greekness" and a series of ancestral links that helped form the patchwork of alliances between city-states.

Each had their own laws and own forms of government. Not all were democracies, and the forms of government and alliance were as varied as the political composition of the states. The only unifying factors were language, religion, and a growing threat from Persia that threatened to engulf the Greek world.

The politically backward but militarily powerful Sparta and the democratic, rich, and culturally vibrant Athens would become the pre-eminent city-states, the only ones capable of taking the lead if the Persians invaded.

RULE OF THE TYRANTS

While progress from the Dark Age to the Archaic Period was characterized by a move toward oligarchies, the seventh century witnessed growing disaffection with aristocratic rule. Far from encouraging democracy, in some cities this resentment encouraged dictatorship.

Below: The personal cost of arming a *hoplite* created a new middle class in Greek society.

Homer referred to the *basilei* who ruled in Dark Age Greece as the "shepherd of his people," but by the seventh century most new city-states were run by aristocratic oligarchies. As a new class of merchants, artisans, and landowners appeared, pressure was applied to these oligarchs to secure economic and political rights. Many of the aristocracy were financially beholden to the rest of the population, and military developments that caused the emergence of the *hoplite* ensured the oligarchs needed the support of the middle class to retain power. The oligarchic system of exacting tributes became increasingly resented as the century wore on, and by 660 many oligarchs were ousted in favor of democratic government or dictatorship.

Although the Greek experiment of rule by *tyrannos* was ultimately unsuccessful, the system had its advocates. A series of later Hellenistic writers gave the term "tyrant" its pejorative element—in most cases, Greek tyrants ruled by popular consent. Most came from the aristocracy or were military leaders, supported by their troops or by financial backers.

The first tyrants appeared around 675, and by the 660s the trend had spread over much of Greece. Corinth, Argos, Miletos, and Megara were among the first *polities* run by tyrants. Tyranny was a particularly popular form of government on the Ionian coast of Asia Minor. Even Athens, which became the epitome of democracy, flirted with tyrannical rule.

The populist Athenian leader Solon was given tyrannical powers during the early sixth century. He canceled "debt slavery," freeing thousands of Attican serfs, and gave the majority of the citizenry a greater say in public affairs. Although it seems bizarre that an

appointed dictator would foster the democratic development of the state, it was a pragmatic solution to a political impasse, where the Athenian nobles and the citizens had been vying for power for decades. Further Athenian dictators followed—Peisistratos and sons Hippias and Hipparchos ruling 545–510 (*see page 67*), but the seeds of democratic change had been sown.

Golden age of tyranny

Successful dictatorships generally occurred in an economically vibrant *polis*, where wealth from colonies and trade had encouraged a vocal middle class. Rural or less financially developed communities tended to retain oligarchic rule, apart from Sparta, which retained its own distinct monarchical system.

Probably the most successful example of tyrannical rule was in Corinth. In about 657, a wealthy aristocrat named Kypselos ousted the oligarchs, a move supported by the city's middle class. His encouragement of colonization and trade created a boom, and his popularity was so widespread that he moved among his citizens without an escort.

In 625, Kypselos was succeeded by his son Periander, who retained control of power in Corinth until his death in 585. Under Periander's administration a slipway (*diolkos*) was built across the isthmus, so vessels could be moved from the Aegean to the Adriatic without having to unload or weather the treacherous southern tip of the Peloponnese. The city prospered on the traffic generated by the portage, and the Corinthians later looked back upon his rule as a golden age.

By the end of the sixth century the age of the tyrants had passed, and politics centered around oligarchic and democratic rule. Despite their later castigation, it was the tyrants in ancient Greece who were largely responsible for the undermining of oligarchic power and who laid the foundations of democratic rule. They encouraged government by popular acclaim, not traditional aristocratic authority, and in most cases they retained power not through despotic rule but by ensuring the continued support of the citizenry. The citizens would soon look to themselves, rather than their supposed betters, for future political leadership.

The slipway to civic wealth

Periander (625–585), tyrant of Corinth, came to be viewed as one of the Seven Sages of Greece, and under his rule the city grew to be second only to Athens as a trading state. However, Periander maintained friendly relations with Athens, even as he negotiated embassies with Miletos and Lydia. He founded several colonies—the most important at Poteidaia in Chalkidike, and Apollonia and Epidamnos on the Adriatic Sea—and conquered the island state of Kerkyra.

As trade with Magna Graecia, the Aegean, and Egypt expanded, Periander had a paved slipway, the *diolkos*, constructed across the narrowest part of the isthmus from Skinos to Poseidonia, connecting the Saronic Gulf to the Gulf of Corinth. On this 10-foot wide pavement of limestone blocks ran the *olkos*, a wheeled vehicle on which ships were borne across the isthmus. This effectively cut over 185 nautical miles from the journey between the Adriatic and Aegean seas and avoided the treacherous weather off the Peloponnese peninsula. Today, stretches of Periander's *diolkos* can still be seen, not far from the great canal finally dug at the end of the 19th century.

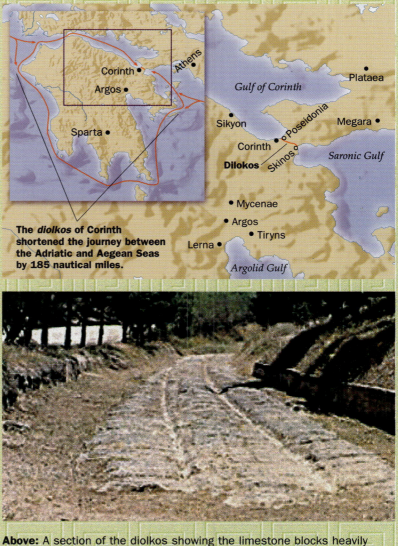

The *diolkos* of Corinth shortened the journey between the Adriatic and Aegean Seas by 185 nautical miles.

Above: A section of the diolkos showing the limestone blocks heavily grooved by the wheels of the ship-carrying vehicles.

GREEK UNITY

The Greeks drew on older cultural or tribal groupings to foster a sense of greater regional unity. Bound by a common sense of cultural and religious identity, it permitted temporary political unity of city-states when they faced invasion by the Persian Empire.

Below: The reconstructed Athenian Treasury stands on the Sacred Way at Delphi. The site provided the warring city-states and shifting league alliances a chance to discuss, negotiate, and trade under the sacred peace. Most city-states had a treasury at Delphi.

Greek identity existed on several levels. The basic unit was the city-state and its hinterland. A villager from Attica, the hinterland of Athens, regarded himself first and foremost as an Athenian, although he might retain some intrinsic pride in his rural locality. Beyond that, he would consider himself a Greek. Colonists in overseas settlements also retained a link with their founding *metropolis*, but shared their identity with the colony. They also considered themselves Greeks, even after several generations overseas.

There was another element to Greek identity. A villager from Attica was not just Athenian, but also Ionian, claiming descent from the older Mycenaean Greeks who had fled the mainland to Ionia during the Dorian invasions that brought on the Dark Age. They were identified by a particular dialect and by their geographical distribution; on the western coast of Asia Minor, in the Aegean islands, in the Chalkidikian peninsulas, and Euboea island. The Athenians were the other Ionian group, claiming descent from Ionian settlers who had returned to Attica during the later Dark Age.

By contrast, on much of the mainland of southern and central Greece and in the southern Aegean, the inhabitants considered themselves Dorian, descended from the peoples who invaded the region in the 11th century. Of these, the Doric-speaking centers were in the Peloponnese, Corinthian isthmus, Crete, and the islands of the southern fringe of the Aegean, stretching from Melos as far as Rhodes.

The Achaeans were the other significant group, whose descendants probably invaded Mycenaean Greece with the Dorians. Although linked to their fellow invaders by cultural and linguistic bonds, they retained their own separate identity. The Achaeans occupied Thessaly in northeastern Greece, Boeotia in the center, and the northern corner of the western shore of Asia Minor (Aeolis and the island of Lesbos). Other distinct dialects set groups apart, such as the Dorian variant spoken in the northwest Peloponnese and western Greece.

These groupings encouraged loose cultural confederations between fellow Ionians, Dorians, or Achaeans, alliances forged through kinship and the common denominator of shared heritage. Ionian city-states tended to support fellow Ionian cities, and

therefore supported Athens over Sparta. This autichthony—a joint claim of cultural superiority through being "true Greeks"—was used to assert the primacy of Athens over its Dorian rivals, and encouraged the enmity of Dorian Greeks. Likewise, the Dorian city-states supported each other, and

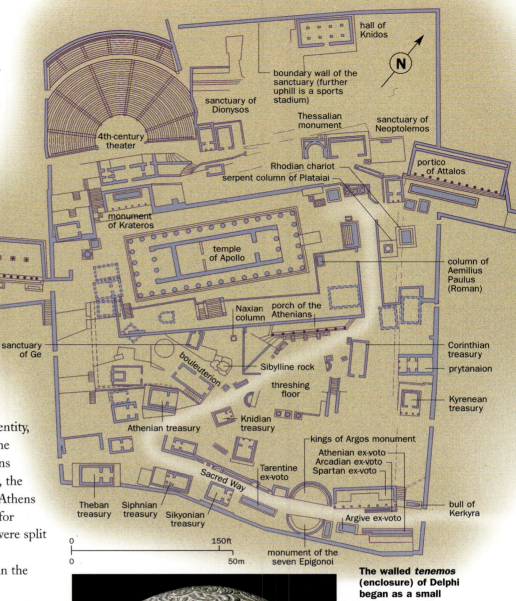

came to rely on Sparta for leadership. The Achaeans were less focused, but tended to look toward Thebes.

Clearly this form of cultural alliance discouraged a greater form of Greek identity, even though all elements shared the same basic language and culture. The divisions went deeper. Within cultural groupings, the Greeks were also sub-divided by tribe. Athens was divided (artificially) into ten tribes for administrative purposes, and Spartans were split into three (the Hylleis, Dymanes, and Pamphyloi). The same pattern applied in the rest of Greece.

Spirit of the Olympians

A higher level of unity only manifested in times of festivity and war. The religious centers at Delphi, Olympia, Isthmia, Eleusis, and Nemea were sacred, and annual panhellenic religious festivals attracted visitors from all of Greece, permitting them to negotiate treaties and trade agreements, or just socialize. Similarly, the Olympian Games, forerunner of the Olympic Games, took place at Olympia every four years, and safe passage to and from the games was guaranteed for the duration of the event, regardless of any wars being fought at the time. This gave the Greeks opportunities to experience unity that was not normally part of their lives. However, no long-lasting political unity was forged.

The real test of Greek unity was to come when the city-states were threatened by invasion from Persia. Only a united Greece could stand against the Persian invaders.

The walled *tenemos* (enclosure) of Delphi began as a small sanctuary on the hillside. During the Archaic period it grew in importance, and became the leading panhellenic political and financial center, the Sacred Way lined by treasuries of the major city-states.

Left: The god Apollo, whose gratest center was at Delphi, is usually depicted riding his sun-chariot. Delphi is therefore rich in images of chariots and charioteers, of which this detail of a youth's head is one of the finest. It was made in about 475, the earliest moment of Classical art.

THE BIRTH OF DEMOCRACY

Athens had tyrannical rule until 508, but the impetus for social and political change gathered, thanks to liberal reforms. After a brief struggle between oligarchs and democrats, the gifted politician Kleisthenes oversaw the true birth of democracy in the Greek world.

During the 590s, Solon—an aristocrat with mercantile connections—was appointed *archon*, the highest office of state in Athens. He was charged with reforming the Athenian state, a task for which he was ideally qualified. He immediately canceled all debts and abolished slavery as a punishment for debt, part of a package designed to free thousands of Athenians from what amounted to slavery.

Solon revitalized the agrarian economy by challenging the power of rural landlords, removing boundary markers, and encouraging the redistribution of land. The *Helliaia* (People's Court) was established, and all Athenians were given the right to bring a prosecution case to it. For the first time, poorer Athenians had a limited role to play in government and they would be unwilling to relinquish this new-found right to the oligarchs.

Despite this appearance of power-sharing, the real beneficiaries of Solon's reforms were the merchants and traders, who now shared power with the aristocrats. Society was divided into four groups based on income, and although high office was restricted to the upper two groups, the basis for democratic reform had been laid. After promulgating his reforms, Solon left Athens and the three main political groups—the Plain, the Coast, and the City—

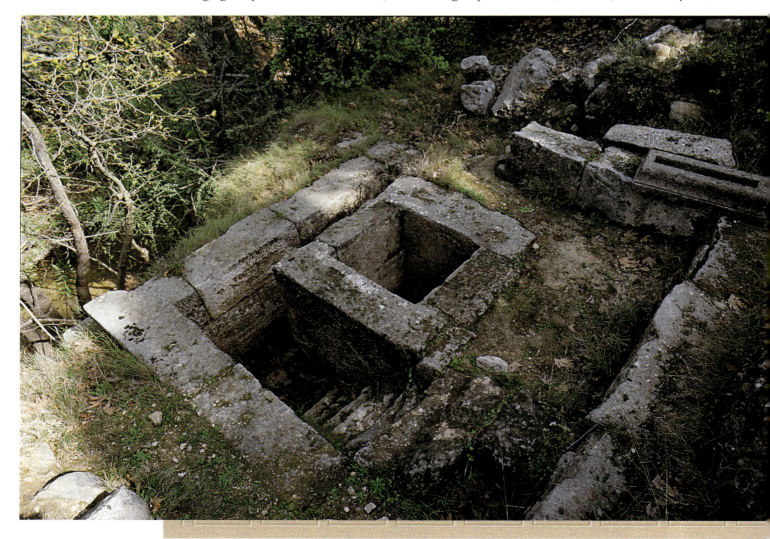

found themselves unable to appoint a new *archon*, resulting in *anarchia* (literally meaning no *archon*).

In 561 Peisistratos, an aristocratic kinsman of Solon, filled the political void by seizing power in a coup. Although the tyrant was deposed twice in the following decade, he retained enough popular support to ensure he could instigate further coup attempts until he secured a hold on Athens in 546. Following his death in 537 he was succeeded by his sons, Hippias and Hipparchos (*see page 67*).

An experiment begins

Peisistratos used the growing prosperity of Athens to launch new civil building projects and was able to maintain his popularity. Hippias was a less gifted politician, although his administration increased Athenian power, drawing the Attican hinterland into the Athenian political fold in an attempt to break down traditional tribal and feudal boundaries. He was less successful in foreign affairs, and proved unable to counter the economic slump brought on by the aggressive expansionism of the Persian Empire. Following the coup attempt in 514 and the assassination of his brother, Athens was split between supporters of the tyrant and the agitators for democratic reform.

A century before (632), the *archon* Megakles, head of the aristocratic family of Alkmaionidai, had brutally crushed a social coup led by the popular Olympic hero Kylon. This time, Alkmaionidai leader Kleisthenes was at the forefront of revolutionary reform. He invited Kleomenes, the Spartan king, to help oust the tyrant, and in 510 Hippias fled Athens for Persia.

A power struggle developed between Kleisthenes and the oligarchic champion Isagoras. When the conservative Isagoras won an election in 508, Kleisthenes abandoned his central political stance and offered power to the *demos* (citizens). Faced with insurrection, Isagoras called on Kleomenes, who sent troops to enforce Isagoras's authority. Kleisthenes and the entire clan of Alkmaionidai was sent into exile.

The Spartans would not tolerate a politicized *demos* and the repressive nature of this conservative military rule irked Athenians, who rebelled, besieged the Spartans in the Acropolis and forced them to surrender. Kleisthenes was hailed as the champion of Athenian democracy and invited back as a hero of political reform. Isagoras escaped to Sparta, but the majority of his supporters were killed or ostracized under a a new measure introduced by Kleisthenes (*see page 77*). The process of democratic reform that followed—dubbed the "Athenian experiment"— set an example to the rest of Greece, and later the world. Many of the political ideals developed by Kleisthenes and his Athenian supporters 2,500 years ago form the basis of sound government today. In these terms, the experiment can be seen as a glowing success.

Time—a public commodity

It is said that necessity is the mother of invention. The division of time into regular, predictable units is fundamental to the operation of society, and the more complex the society, the more important awareness of time becomes. In giving Athenians greater personal freedom, democracy made the citizens more aware of the importance of governing their lives by a timescale that was common to all, not just a privileged few. The obvious motive power for public devices was water.

The simplest form of water clocks were used to time orators' speeches, which—like politicians everywhen—must often have meandered on for too long. This timing device was constructed of two pots, one placed on a rock above the other. A measured amount of water poured into the top pot promptly emptied through a spout at the urn's base into the lower container. When the water ran out from the upper pot, the orator's speech had to end.

The philosopher Plato (430–350 BC) was said to have invented a water clock with an alarm. Later Greek scientists, such as Archimedes, developed complicated models of the heavens that illustrated the movements of the sun, the moon, and the planets against the fixed position of the stars. Shortly after Archimedes, Ctesibos created the *clepsydra* in the second century BC. A more elaborate version of the common water clock, the *clepsydra* was quite popular in ancient Greece, and some were considerable constructions, like the one shown.

Above: A simple water clock for timing public demagogues. The foundation remains of the mid-4th century *clepsydra*, **facing page**, are from Amphiaeiron. The well was fed by underground pipes.

THE DEMOCRATIC SYSTEM

In 508, Athenians adopted a democratic form of government. The "Athenian experiment" was to be repeated throughout much of Greece, a form of government that was both ahead of its time and a proud reflection of Greek civic spirit.

Kleisthenes introduced true democratic government to Greece by reorganizing the Athenian constitution and giving every free Athenian man the right to vote. This instituted the *ekklesia* (assembly of the people) who ran their own affairs. Giving citizens the vote and the right to run for political office was only the start of Kleisthenes' reforms. The whole structure of government would be changed.

Attica was divided into 170 *demes* (communities), each with its own *demarchos* (mayor) and local government. All eligible voters were listed according to their *deme*, even if they moved to another part of the state.

The autocratic Kleisthenes understood the importance attached to old tribal loyalties, so he sought to revise these along political lines. He abolished the four old Ionian tribes that had dominated Athenian and Attican political life for centuries and introduced ten new *phyle* (tribal groups), each named for an Attican hero. These became political units, as each tribe was allocated *demes* in approximately equal proportion. This created ten political blocks, each containing approximately 17 local *demes*.

The *demes* in each tribe were further divided into thirds (*trittyes*), based on three geographical groupings: city, coast, or plain (inland Attica). This elegant division ensaured that each *deme* contained a representative cross-section of the community, urban and rural. Because the *phyle* were not based in any one region of Attica, they had to co-operate with other similar *phyle* in different locations in order to safeguard their collective welfare. The map on the left helps to understand this complex development. It was an ingenious system, and the basic structure served Athens well throughout the ancient Greek period. It also served as the basis for Athenian military organization.

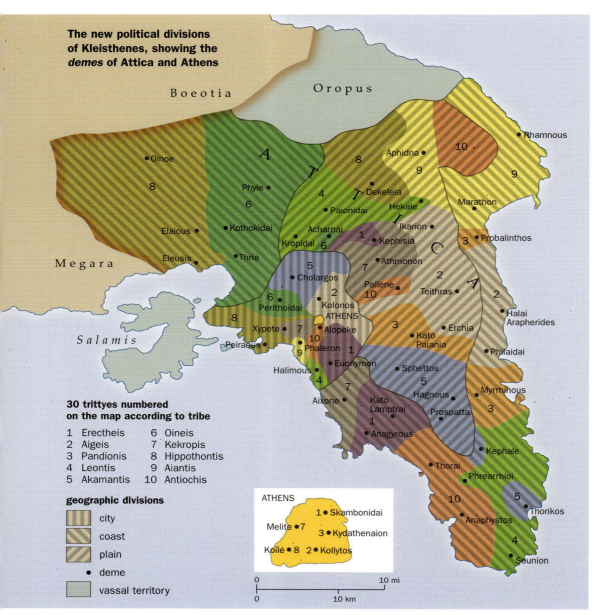

The new political divisions of Kleisthenes, showing the *demes* of Attica and Athens

30 trittyes numbered on the map according to tribe

1 Erectheis	6 Oineis
2 Aigeis	7 Kekropis
3 Pandionis	8 Hippothontis
4 Leontis	9 Aiantis
5 Akamantis	10 Antiochis

geographic divisions

- city
- coast
- plain
- • deme
- vassal territory

The Council of Five Hundred

The *ekklesia* (assembly, from which we derive the word "ecclesiastic," meaning a member of an assembly) was a political body that ensured every citizen the right to vote on any major issue affecting Athenian life. Meeting on the Pnyx (*see diagram, page 107*), vital decisions such as the allocation of public money, declaration of war, or the forming of an alliance were put to the vote. However, of an Attican population of approximately 250,000 in 500 BC, only about 40,000 were citizens; and of these only some 6,000 regularly attended *ekklesia* meetings. The remaining 210,000 were under-age, women, *metics* (resident foreigners), or slaves. Clearly, even a reduced gathering of 6,000 was too large to ensure the smooth running of Athens. Consequently a *boule* (the Council) of Five Hundred was created to govern the city. This was composed of 50 men (a political block known as a *prytani*) elected as representatives from each of the ten Attican tribes (*refer to the map on the left*).

Every 36 days (the political month was divided into ten units), a new group of *prytaneis* was selected on a tribal basis, and every day a new president of the *boule* was selected from among his tribal peers. Although the city's governing body, the *boule* had to submit any major decision to a meeting of the *ekklesia*.

The aristocratic post of *archon*, or chief governing officer, continued as a means of allowing the old ruling families some part in the new government, but their role was of civic and diplomatic figurehead, rather than arbiter of policy. They were accountable to the *ekklesia*, as were all employees of the state, including its army, navy, and civil servants.

Under the guidance of Kleisthenes, Athenian democracy came of age, and once observers discovered the experiment worked, several other Greek states adopted constitutions based on the Athenian model. As Athens prospered, the benefits of democratic rule became even more apparent, but the resilience of the Athenian state was about to be tested in a war that threatened to engulf the entire Greek world.

Although not a struggle between Greek democracy and Persian autocracy, the Greek and Persian wars hastened the move toward democratic government in Greece, since Athens emerged as a major power during the struggle.

Ostracism—the removal of trouble-makers

Among the various institutions introduced by Kleisthenes, ostracism was one of the more controversial, although historical evidence suggests the Athenians took to it willingly. Previous governments had removed trouble-makers by traditional methods: execution, banishment, or plain assassination. Under the new democratic movement, Kleisthenes made the Athenian Assembly responsible for voting once a year to send one troublesome citizen into exile for ten years. The votes were cast by scratching the name of the candidate on *ostraka* (potsherds, broken fragments of pottery), from which the word "ostracism" derives.

In each year before the eighth *prytani*, the *demos* voted on whether to hold an ostracism. If the result was positive, the Agora was fenced off, leaving ten openings through which the *demos* entered according to their *phyle*, depositing their inscribed *ostraka*. The members of the *boule* then made the count. A minimum of 6,000 votes was required for a citizen to be exiled, and the unlucky person had to leave Athens within ten days.

While this system gave power to the the populace, it had the effect of weakening Athens, since the ostracized frequently included some of the most talented political and military leaders, such as Themistokles and Alkibiades.

Left: An *ostrakon* voting for the exile of Themistokles (c.471), the brilliant naval commander who saved Athens from the Persians, but fell foul of ambitious opponents who had themselves been ostracized earlier.

THE RULE OF LAW

Legal codes developed in the sixth century, a by-product of the democratic system of government. For the first time Greek citizens had a chance to seek legal redress for their grievances, since previously temple priests and secular oligarchs with an agenda of their own had been the arbiters of justice.

One of the earliest examples of Greek law comes from a stone inscription dating from the fifth century found in Gortyn, Crete, but it is clear that such codes existed at least a century before. The Gortynian inscription is one of the longest and best-preserved examples of a Greek legal code, although its archaic style appears similar to those found in early Hebrew law, as reflected in the Bible.

Set punishments were proscribed for crimes, and caveats added to suit circumstances. This was the form of codification adopted in the Athenian legal code promulgated by Draco

Another form of legal inscription was more religious in nature, invoking dire threats and curses, rather than set punishments. For example, the small city of Teos in Ionian Asia Minor recorded that, "Whosoever works wicked magic against the Teians, their city, or any persons, death will become him and his kin. Whosoever hinders the import of [Teian] grain, death will become him and his stock."

Although the sentiments did not survive, this form of legal writing formed the basis for later laws because it laid out precisely the punishment for a particular misdemeanor. The sentence was not in doubt, especially when conditional clauses were added to cover mitigating circumstances, partial blame, and other factors.

The first legal inscriptions in the seventh and sixth centuries were probably written by temple clerics, but by the mid-sixth century the task devolved into the hands of civil rather than religious officials. This marked the transition

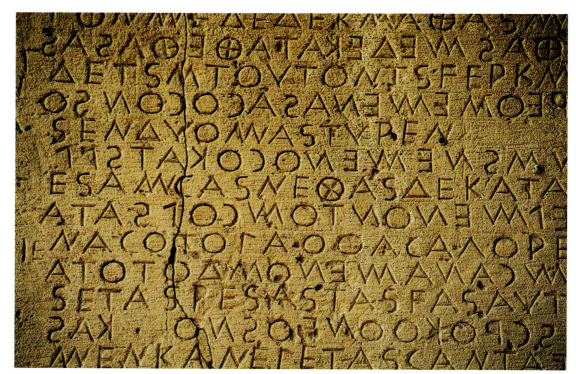

Right: Detail from the the Gortyn law code, southern central Crete. One of the longest and best preserved of early Greek alphabetic inscriptions, the 600 lines were inscribed in the fifth century. During the first century, they appear to have been incorporated into a theater and later became part of a mill's water channel, where they were discovered in the 19th century AD.

around 630, although we know little of its nature apart from its "draconian" severity. This apparent severity was misleading, since it is clear that most Greeks saw the law as a constantly evolving series of guidelines, as reflected by subsequent Athenian codices.

from a series of laws that were literally cast in stone to a legal system that was subject to review, a continual process of elaboration through example, practice, and changing perceptions.

Trial by jury

These codes provide us with a rare glimpse of Greek society and the morals that guided it. The code discovered at Gortyn represents an early Dorian legal system, containing some 600 lines of inscription, detailing the legal differences between free men, citizens without legal status, serfs, and *helots* (slaves). This structured social system was the foundation of Spartan society, a declaration of the rules that bound the *helots* to lives of servitude.

While there was some latitude for circumstance or the intercession of adjudicators, it was largely a legal code centered around statute and example, rather than a changeable legal framework. This suited Spartan society, which rested on the subjection of *helots* by the military elite. Despite this, it also outlined the rights of *helots*, including their privilege to own property under certain circumstances. Elsewhere in Greece, the codices permitted greater flexibility and became increasingly less

draconian following the adoption of democracy.

The principal reason for clear laws was the lack of lawyers or judges. Instead, any citizen had the right to bring a charge against another and present the case to the city's governing body. If there was a case to answer, a jury was selected at random from eligible citizens using a *kleroteria*, a form of random selection machine. The prosecutor and defendant presented their cases to their peers.

The jurors were presented with two bronze disks, one hollow, used if the juror decided the defendant was guilty, and a solid disk, which denoted innocence. A simple majority decided the fate of the plaintiff, and justice was administered by city officials. Punishments included death, mutilation, imprisonment, house arrest, fining, and exile.

The Greek judicial and legal system continued to evolve, surviving until the arrival of the Romans in the second century, who replaced the system with their own.

Above: Early Greek laws were codified by officers of the sacred precints and literally "cast in stone." This example carved on a stone plinth comes from Delphi.

CHAPTER 7

WAR WITH PERSIA

Historians generally assume that the Archaic Age lasted from about 750 to 480, a time when the city-states were established and the Greeks spread throughout the Mediterranean. It was an age of cultural and political renaissance; seminal examples of Greek art, architecture, and writing date from this vibrant period.

But suddenly, Greek civilization found itself under threat of extinction. A new power to the east threatened to quash the city-states through overwhelming military force. In 546, the Persian king Darius conquered the Lydian kingdom of Asia Minor to create a Persian Empire that stretched from the Aegean Sea to the Indian Ocean. He then turned against the Ionian Greek cities on the western shore of Asia Minor. The Athenians offered support to their fellow Greeks, but the Persian juggernaut proved unstoppable. By 510, the Ionian coastal cities and islands were in Persian hands.

Darius next turned his attention to the troublesome Greeks. He crossed the Bosphorus

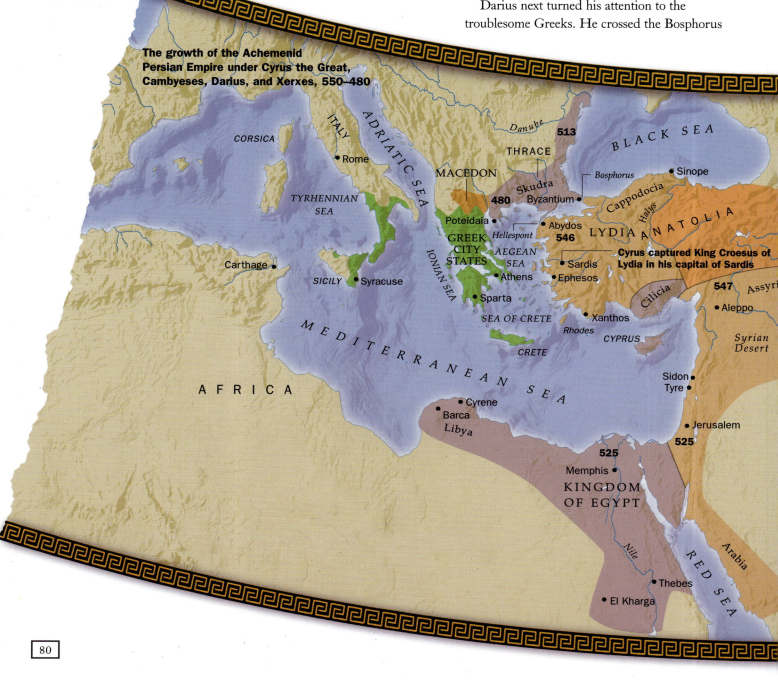

The growth of the Achemenid Persian Empire under Cyrus the Great, Cambyeses, Darius, and Xerxes, 550–480

into Europe and marched on Greece through Thrace and Macedon, which were both brought under the Persian heel. Next came Thessaly, but a revolt in the Ionian city of Miletos temporarily halted Persian expansion. Despite Athenian help, the revolt was quashed in 494.

Darius decided he had to crush Athens to prevent further interference. The stage was set for the Persian Wars, a series of campaigns that pitted Athens and a handful of her temporary Greek allies against the might of the Persian Empire. Persian ambassadors demanded that the Athenians send the Persian king earth and water, symbols of subjugation. The request was refused; war seemed inevitable.

At first, Darius only planned to send a punitive expedition to force Athens to submit. After losing a fleet in 492 in a storm off the Chalkidikian headland of Mount Athos, the Persian king gathered another fleet and another army. Athens struggled to gather allies—old enmities between Athens and Sparta hindered widespread co-operation. Athens would have to face the Persians virtually unaided.

This was the situation in 490, when the Persians launched their attack on Athens. What followed over the next 11 years was a contest between David and Goliath; between Greek civilization and that of the eastern potentates of Media and Persia. Ironically, the Persians achieved the impossible by uniting the Greeks against a common enemy—Spartans, Thebans, and Athenians fought alongside each other as the city-states set aside their rivalries in a battle for survival.

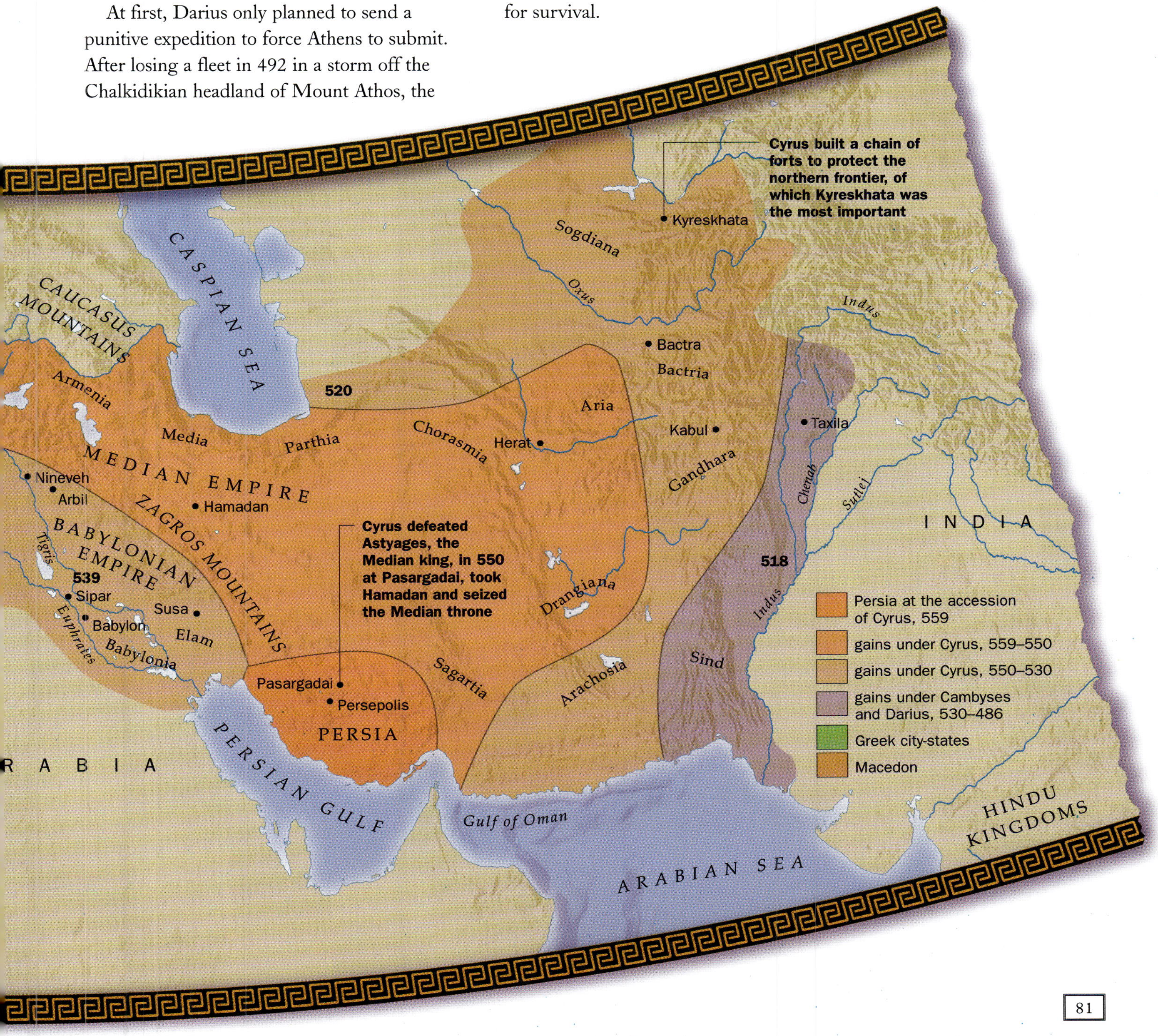

Cyrus built a chain of forts to protect the northern frontier, of which Kyreskhata was the most important
Kyreskhata
Sogdiana
Oxus
CASPIAN SEA
CAUCASUS MOUNTAINS
Indus
Bactra
Bactria
520
Armenia
Aria
Media
Parthia
Chorasmia
Herat
Kabul
Taxila
MEDIAN EMPIRE
Gandhara
Nineveh
Arbil
Hamadan
Chenab
Sutlej
INDIA
BABYLONIAN EMPIRE
ZAGROS MOUNTAINS
Tigris
539
Cyrus defeated Astyages, the Median king, in 550 at Pasargadai, took Hamadan and seized the Median throne
518
Sipar
Susa
Babylon
Euphrates
Elam
Babylonia
Drangiana
Indus
Sind
Sagartia
Arachosia
Pasargadai
Persepolis
PERSIA
ARABIA
PERSIAN GULF
Gulf of Oman
ARABIAN SEA
HINDU KINGDOMS
Persia at the accession of Cyrus, 559
gains under Cyrus, 559–550
gains under Cyrus, 550–530
gains under Cambyses and Darius, 530–486
Greek city-states
Macedon

THE PERSIAN THREAT

The Persian Empire of Cyrus stretched "beyond the edge of the known world," and had more troops, wealth, and resources than anything the Greeks could imagine. Cyrus would soon want Greece on his list of subject territories.

Below: Detail from the so-called "Vase of Darius" shows a Greek version of the Great King seated on his throne receiving an ambassador.

As Greece emerged from its Dark Age, the Assyrian Empire to the east reached the peak of its power. Although it prospered under King Ashurbanipal (r.668–27), the empire disintegrated after his death. Assyrian territory was partitioned by the Medians and the Babylonians. Under King Cyaxares (r.c.625–585) the Median Empire became the dominant power in the Middle East, stretching from Iran to Anatolia.

In 550, Persians under Cyrus the Great revolted against their Median overlords, conquered the empire, and assimilated the Median aristocracy and government into a new Persian state. The Achemenid Persian Empire—named after the founder of the Persian royal dynasty—was ruled by Cyrus (as Cyrus II, r.559–30), who expanded his domains by conquering Lydia (Asia Minor) in 546, Babylonia (most of the Middle East) in 539, then Bactria (northern Iran) and Gandhara (now Afghanistan). By the start of the fifth century, Cyrus II's empire stretched from the shores of the Aegean to the Himalayas and from the Caspian to the Red Sea.

Although the conquest of the Lydian Mermnad dynasty in Asia Minor had been

relatively straightforward, it brought the Persians into contact with Greek colonies on the southern shore of the Black Sea. It also meant that their troops lay before the Greek city-states of Ionia, on the Aegean coast of Asia, and the Persian fleet threatened the Ionian islands off the Asian shore.

Great cities such as Miletos, Halikarnassos, and Ephesos fell one after the other. The Ionians had called on the Greek mainland for help, but despite the presence of Athenian and Euboean warships and *hoplites*, the Persian conquest continued. Cyrus moved east after his Aegean conquests, entering Babylon at the head of his army in 539.

The mightiest army

Cyrus spent the last eight years of his life reorganizing his heterogeneous empire, dividing it into approximately 20 provinces.

c.750	750–480	700–600	550	546–39	538	525	512
Greeks adopt a new alphabet, adapted from Phoenician writing	The Archaic Age	Development of the elite *hoplite* infantrymen	Persia rebels against the Median Empire and takes its territory	Persia conquers territory in Asia Minor and Middle East, expanding the empire	The Persian Empire conquers Babylonia	Persia conquers Egypt	Macedon annexed to King Darius's Persian Empire

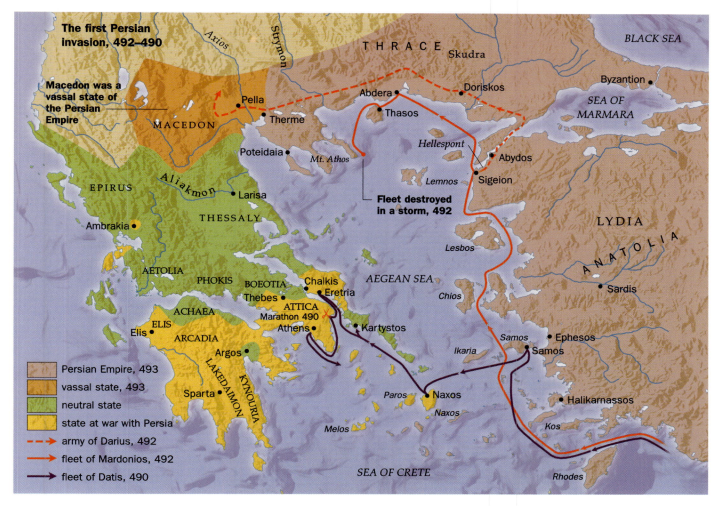

The first Persian invasion, 492–490

Macedon was a vassal state of the Persian Empire

Fleet destroyed in a storm, 492

Persian Empire, 493
vassal state, 493
neutral state
state at war with Persia
army of Darius, 492
fleet of Mardonios, 492
fleet of Datis, 490

Each was ruled by a *khshathrapavan* or *satrap*, regional governors who acted as military leaders as well as administrators. Cyrus ruled his empire from a palace at Pasargadai, a city he founded in 540. This remained the empire's capital until 522, when Cyrus's son, Cambyeses (r.530–22), moved to nearby Persepolis.

In 512 Cambyeses' successor, Darius the Great (r.521–486) invaded Thrace by crossing from Asia into Europe over a pontoon bridge designed by the Ionian Greek engineer Mandrokles of Athens. Darius campaigned against the Scythians beyond the Danube, then moved into Macedon, which reluctantly acknowledged Persian suzerainty.

While Darius campaigned against Greek rebels in Asia Minor, his son-in-law Mardonios tried to move south against mainland Greece, but was thwarted when he lost his fleet in a storm. Darius concentrated his forces in Asia Minor and prepared to launch a punitive amphibious expedition against Athens and her allies in 490.

The Great King had immense resources available to him. The heterogeneous appearance of his army was misleading, since it was administered by highly efficient staff and supported by a bureaucratic network that ensured it wanted for nothing. Spearheaded by the Immortals, or Persian Guard, the army consisted of 30 army corps, each drawn from a different region of the empire. It included Parthian and Median cavalry, Cypriot slingers, Indian bowmen, Iranian and Bactrian spearmen, and even Libyan skirmishers.

Although the Persian army's polyglot nature caused command and communication problems, its sheer size was awesome. Darius could call on 150,000 men, supported by 650 warships. The Greeks were outnumbered by a ratio of approximately three to one in troops and three to two in warships, and then only if the city-states united. Even when faced with such a threat, the Greeks found it virtually impossible to combine their resources.

510	494	490	480	480	479	460–454	449
Ionian islands and coastal cities are integrated into the Persian Empire	Athens' assistance to Miletos city's revolt earns Persia's enmity	A small Athenian army defeats the Persians at Marathon	Spartans block an invasion at Thermopylai, but the Persians find another route	Persians raze the abandoned Athens, but are driven away, their fleet massacred	Athens is torched again, but a combined Greek army defeats the Persians	Athenian troops support Egypt against Persia but are defeated	Athens and Persia sign a peace treaty

MARATHON

In 490, Darius launched a fleet of 600 ships across the Aegean, conquering each island in turn. Finally the Persians landed in Attica, where they met an Athenian army and fought the first battle of the Persian Wars.

The Persian expeditionary force of 21,000 soldiers gathered on the Ionian island of Samos, under the joint leadership of Median general Datis and the king's brother-in-law, Artaphernes. According to the Greek historian Herodotos, their mission was to "reduce Athens and Eretria to slavery, and to bring the slaves before the King." The exiled Athenian dictator Hippias, son of Peisistratos (*see pages 67, 71*), agreed to act as a puppet ruler and accompanied the expedition, together with a unit of mercenary Greek troops.

The force moved southwest through the Cyclades to the island of Naxos, where all buildings were destroyed. To the northwest many inhabitants of Delos fled before the invaders, but Datis sent messages of peaceful intent. After all, he argued, Naxos was an Athenian ally, while Delos was a non-belligerent. After appeasing the islanders by making offerings at the Delphic temple of Apollo on Delos, the Persians continued to the island of Euboea, north of Athens, collecting hostages from each island community they passed.

On Euboea the small city of Kartystos refused to submit. It was besieged and its civic buildings were put to the torch. The Persians advanced on Eretria. Once again, the city refused to surrender, and held for a week before an insider was bribed to open the gates. Once again, the Persians destroyed the temples and civic centers, and enslaved the population.

Hippias recommended the Persians land at Marathon, on the northern coast of Attica—far enough from Athens to ensure an unopposed landing, with a long beach capable of harboring the entire fleet. The plain beyond was open enough to allow the Persian cavalry to operate effectively. Since the Athenians had few horsemen, this was considered a vital element.

The opening victory

It had been hoped that Athens would be betrayed by sympathizers, bought by Persian silver. Consequently, Datis and Artaphernes waited in their camp for an insurrection that never happened. Every day they remained idle gave the Athenians time to rally their forces and their allies.

Athens' 10,000 *hoplites* had been watching the Persians from the hills overlooking the Plain of Marathon, and had sent messages to other states asking for help. The Spartans refused to move until August, after a religious festival, an excuse which probably meant they were waiting to see what developed. Although a few hundred volunteers from Plataia arrived, the Athenians stood alone. The *polemarchos* (war *archon*) Callimachos led the army, while the gifted Miltiades co-ordinated Athenian strategy.

Before the Spartans could arrive to reinforce the Athenians, Datis and Artaphernes decided it was time for action. Hippias had made contact with some of his supporters in Athens, who offered to betray the city if the Persians arrived. A plan was laid that involved pinning the Athenians at Marathon while the bulk of the Persian army sailed around Attica to capture Athens, which was virtually undefended.

As Datis disembarked the bulk of the cavalry and a large division of infantry under cover of darkness, spies informed Miltiades of developments. The Athenians decided to strike while the enemy was divided, hoping to defeat Artaphernes on the plain, then return to Athens to intercept Datis. The attack, which concentrated Athenian forces on the enemy's wings, took the Persians by surprise. The Persian flanks gave way and Artaphernes' men conducted a fighting retreat toward the beach.

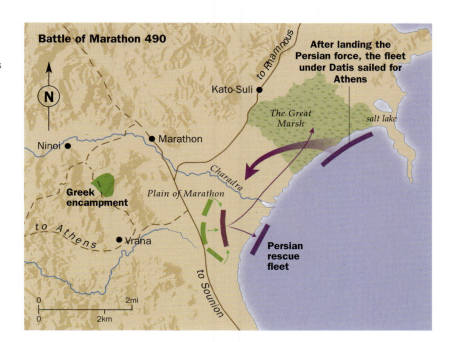

Battle of Marathon 490

N

to Rhamnous

Kato-Suli •

The Great Marsh

salt lake

Ninoi •

• Marathon

Charadra

Greek encampment

Plain of Marathon

to Athens

• Vrana

Persian rescue fleet

to Sounion

0   2mi
0   2km

After landing the Persian force, the fleet under Datis sailed for Athens

The Athenians raced through the Persian camp, trying to prevent the Persian fleet from coming to the rescue. In the short and bloody battle, over 6,400 Persians were killed in the marshes and on the beach, while Athenian losses totaled 192.

The Athenians raced back to Athens to prevent Datis from landing. Realizing the campaign had been lost, Datis collected what survivors he could—including Artaphernes—and returned to Asia. Athens had been saved for the moment, but when the Persians returned, it would not be a mere expedition, but a full-scale invasion force.

Facing: A copy of the memorial stela erected originally in about 500 stands near the Athenian grave mound on the site of the Battle of Marathon.

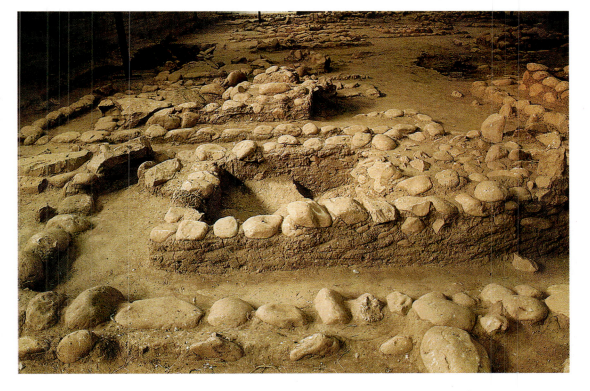

Left: In the massacre of Persian forces at Marathon, the Athenians lost only 192 men. Their collective tomb still stands close the battle site.

THERMOPYLAI

When he died in 486, King Darius was planning an invasion of Greece from the north. His son Xerxes (486–65) took up the challenge, but was delayed by events in Egypt. By the winter of 481–80, his preparations were complete.

Right: Erected in the 1950s, the Leonidas monument stands guard over the Pass of Thermopylai, seen looking west (**facing**).

Below: Detail of a relief sculpture from Persepolis showing King Xerxes seated on his throne.

At Sardis, in northwestern Asia Minor, Xerxes assembled an army of about 200,000 men, spearheaded by his elite corps of 10,000 Immortals. Greek chroniclers later claimed that Xerxes' army was so large that his men "drank the rivers dry." Like the army of Darius before them, the Persians crossed into Skudra (Thrace) on pontoon bridges, escorted by a fleet of supply boats. Not wishing to risk another fleet off Mount Athos, Xerxes ordered a canal to be dug across Acte, the finger of land that led to the storm-tossed mountainous cape.

The Greeks' reaction to the invasion was mixed. Some northern states opened their gates to the Persians, while others declared their neutrality. While the Greeks argued among themselves, the Persians advanced. King Leonidas of Sparta was appointed head of a coalition of Greeks determined to resist the invader, but Spartan involvement antagonized several city-states. Eventually a force of just over 5,000 Greeks marched north into Thessaly, hoping to block the Persians in the Thessalian passes. They were too late and, in danger of being outflanked, they retreated southward.

Leonidas elected to halt and meet the Persians at the Pass of Thermopylai (the "hot gates"), a narrow coastal strip between an inlet of the Aegean called the Malian Gulf and the impassable Lokrian mountains. By mid-August Xerxes' army had reached the pass, but the fleet was unable to link up with it, due to the presence of the Athenian navy guarding the northern entrance to the gulf.

Unable to use his ships to bypass the Greek position, Xerxes had no choice but to attack it.

While the two fleets fought a series of inconclusive skirmishes off Artemisium, on the northern coast of Euboea, Xerxes launched two frontal attacks over two consecutive days, using his veteran Median troops, and then a volunteer corps. The Persians were unable to overwhelm their opponents with sheer numbers due to the Pass of Thermopylai's restrictive frontage, and the attacks failed.

The Spartans' last stand

Man for man, the Greeks had proved themselves to be better armed, trained, and equipped. The brunt of the Persian attacks fell upon the elite contingent of 300 Spartan soldiers, the toughest troops in the Greek force.

Xerxes made other unsuccessful attempts to dislodge the defenders, and Persian losses mounted. Meanwhile a severe storm had reduced the Persian fleet by about a third to approximately 700 warships. Unsure how to break the impasse, Xerxes seized the opportunity offered by a local informant named Ephialtes, who appeared in the Persian camp and said he could show the invaders a route that bypassed Thermopylai. Xerxes dispatched his general Hydarnes at the head of a 10,000-man corps along Ephialtes' route.

A Greek blocking force was swept aside, but the alarm was raised and the majority escaped the closing trap. Leonidas and his 300 Spartans elected to remain in position to buy time for their allies to escape. Cut off from all hope of rescue, the defenders all died in a last stand. Their actions saved the remnants of the Greek army from pursuit by the Persian cavalry.

Xerxes had fought his way into the rich lands of Greece, but at a high cost in time and men. Not only did the Spartans gain time for their allies to escape, their stand also renewed the courage of the faltering Greek confederation. Although the Persian advance continued, the Greeks would no longer acquiesce to Xerxes' demands. The honor of Leonidas and his Spartans had to be avenged.

Today the site where the 300 Spartans made their last stand is marked by a monument, bearing this simple epitaph penned by the Greek poet Simonides:

Tell them in Lakedaimon, passer-by,
That here, obedient to their command, we lie.

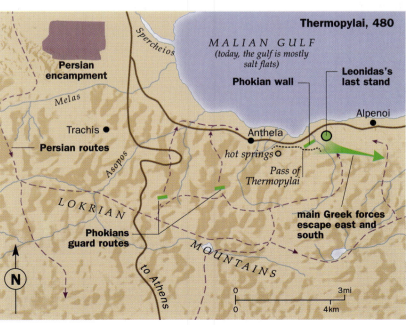

Thermopylai, 480

MALIAN GULF
(today, the gulf is mostly salt flats)

Persian encampment

Phokian wall

Leonidas's last stand

Melas

Spercheios

Alpenoi

Trachis ●

Anthela

Persian routes

hot springs ○

Asopos

Pass of Thermopylai

main Greek forces escape east and south

LOKRIAN

Phokians guard routes

MOUNTAINS

to Athens

N

0   3mi
0   4km

THE WOODEN WALLS OF ATHENS

After Thermopylai, central Greece lay open to the Persian invaders. While a few Athenian defenders held the Acropolis, Athens was abandoned to the "barbarians." Under the guidance of the naval commander Themistokles, the Athenians sought revenge, staking everything on a climactic sea battle.

In the late summer of 480, Xerxes and his Persian army of nearly 200,000 men marched through central Greece, conquering everything in their path. Thebes surrendered, offering "earth and water," as did Delphi, Elatea, and other, smaller Boeotian cities, until by September the Persians stood before the walls of Athens.

The battered Athenian fleet lay offshore, between Athens' port of Peiraeus and the island of Salamis to the south. The *boule* asked advice of the Oracle of Delphi. The reply came back: "Zeus… grants to the Triton born [Athenians] a wooden wall alone to remain unsacked." Themistokles interpreted this to mean the triremes of the Athenian fleet would be their bulwark, and that there was no point in attempting to defend the city. He then organized what appears to have been a well-planned evacuation of the population to the island of Salamis.

While refugees crowded onto the island, the bulk of the Athenian army retreated west to join the rest of the hastily assembled Greek coalition force on the isthmus of Corinth. A small force of *hoplites* stayed behind to defend the Acropolis, the sacred and political heart of Athens. The city was left to the Persians.

The Acropolis was soon besieged, and after a short time the defenders were overwhelmed and massacred. The city's temples were ransacked and burned, and Athenians watched their city go up in smoke from the safety of their island sanctuary.

Although the Athenians were in the majority, other city-states contributed squadrons to the Greek fleet, bringing it to about 350–380 triremes. The Persian fleet of around 500 mainly Egyptian, Ionian, and Phoenician triremes anchored to the west and waited for orders. By various ruses, Themistokles tried to provoke the Persians into battle, since only a decisive victory could reverse the situation. Xerxes also sought a fight—by destroying the Greek fleet, he could bypass the defenses at Corinth and conquer Sparta.

A sea choked with wrecks

The Persian king gave the order to attack and had his throne set up on the shore, where he could watch the spectacle. Prior to their attack, the Persians occupied the island of Psyttaleia, between the two fleets, so they could protect friendly sailors and kill enemy survivors. The Greeks drew back, forming the core of their fleet in the Salamis channel, with a small squadron left in Ambelaki Bay to the south, where they could sortie against the enemy rear.

Like Thermopylai, the Greek dispositions gave the enemy no room to deploy its superior numbers. A brutal jostling mêlée ensued, in the full view of Xerxes and the Persian army on the north (Attican) shore and the Athenians on the southern (Salamis) side of the channel. The Greeks managed to stay in line abreast, while the Persian fleet became entangled through sheer numbers and the problems inherent in maintaining formation in unfamiliar tidal waters and a rising breeze. The Greeks repeatedly rammed helpless Persian ships, adding to the chaos.

The battle slowly swung in the Greeks' favor. Increasing numbers of Persian triremes tried to escape, only to be caught in the flank by the squadron hidden in Ambelaki Bay. Athenians recaptured Psyttaleia and massacred the Persian garrison. Little quarter was given on sea or shore as the Persian fleet found itself caught in a trap.

The final battle took place off the shore of Mount Aigalos, where Xerxes watched the destruction of his fleet. As one witness, Aeschylus, wrote: "Crushed hulls upturned on

the sea so thick you could not see the water, choked with wrecks and slaughtered men, while the shores and reefs were strewn with corpses."

The war had not been won, but the Persians had been dealt a crippling blow. They retreated north, leaving the ruins of Athens to its citizens. The Persian fleet was beaten, but its army remained intact, and would return.

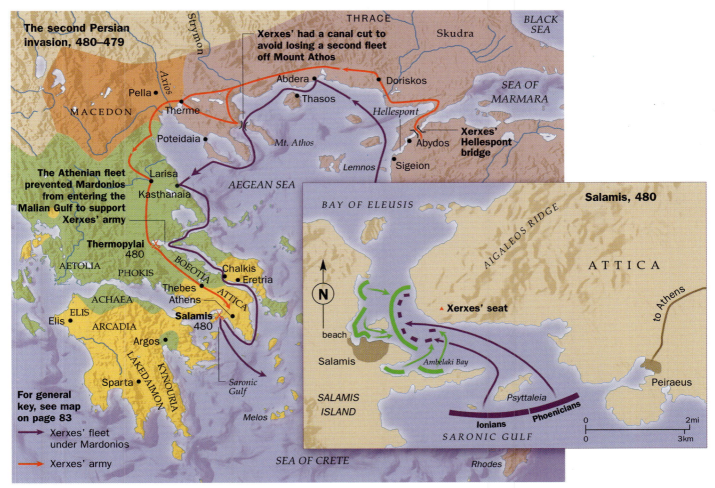

The second Persian invasion, 480–479

Xerxes' had a canal cut to avoid losing a second fleet off Mount Athos

The Athenian fleet prevented Mardonios from entering the Malian Gulf to support Xerxes' army

Xerxes' Hellespont bridge

Thermopylai 480

For general key, see map on page 83

→ Xerxes' fleet under Mardonios

→ Xerxes' army

Salamis, 480

BAY OF ELEUSIS

AIGALEOS RIDGE

ATTICA

Xerxes' seat

to Athens

N

beach

Salamis

Ambelaki Bay

Peiraeus

SALAMIS ISLAND

Psyttaleia

Ionians   Phoenicians

SARONIC GULF

0   2mi
0   3km

PLATAIA: THE LAST BATTLE

The Greeks gained heart from the Persian retreat, but nobody was in any doubt that the enemy would return in the spring. Both sides prepared for a final battle to decide the fate of Greece. A coalition led by Spartans prepared to fight, hoping battle would come before rivalries split them apart.

In the winter of 480–79 the Greeks debated over how to deal with the expected Persian invasion. Sparta and her Peloponnesian allies knew that they could hold the isthmus of Corinth against any attack, since the Persians had lost their ships. Athens and the city-states of central Greece had already been invaded and insisted on a defense that would safeguard their cities.

The Persian commander Mardonios was also busy, trying to isolate Athens with offers of peace and treaties. With the Athenian fleet neutralized, Mardonios could take the war to Sparta. The Athenians refused to be bought. With the spring, a Persian army marched south through Thessaly and Boeotia into Attica. Again, Athenians sought the refuge of Salamis. Again, Athens was put to the torch.

Finally, the Spartans agreed to co-operate, and a combined Greek army marched from the isthmus of Corinth to Megara, forcing the Persians to withdraw from Athens toward their supply lines in the northwest. The countryside of Boeotia south of Thebes was good, flat cavalry country, and Mardonios hoped to draw the Greeks onto the plains. While Persians drew up for battle near the town of Plataia, Greeks under the command of King Pausanios of Sparta came down from the mountains and encamped in the foothills south of their enemies.

Accounts of the rival sizes of the armies vary, but it is probable the Persians mustered around 50,000 men, while the Greeks advancing toward them numbered about 35,000. The *hoplites* were superb heavy infantrymen, but the Persians and their northern Greek allies were strong in skirmish troops and cavalry. Each troop type had advantages and limitations.

Feigned retreat

The Greek army consisted of Spartans, Athenians, Corinthians, Megarans, and contingents from 20 smaller city-states. The Persians—including Medes, Bactrians, and Indians—were supported by 15–20,000 Greek allied contingents recruited from Boeotia, Thessaly, Macedon, Lokris, and Phokis, all occupied states in northern or central Greece. This was not strictly a battle between Greeks and Persians, but a struggle between two ideologies, one imperial and the other federal.

The Persians stood in good cavalry land, the Greeks in ideal infantry terrain. Whoever attacked the other would give up the advantage of suitable terrain. Mardonios made the first move, using his Persian cavalry to skirmish with Greeks in the foothills of the Kithaireon (now known as Asopus Ridge), hoping to lure them onto the plain. The Greeks were shaken, but their formation held and they remained in place. The Persians also isolated and destroyed a supply convoy.

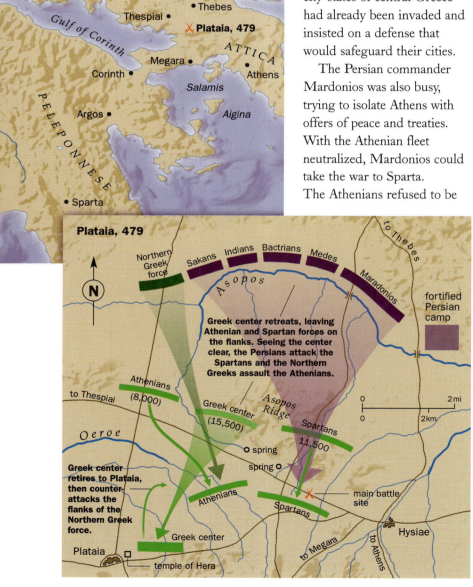

Pausanios must have been unnerved, particularly when Persian cavalry scouts reached the passes behind him. This was a psychological as much as a military contest, and the Spartan refused to be drawn. Having cut the supply line, Mardonios expected the Greeks to retreat, and Pausanios knew that. He organized a retreat toward the mountains, but left his flank forces of Athenians and Spartans in place.

The action paid off, tempting Mardonios into a general engagement against the Greek line, sending his Persians against the Spartans and the Greek center, while his Greek allies attacked the Athenians. The limited Greek frontage forced the Persians to attack in deep formations, and when Mardonios fell at the head of his cavalry, the Persian left flank crumpled, followed by the rest of the army. Only the Boeotians remained, and 300 *hoplites* of their Sacred Band fell in battle against their old enemies, the Athenians. The Persian cavalry prevented the retreat turning into a complete disaster, but the Persians limped off as darkness fell.

Thermopylai had been avenged and the Persians made no further attempt to invade Greece. The theater of war retreated to Asia Minor until peace was made in 449. The Greeks had displayed unity, but also fought with each other. Within decades, this internecine rivalry would lead to a full-scale war between the two great powers of the Greek world.

Above: Detail of Persian soldiers from Persepolis

Below: Detail showing a weary Greek warrior resting, his helmet sitting atop his shield.

CHAPTER 8

SOCIETY AND EVERYDAY LIFE

To the ancient Greeks, a community based on the *polis* was the only civilized form of society, despite differences in city-state politics, wealth, and size. Some were administrative centers that controlled an extensive hinterland, while others' authority was limited to a few miles. Differences in society were political rather than social: the majority shared the same social structure, composition, and values.

This said, our largest problem with the reconstruction of life in ancient Greece lies with the sources available to us. For the most part, Greek historians concentrated on recording social patterns in Athens and Sparta. Even here, the two were portrayed as extreme examples of democratic government or militaristic kingdom. Writers emphasized the differences between the two, rather than presenting them as examples of Greek society in general. Given the unusual circumstances in Sparta, we have to regard Athens' social organization as representative of non-tribal Greece, although in several respects it was unique.

Archaeology can also support our understanding of the subject, since the ruins of homes, marketplaces, and even entire cities across Greece can help us determine the extent to which the Athenian model reflected the social organization of the rest of the region.

The *polis* as a political, administrative, and social unit affected every element of life in Athens. The *agora* was a meeting place more than a commercial district. Athenian males mingled with their peers there on a daily basis, or attended events in grand civic or religious buildings.

By contrast, the typical home was a small, unprepossessing dwelling, where Athenian women spent their lives in isolation, permitted to run a household but rarely allowed to mingle with people outside of the home. Even here the Athenian man entertained male guests in a suite separate from the rest of the house. The only female guests who were usually permitted to join these all-male gatherings were *hetaira*, the female companions that were akin to the geishas of Japan.

Home and family therefore played a secondary role to the *polis*, and although Athens was the personification of democracy, the city was split by gender and social standing, and between Athenians and *metics* (foreigners). Although the incidence of slave ownership varied from region to region, most Greek households, farms, or businesses relied on slaves for the smooth running of life and business.

Recreation and education were virtually exclusive male preserves. Sporting events and athletic festivals held great importance in the Greek calendar, and together with frequent religious festivals and political gatherings, they provided a welcome distraction from everyday life and a focus for displays of civic pride.

This notion of belonging to a greater civic whole remained at the core of Greek society until the collapse of the city-states during the Hellenistic era. And the legacy of this civilizing spirit has endured into modern notions of civic duty, civic pride, and even in the communal support of local sporting teams. Like many aspects of ancient Greece, the better elements of its civilization were examples for later generations.

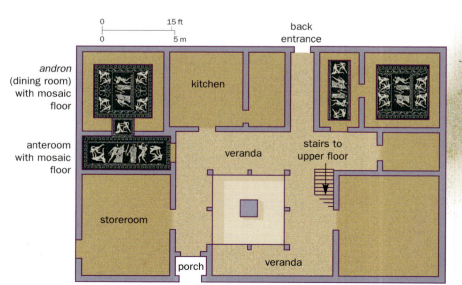

Houses at Olynthos in Chalkidike are among the best preserved. This plan and reconstruction show the ground and upper floor of the "Villa of Good Fortune." The mosaic floors were made from black and white pebbles (although the patterns shown in the plan are only representative, not accurate to the originals). The room next to the kitchen doubled as a chimney. Smoke was drawn through a row of holes in the wall placed near the ceiling and vented from holes in the tiled roof.

0   15 ft
0   5 m

back entrance

andron (dining room) with mosaic floor

kitchen

anteroom with mosaic floor

veranda

stairs to upper floor

storeroom

veranda

porch

EDUCATION AND THE YOUNG

Education was an important part of parental and civic duty. After a relatively care-free early childhood, boys were schooled to become model citizens—statesmen or soldiers—while girls were prepared only for marriage.

Below: Fragments of a red-figured vase show a school at work. To the left, one youth is learning music, which played an important part of ancient Greek education and was frequently combined with physical education. On the right, another boy learns the alphabet while under the eye of his seated paidagogos.

In a Greek family, only male offspring could continue the family line. Following matrimony, a girl was expected to sever virtually all family connections, owing her future happiness exclusively to her new husband. Consequently, although all children received a rudimentary education, only males benefited from extensive schooling. Artistic and literary evidence suggests that the majority of young children (of both genders) were protected from the cares of adult life, and decorative arts often depict very young children playing.

In Athens, pupils were schooled to become productive

members of a democratic society. Given the pressures imposed on all male citizens to take an active part in debate, justice, and local or city government, it seems likely that there was an extremely high literacy rate, although this level of education was probably lower in the city's hinterland.

There was no state-run education system, so for those families unable to afford the cost there was an apprenticeship system. This encouraged youngsters to improve their education while they learned a vocation, schooled by a master

craftsman or merchant. Apprenticeships, of at least six years, were usually begun at 12 years of age. Typical trades that relied on an apprenticeship system included builder, merchant, potter, carpenter, and shipwright.

Privileged school network

For the male offspring of wealthier citizens, the options were far more appealing. When he was about seven the boy was removed from his nurse and given to the care of a *paidagogos*, a selected household slave who accompanied him everywhere and could mete out punishment if he behaved badly. The *paidagogos* took the boy to school and stayed with him to ensure he paid attention and worked hard. There was a law forbidding children to be on the streets in the hours of darkness, so classes took place from about half an hour after sunrise until half an hour before sunset. Classes—held in teachers' private houses— taught basic reading, writing, and mathematics.

Since music was an important part of life in ancient Greece, boys were also taught to sing and play the lyre and flute.

For girls, their education stopped at the point their brothers left for school. Slaves often taught the finer points of deportment, the skills required to run a household, and the expected forms of social behavior. Although schools did exist to

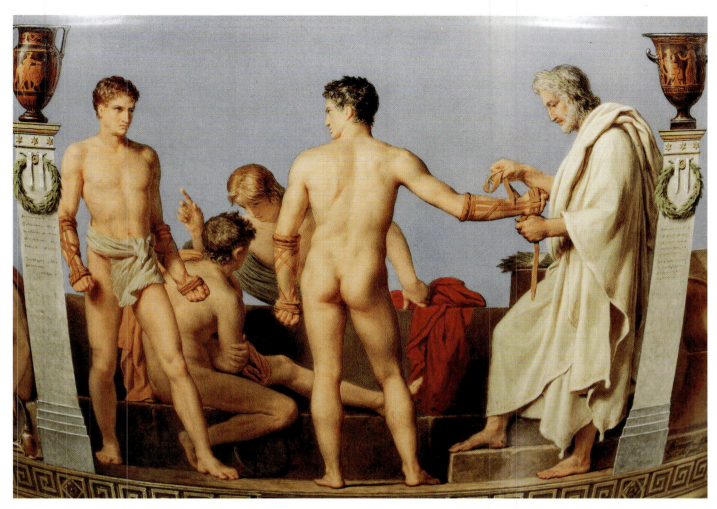

teach these skills to girls, little is known about their curriculum and the prevalence of their use.

Once a boy reached the age of 12, his schooling was expanded to include physical education, which now took precedence over any other subject. Academic classes were held under an arcade surrounding the *palaistra*, an open-air sports ground, which took its name from *pale* (wrestling). A *paidotribes* taught gymnastics and other physical exercises—with the aid of a long stick when necessary—which were done with the youths stripped naked. Limbering up was done to music, followed by sports such as wrestling, running, and discus and javelin throwing. With exercises concluded, the class retired to the bath house to clean up. The combined baths and *palaistra* were collectively known as a *gymnasion*, from the Greek word *gymnos*, meaning "naked," and every important Greek city at least one.

Older youths might also attend an academy for tutoring in the finer disciplines, such as appreciation and participation in music, culture, science, and the arts. This was probably an exclusively Athenian institution, reflecting a society that emphasized cultural development.

Schooling lasted for about 12 years, ending at the age of 18, at which point the young man was eligible for military training and special education in religious and political duties. Youths of this age, known as *ephebes*, were subject to the rigors of army life. For most, this military experience lasted for one to two years, after which the youth was considered a fully fledged citizen of the *polis*. There were exceptions to this liberal system, most notably in Lakedaimon, where the Spartans ran a much different educational regime (*see pages 142–3*), but Athens formed the model.

If the *ephebe* continued academic education in parallel with military instruction, the process was administered by sophists hired for the purpose. These roving tutors advised on the skills considered vital for civic advancement and statesmanship: oratory, persuasion, rhetoric, reasoning, philosophy, and logic.

By the fourth century this sophist education had spawned institutes of higher learning, the most famous of which was the Academy run by Plato. The result was a breed of skilled young civic leaders, eager to further their political and military careers through the advancement of the city-state. These leaders helped shape ancient Greece and shared responsibility for its successes and failures.

Above: Greek youths prepare for a boxing match at the *palaistra*. The illustration on this Etruscan-style vase is one of several entitled *The Physical Education of the Ancient Greeks*. It was painted in Sevres between AD 1827 and 1832.

DAILY LIFE

Possessions and daily routines were not particularly varied, but all were designed to complement the climate and lifestyle in a city-state. For the wealthy, luxuries could be imported from overseas and a round of social gatherings broke up the routine. For the less fortunate, life was a repetitive cycle.

As the best documented city-state, much of our knowledge of everyday life in ancient Greece comes from accounts of Athenian society. Since her democratic form of government was applied to much of the rest of Greece, we have to assume the Athenian picture reflected life in most city-states, with the obvious exception of Sparta.

businesses, allowing citizens to conduct their affairs and socialize in one venue.

Ancient Greeks mostly relied on foodstuffs produced in the hinterland of the *polis*, although maritime cities like Athens also imported luxury goods and even basic foodstuffs. The most abundant crops were cereals (mostly barley), olives, and grapes, the latter mainly used for wine production. Beans, figs, and other vegetable crops augmented the basic diet, while olives were both food and pressed for oil.

Animal husbandry was a subsidiary farm activity and—although cattle, sheep, pigs, and even goats were raised for slaughter—meat was

Above: Woollen (or flaxen) tunics (*chiton*), short for men, ankle-length for women were the basic clothing, complemented by cloaks (*himation* and the shorter *chlamys*) and hats. Footwear ranged from light sandals to sturdy walking boots.

Unless involved in trade or military service, most male citizens spent at least their leisure hours in the company of their peers, in the *agora*. Business was conducted, friends met each other, and political matters were debated. The business and social center of the city-state, the *agora* was also a venue for public debate and philosophical discussion. It was surrounded by shops and

a luxury. Dairy cattle and goats were commonplace, reared for milk and cheese production, as were fish, cooked from fresh or in some cases eaten in a dried form.

Typically Greeks ate three meals a day, in the early morning, at midday, and in the evening.

Breakfast was normally a light meal—bread dipped in wine or a lump of cheese were common at all levels of society. Lunch was a little more substantial, often including olives, cheese, bread, and wine.

Women excluded

The evening meal was the primary repast of the day. Among the wealthy, dinner often involved inviting male friends home for a meal, or even eating at a "dining club," the equivalent of a restaurant. Evening meals were eaten while reclining on a couch, and slaves brought food, wine, and finger bowls to the diners. Women were excluded from formal dinners, except as slaves or as "companions" for men.

Inevitably these *symposia* (banquets) involved the drinking of wine, often diluted with water, since Greek wine of the period was akin to a wine syrup (in some cases, dilution could be as much as 20 parts of water to one of wine). Musicians, dancers, and consorts of both sexes could provide entertainment for the diners, and were often called upon to provide more intimate distractions as the evening wore on.

The most common form of dress was the *chiton*, a cloth tunic pinned at the shoulder, extending to the knee for men and the ankle for women. The arms were left bare, as was the head, although hats or cloaks (*himation*) provided extra protection from the elements when required. Women also wore a *peplos* over the *chiton*, a long flowing robe that ranged in design from the plain and simple to the highly decorated.

Men working at a trade frequently wore a short skirt, belted at the waist, while a longer version was sometimes worn in the evening, extending from the waist to the ankles. Unlike later civilizations, nudity was not considered scandalous, among males at least. Male nudity at sporting events, the baths, or in the home was commonplace.

Above all, clothing, diet, and routine were all influenced by the cultural emphasis on practicality, and were suited to the environment of the Greek city or landscape.

Above: A selection of everyday objects used in the fifth century. They include an amphora for wine, plates, jugs, and a small domestic shrine in the background.

THE ROLE OF WOMEN

Women were second-class citizens, lacking any legal rights, political say, or even freedom. Instead they were considered the property of their father or husband, and were treated accordingly. Despite this, women influenced the development of Greek civilization.

Below: A man is entertained by a girl as he reclines in this fourth-century red-figured plate. He appears to be commanding her to either start or stop dancing to his accompaniment on the pipes in his left hand. This is not a marital scene; ancient Greek men were not usually entertained by their wives, only by *hetaira* (female companions).

In ancient Greece, women were considered the property of their father, and later of their husband, with no legal and few social rights. The *kyrios* or head of the household (the father, husband, or other male relative) legally owned the women in his home, and this legally supported ownership was passed from father to husband when a girl married.

Women had no political voice, and with few exceptions they were unable to own or inherit property. Even the marriage process was a legal exchange in which the betrothed girl had no say. Marriages were transactions between *kyrios*, an "arranged marriage" where a girl, often as young as 12, could find herself the wife of a man three decades her senior. This age difference was considered the norm, and helped reinforce the authority of the *kyrios* over his bride.

The role of a wife was to run the household,

take care of children, manage servants, and attend to the husband's needs. She was a virtual prisoner within her home, and rarely left its confines except during religious festivals and other special occasions. Wives of less wealthy citizens were marginally more fortunate, since they had the opportunity to leave the house to buy provisions at the *agora* and meet women outside their own family. Some even worked outside of the home as servants or craftspeople.

The *hetaira* was an exception. Among men, a *hetairos* was a male companion, and the use of the word in a feminine form implies that female companions were expected to be sociable in a way that wives were not: versed in poetry, music, dancing, and intelligent conversation. *Hetaira* were not prostitutes in the modern sense, more like courtesans—although the "oldest profession" was present in ancient Greece. Such skills were considered unnecessary for the majority of Greek women. This betrays a preconception about intellectual abilities that seems ridiculous in the Western world today. At the time, however, viewing women as a form of second-class citizen akin to slaves was the norm. Even the celebrated philosopher Aristotle wrote that the ability to think was not found in slaves, nor in women.

Extra-marital companions

Even within the home, a woman's place was strictly delineated. While a man could invite guests to his home and entertain, a woman could not. In all strata of society, when callers or guests arrived, the women of the household would retire to their chambers, which were out of bounds to all but the *kyrios*.

While couples could and did enjoy each other's company, men were free to pursue relationships with other women, or with men. There was no social stigma over homosexual liaisons, and men were more likely to consort with *hetairos* or *hetaira* than with their wives, who were viewed as little more than a partner who would produce and raise an heir. Indeed, an all-male relationship that involved the spiritual and cultural guidance of a younger man by an older mentor was encouraged, and the virtues of such a relationship were extolled

by numerous contemporary writers. Extra-marital relations were considered an acceptable and commonplace addition to marriage, but only on the part of the man. Even the hint of an affair on the part of a woman was considered scandalous, and the husband was expected to beat his spouse into line; or worse.

The only power a woman had was through the gentle persuasion of her husband, a skill that was immortalized by the comedies of Aristophanes.

In *Lysistrata*, women collectively decide to withhold marital favors from their husbands, in order to force the men to abandon a war.

As in any age, a relationship depended on two parties, and however downtrodden she might be, a woman in ancient Greece had the same attraction to her spouse as women in any other age. By building on the strength of marital relationships, women could wield "behind the scenes" power.

Above: This first-century head of a woman already shows the matronly qualities that would be admired by Romans in their wives. This looks like a person determined not to be ignored.

METICS AND SLAVES

In Athens, a *metic* was a foreigner; a non-citizen with only limited rights. They included merchants and craftsmen without whom the Athenian renaissance would never have taken place. Similarly, a significant portion of the population were slaves, lacking even basic rights.

Large communities of foreigners lived and worked within the bounds of Athens and other Greek cities. These non-citizens, known as *metics*, formed an essential part of the city-state—Athens alone contained a community of 25,000. The majority were merchants, traders supervising the shipping and import businesses that helped Athens grow rich. Prominent *metics* also included artisans, physicians, philosophers, teachers, and leading artists, all of whom helped Athens develop, and without whom the cultural and social boom that followed the Persian Wars would not have taken place.

Metics were denied the right to own property or land, and were unable to vote in the *ekklesia*. But they paid taxes and could employ slaves

Right: Marine archaeologists inspect the woodwork of the Kyrenia wreck, dated to the first century. While most Greek men were concerned largely with matters of politics and warfare, commerce and mercantile trade was left in the hands of foreigners, or *metics*. Sailing the Mediterranean in ships built the same way as the Kyrenia wreck, *metic* captains and merchants ensured a constant flow of goods between the far-flung colonies and the Levant, Palestine, and Egypt.

(but not free citizens) and engage in trade. They were called upon for military service in times of dire emergency.

The number of *metics* increased during the fifth and fourth centuries, and the elitist Athenians coined the nickname "barbarian" for non-Greek *metics*, due to the "bar-bar-bar" of their foreign speech. Most barbarians were Thracians from the north, Lydians and Carians from Asia Minor, and Egyptians and Phoenicians from the east.

While Athens was considered a democracy, social mobility was linked to money, so citizens were grouped according to their perceived income, from aristocrats (which included wealthy merchants), through the middling *hoplite* classes, to the *thetes*, or lower social and economic class. Despite their lack of political and economic rights, *metics* were accepted as virtual equals.

Below these levels were the slaves, who formed a vital part of the economic and social structure. Historians have estimated that there were as many as 100,000 slaves in Athens and Attica in 431—approximately 50 percent of the entire population, although estimates vary considerably.

A vital cog of society

Slaves were captured in overseas raids or wars, or simply brought to a *polis* by regional slave traders. The growth of slavery came through the increasing wealth of the city-state and the efficiency of the agrarian system that supported it. The growth of trade and the transformation of agriculture created a demand for cheap labor, and slave traders were eager to supply it.

Slaves came from all over the ancient world, but particularly fertile slave trades emerged around the shores of the Black Sea, in Thrace, in the Middle East, and along the coast of Asia Minor. Even fellow Greeks were likely to be enslaved if ill fortune or capture placed them at risk. Greek literature is filled with references to the risk of capture, the fate of the slave, and hopes dashed through enslavement. However,

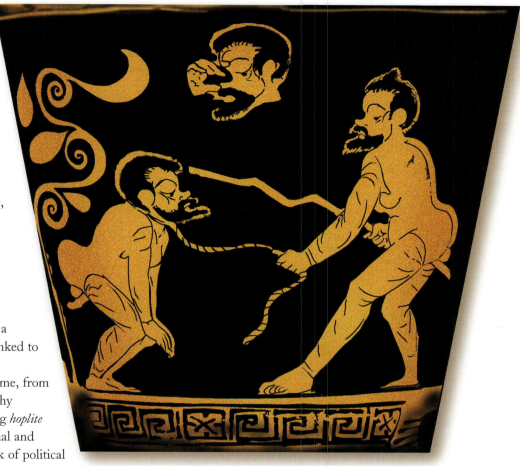

there seemed to be no moral opposition to slavery as an institution—Greeks regarded slavery as a vital part of the economic and social fabric of society.

Slaves could be employed as household servants, laborers, stevedores (to unload cargo), farm workers, and miners. Slaves employed in the silver mines of Laurion, at the southern tip of Attica, worked in horrendous conditions and life expectancy was short. However, most slaves in Athens appear to have been well treated, even accorded minimal rights under Athenian law. Some slaves earned an income, and their ranks included highly skilled craftsmen, whose services could be bought from their masters.

This was not the case in Sparta, where *helots* far outnumbered the citizenry. Spartans kept their slaves in place with a brutality that was considered excessive elsewhere in Greece and their system should be viewed as an anomaly.

In most cases, relatively well-treated slaves constituted a vital part of society, and their work was rewarded with a tolerable standard of life. Without a productive slave workforce, the social and economic structure of ancient Greece could not be maintained, so it was in everyone's interests to ensure that slaves remained appeased and efficient.

Above: There are few ancient Greek artifacts that depict slaves or slavery, and when slaves are shown, it is usually in a comedic manner, as in this example. The image on the vase painting re-enacts a scene from an Athenian comedy. Slaves were frequently the butt of jokes in plays, or used for comic relief.

SOCIAL STRUCTURE OF THE POLIS

Ancient Greeks considered their way of life the epitome of civilization—the *polis* was the ideal social and political unit. Between the city-state and the home the Greeks created additional levels of social structure, which helped provide religious, neighborhood, and familial identity.

The home was an important element of Greek life, the place where a family was reared, women were isolated from much of their surroundings, and men entertained their peers. Evidence concerning the importance of the home is provided by surviving legal documents, works of literature and drama, and archaeological remains. Vital elements of the story are missing, such as the thoughts of women and the manner in which society regulated the lives of the poorest citizens.

The city-state was multi-layered. The smallest unit was the *oikoi* (family). These social units of home and family were the building blocks of society. The *polis* laid down responsibilities for all members of the *oikois* and protected the sanctity of family and home by legislation. To become a citizen, a child had to be a legitimate member of an *oikoi*, born within the city to parents who were accepted citizens.

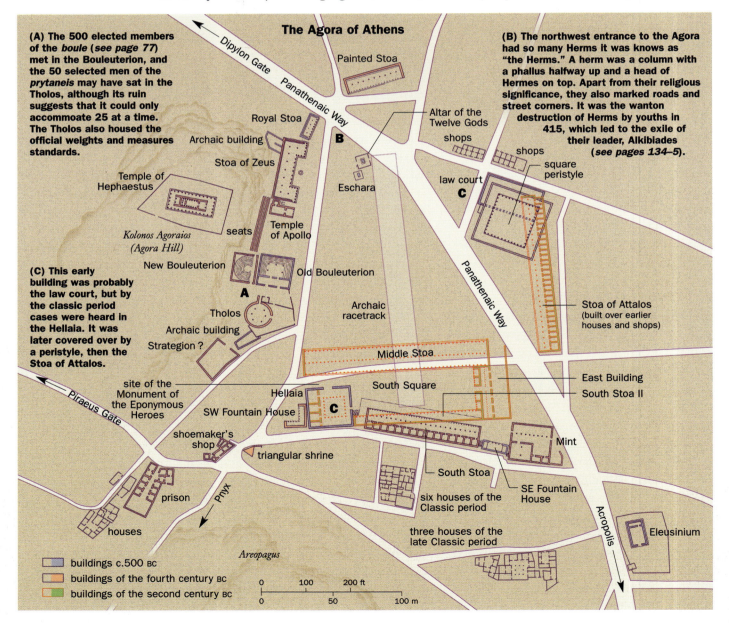

The Agora of Athens

(A) The 500 elected members of the *boule* (see page 77) met in the Bouleuterion, and the 50 selected men of the *prytaneis* may have sat in the Tholos, although its ruin suggests that it could only accommoate 25 at a time. The Tholos also housed the official weights and measures standards.

(B) The northwest entrance to the Agora had so many Herms it was knows as "the Herms." A herm was a column with a phallus halfway up and a head of Hermes on top. Apart from their religious significance, they also marked roads and street corners. It was the wanton destruction of Herms by youths in 415, which led to the exile of their leader, Alkibiades (see pages 134–5).

(C) This early building was probably the law court, but by the classic period cases were heard in the Hellaia. It was later covered over by a peristyle, then the Stoa of Attalos.

Dipylon Gate
Panathenaic Way
Painted Stoa
Royal Stoa
Archaic building
Stoa of Zeus
Temple of Hephaestus
Altar of the Twelve Gods
shops
shops
square peristyle
law court
Eschara
Kolonos Agoraios (Agora Hill)
seats
Temple of Apollo
New Bouleuterion
Old Bouleuterion
Tholos
Archaic building
Strategion ?
Archaic racetrack
Stoa of Attalos (built over earlier houses and shops)
Panathenaic Way
Middle Stoa
East Building
South Stoa II
site of the Monument of the Eponymous Heroes
Piraeus Gate
Hellaia
South Square
SW Fountain House
shoemaker's shop
triangular shrine
Mint
prison
Pnyx
South Stoa
SE Fountain House
Acropolis
houses
six houses of the Classic period
Eleusinium
three houses of the late Classic period
Areopagus

buildings c.500 BC
buildings of the fourth century BC
buildings of the second century BC

0   100   200 ft
0   50   100 m

Children were named using an identifying first name and a patronymic.

Males became members of a local *phratry* (brotherhood), a social group at neighborhood level. In Athens this was based on the tribal system and fully integrated into government structure. Above that was the *deme* (or city district). Members of a *oikoi* were associated with a particular *deme*, even if the family moved to another part of the city. These were further building blocks on the path to civic involvement and identity with the *polis*.

Some city-states relied on a large slave population, or like Athens could draw on a large agricultural hinterland. Some were more involved in trade than others, while some were ports, and each had a set of dependent colonies overseas. Imports varied with location, as did the religious nature of the *polis* and its emphasis on military or naval power. Economies varied significantly—cities such as Athens were extremely wealthy, while smaller centers struggled to avoid urban decline.

The ties that bind

The majority of city-states shared certain features. The basic elements were the walled city itself, a hinterland surrounding it, and at its heart an *agora* and an *acropolis* or other civic and military center. The location of these centers permitted daily access by the citizenry. Meeting in the *agora* was a male pastime; while women did walk in *agoras*, they could not mingle with men and tended to be chaperoned by servants.

These visits were strictly fleeting; after a brief foray into the city, a woman would return to tend her home.

Apart from this division, the city-state was largely a democratic institution. Debate, political assemblies, and proclamations were made in the open, as part of a participatory form of government. By dividing the citizenry into tribes, and then into *phrateres* or local administrations, the city-state was governed at regional as well as city level.

The home and family remained the core of essentially private life, outside the gaze of the city. Beyond that, an ever-widening series of forums—local, tribal, and city—meant that citizens were required to maintain an active interest in the affairs of publicly aired government. The *polis* was a network of communities or associations, each governing themselves and participating in the governance of a higher body. Ties of family, kinship, tribal and religious associations, and friends all influenced the shape of the city-state and ensured that through participation in government, individual rights and freedoms were maintained through an active participation in the democratic process by the entire body of eligible citizens.

This essential dichotomy of freedom and civic service epitomized the role of the Greek citizen throughout the Classical Age, and formed the basis for the ideal government outlined by Greek writers and thinkers, such as Aristotle and Plato.

Below: The expanse of the Agora viewed from the hill in front of the Theseion, looking southeast toward the Acropolis. The Stoa of Attalos is the long arcaded building on the left. It was fully restored during the 1950s to become a museum. In the center can be seen the remains of the Middle and South Stoas.

CHAPTER 9

ATHENS AND THE CLASSICAL GREEK AGE

Athens emerged from the Persian Wars in 480–479 as the leading power of the Greek world. Although the city lay in ashes, Athenians were regarded (or were successful in persuading others to regard them) as the leaders of the Greek coalition against the Persians. Once the threat of invasion had subsided, this perceived supremacy enabled Athens to pursue imperialistic ambitions. This arrogance resulted in the increasing enmity of Sparta and her Peloponnesian allies, but Athens ignored her neighbors and continued to expand political and economic boundaries to build a loose empire that covered much of the Aegean.

During the fifth century Athens was rebuilt, largely at the expense of her new allies. The new civic buildings were perhaps the most spectacular examples of their kind in Greece. These tangible expressions of power were matched by an equally dramatic exuberance. For over a century, Athens was the cultural, political, and artistic center of the Greek world, and the city's merchants were every bit as adventurous as their civic leaders.

Athenians were riding high on a political and economic bubble, buoyed by an influx of tax money and the ascendancy of trade in the region. Artists, architects, sculptors, philosophers, and writers also thrived in a city where the desire for civic splendor resulted in a constant stream of cultural and architectural projects. The beautiful *polis* created out of the ruins was a fitting tribute to the spirit of a resilient people. This was a golden age, when Athens, supported by her victorious fleet and army, was able to dominate the Greek stage, and spread the Athenian message of democracy and enlightenment throughout the region.

This was not achieved without a struggle. The Athenian military, victorious in the war against Persia, was now in need of reform. It had exchanged its role of a localized defensive body for that of a considerable force policing the seas, garrisoning cities, and even launching punitive overseas campaigns. While the city was protected by massive new defensive walls (*see the following page*), the true guardian was the navy, and itself a reflection of the importance of maritime trade to the Athenians.

Under the guidance of Themistokles, Athenian domestic and foreign policies merged into a strategic vision that placed Athens at the heart of a maritime mercantile empire, changing the role of the *polis* from regional center to super-state.

Despite the achievements, many city-states viewed Athens and her democratic government with suspicion, and Athenian prosperity and self-confidence encouraged the envy and enmity of some Greek states. Sparta was the chief opponent and, as both powers gathered allies around them and formed their defensive blocs, the likelihood of a war between the states increased. When it came, this war would test the resolve of Athenians to the utmost, ultimately draining all its human and material resources.

ATHENIAN NAVAL SUPREMACY

Athens had been the architect of Xerxes' downfall, so it is not surprising that Themistokles should encourage his fellow citizens to view themselves as the masters of Greece. He set in train plans to glorify the battered city and ensure her future dominance.

Owing to the mountainous nature of the Greek mainland, sea travel was the only feasible mode of transport. It follows that whichever state controlled the sea-lanes would dominate trade. Themistokles had made Athenians recognize the value of being powerful at sea, so—as they rebuilt their city in the aftermath of the Persian Wars—money was also made available to construct a large war fleet.

After the first Persian invasion of 490 and the victory at Marathon, Athens had launched a revenge attack on Aigina for the island giving aid to the Persians. However, when Aigina defeated them, Themistokles was forced to rethink naval policy. He needed a larger fleet, with more powerful ships. By the time of the second Persian invasion in 480, Athens already had a substantial navy. At Salamis it numbered 200 ships and only a further 190 from all other Greek states. Athens' *boule* noted this ratio, and the naval imbalance influenced its future decisions. Salamis had proved to be a strategic

turning point, since without the Athenian fleet, all of Greece would have fallen to the Persians, including Sparta.

The formation of the Delian League in 477—intended to bond the naval powers of the Aegean into one political unit—effectively handed control of the sea over to Athens. She had the largest navy in the Aegean—strong enough to cause the Phoenicians, who had been the dominant maritime power in the eastern Mediterranean before the Persian Wars, to suffer as far away as Carthage. By contrast, Chalkis on Euboea boasted a fleet of only 20 triremes, while Aigina could muster 30. Smaller states and islands contributed even fewer vessels.

Eroding native resources

This naval dominance over her allies meant that Athens ruled the league; and the arbiter of Athenian policy was the fleet. During the 460s it underwent a major expansion. Service in the galleys came to be seen as an honor for young Athenians. When the aristocratic Kimon offered to take his turn rowing in a war galley, a flock of

The Long Walls ordered for the defense of Athens and Peiraeus by Perikles were inspired by similar, though smaller, walls linking Megara to its harbor of Nisaia. Athens had helped defend Megara in 460. At first only two walls were built, one to the north running from the Pnyx Hill to Peiraeus, the other from the Museion Hill to Phaleron. Later, Perikles ordered a third wall to form a corridor with the North Wall. This rendered the Phaleron Wall redundant. The Long Walls were demolished in 404, as part of the peace treaty with Sparta, but the North and South Walls were rebuilt less than a hundred years later.

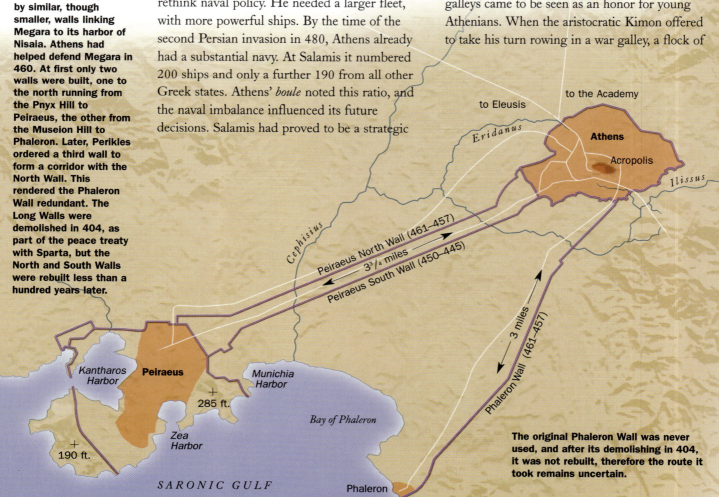

The original Phaleron Wall was never used, and after its demolishing in 404, it was not rebuilt, therefore the route it took remains uncertain.

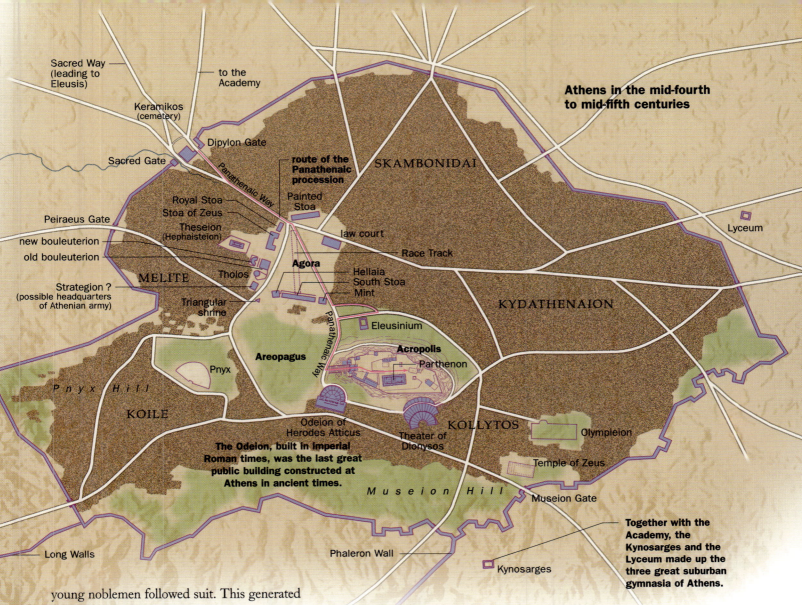

Athens in the mid-fourth to mid-fifth centuries

Sacred Way (leading to Eleusis)
to the Academy
Keramikos (cemetery)
Dipylon Gate
Sacred Gate
route of the Panathenaic procession
Painted Stoa
SKAMBONIDAI
Peiraeus Gate
Royal Stoa
Stoa of Zeus
Theseion (Hephaisteion)
Panathenaic Way
law court
Lyceum
new bouleuterion
old bouleuterion
Tholos
Agora
Race Track
Strategion ? (possible headquarters of Athenian army)
MELITE
Triangular shrine
Hellaia
South Stoa
Mint
KYDATHENAION
Eleusinium
Areopagus
Acropolis
Parthenon
Pnyx
Pnyx Hill
KOILE
Panathenaic Way
Odeion of Herodes Atticus
Theater of Dionysos
KOLLYTOS
Olympieion
Temple of Zeus
The Odeion, built in Imperial Roman times, was the last great public building constructed at Athens in ancient times.
Museion Hill
Museion Gate
Together with the Academy, the Kynosarges and the Lyceum made up the three great suburban gymnasia of Athens.
Long Walls
Phaleron Wall
Kynosarges

young noblemen followed suit. This generated widespread pride in the Athenian navy and in the policy of military and naval service that embraced all elements within the city-state. By 420 Athens had over 350 triremes, a fleet that dwarfed those of Sparta (never to this point great sailors) and her Peloponnesian allies.

On land, however, it was a different story. Sparta was by far the stronger of the two. In the event of war, the strategic imbalance on land and at sea predicated a protracted struggle, since neither side would be able deliver a decisive blow. This inherent problem came to the fore during the Peloponnesian War.

Massive Athenian naval expansion was not without its drawbacks. The most severe effect arose from the quantity of timber required to build and maintain such a large fleet. Athenian shipyards stripped Attica and Athens' allies of all suitable trees. With the deforestation of central Greece, it became necessary to import timber from the Black Sea coasts, which in turn forced Athens to expend more resources to ensure the security of northward sea lanes

through the Aegean Sea.

Timber was not the only new import requirement. The loss of so many trees in central Greece led to increased soil erosion and, consequently, a decline in food production. In the bid for supremacy, Athens had left the people vulnerable to famine in the event of a blockade in a war. With her mighty navy, one could see this as a possibility, and yet that is exactly what happened in the war that soon followed.

Athens maintained control of the sea until the last years of the Peloponnesian War, and although her ships and sailors earned a well-deserved reputation for excellence, the fleet proved unequal to the task of keeping enemies at bay.

Below: Plan and elevation of the Pnyx, a platform for *ekklesia* meetings built in 404, and later enlarged (red line) in 330–26.

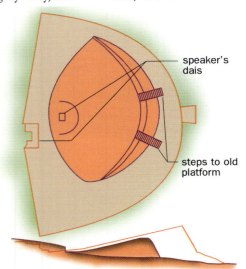

speaker's dais

steps to old platform

ATHENS AND THE DELIAN LEAGUE

Within two decades of the Persian War, Athens had expanded her fleet, then used it as a tool to encourage allies to join an Aegean coalition. Deprived of self-determination, the allies became little more than subject provinces in a new "democratic empire."

Below: Centrally placed in the Cyclades, the island of Delos was sacred to Apollo from a time before Homer. For a while, it was the treasury of the Delian League until Athens removed the money.

The defeat of the Persians in mainland Greece and Thrace had not removed the threat, especially to the Greek islands in the Aegean and on the Ionian coast. A defensive alliance was the logical step to prevent further Persian attack and Athens was the obvious candidate to lead this initiative. It was not just the demonstrated success of its new navy, but the city's democratic government and emphasis on culture (*paidaia*) was a model other Ionian

Greeks, effectively portraying Athens as the *metropolis* for all other Ionian cities (when the case was really the reverse, since Athenians had most likely emigrated from Ionia after the Dorian invasions quietened down at the end of the Dark Age). Above all, the politicians could play on the undisputed fact that Athens had distinguished herself in the war against Darius; Athens had been sacrificed to thwart Xerxes; and Athens had orchestrated the great naval victory at Salamis. Moreover, it was Perikles, Themistokles' gifted young protégé, who was commanding Athenian forces in pursuit of the Persians in Egypt on the behalf of all Greeks.

These factors came to the fore in 477, just four years after the repulse of the Persian invasion. Athenian politicians and commanders

states wanted to emulate.

Athenian orators emphasized this shared Ionic ancestry at every opportunity prior to the establishment of what would be called the Delian League. Themistokles and his colleagues accented the importance of Eleusis in Attica as the religious and cultural focus of all the Ionian

met with their counterparts from overseas colonies, Ionian cities, and most of the Aegean islands at a large gathering on the island of Delos, a site sacred to Apollo. The result was the formation of the Delian League, an alliance of Aegean city-states that included the cities of the Ionian coast of Asia Minor, the islands of the central and northern Aegean, the Chalkidikian coastline, and the Thracian and Asian shores of the Sea of Marmara. Leading members of the league besides Athens included Rhodes, Miletos, Naxos, Samos, Mytilene, the Chersonesos, Euboea, Boeotia, Lokris and Phokis. The members shared a common military policy, but it was clear from the first that this was to be determined by Athens. The war against Persia continued, with minor campaigns in Asia, Cyprus, and Egypt.

Enforced membership

Under the pretense of increased security, in 454 the league's treasure was removed from Delos to Athens. This act marked the political reality of Athens' increasing domination. The treasure represented an astonishing fund, but a substantial amount went toward Athens' civic building projects. Themistokles justified what was effectively a theft by claiming that the payments

frontiers and underlined Athenian supremacy. Kimon took the Persian-held city of Eion in 475 to bring the entire Chalkidikian coast within the Delian hegemony. And when, two years later, he destroyed the piratical island base of Skyros, Athens gained complete control over the Aegean Sea. This permitted safe transit of merchant ships to Athens from Thrace, the Black Sea, and northeastern Asia Minor. Athenians captured the last Persian-held towns on the Aegean coast of Asia Minor, a campaign that culminated in victory over the Persians at Eurymadon (468).

Empire secured, Athens became increasingly arrogant; allies were treated as subjects. When Naxos elected to withdraw from the league in 470, a fleet was dispatched to force the island to return to the fold. Other withdrawal threats were also treated as rebellion and similarly crushed. But with the Persian threat diminished, the financial burden of supporting Athens became too much for some allies to bear. Athens chose to

Below: The avenue of Archaic period lions of Delos was once part of a thriving city. Much of the statuary has been removed, to Athens, Venice, and elsewhere. As Athens dominated the Delian League, so Delos came under the control of Athens, until 314, when the island became independent. Again, it established itself as a center for banking and maritime commerce.

were a combination of *phoros* (donations) to the goddess Athene and administrative charges levied on their league allies.

Through substantial increases in the navy, Athens came increasingly to dominate the Delian League. A series of military and naval campaigns extended and secured the league's

ignore the rising wave of resentment at its own cost. In 447, Boeotia pulled out, followed quickly by Phokis and Lokris, while Megara and Euboea rebelled with Spartan help. In the end, Athenian arrogance proved to be a costly mistake, a factor in the descent into a war the Greek world could not afford.

THE ATHENIAN RENAISSANCE

After watching their home burn at the hands of the Persians, Athenians grasped the opportunity presented and rebuilt the city in a way that reflected the its pre-eminence. Under the guidance of Themistokles, Athens became the most splendid urban center in Greece, a stone symbol of Athenian efficiency.

The Classical Age of Greece is usually defined as the period between the end of the Persian invasion in 480 and the death of Alexander the Great in 323. This period marked Athens' transformation into a major power and its development into the leading cultural center. The rebuilding of Athens led directly to its architectural and cultural renaissance, a period when Athens led the Greek world in artistic innovation. Builders, sculptors, and painters achieved mastery of their materials, developing and introducing

Below: The Acropolis of Athens as it appears today. Few of the peripheral buildings from the Classical Age still stand.

techniques that transformed the appearance of the greatest *polis* in Greece.

After masterminding the Persians' defeat at Salamis, Themistokles encouraged wounded Athenian pride to view the city's devastation as a challenge rather than a disaster. His persuasive arguments resulted in a vast allocation of the state treasury to spearhead the reconstruction of Athens along greater, more grandiose lines. There was one exception in the Themistoklean scheme. The Persians had destroyed the unfinished Parthenon, and Themistokles wanted the ruined temple on the Acropolis left as a monument to Persian savagery. Since this negative sentiment was not in keeping with the times he himself had engendered, he was persuaded to order its replacement with a larger edifice. The Acropolis in general and the Parthenon in particular came to symbolize Athens' rebirth and its new-found position as the foremost *polis*.

490	480	c.479–400	477	475	470	468	460–405
Athens and Sparta defeat Persia at Marathon	Beginning of Greece's Classical Age	Athens, twice devastated, is rebuilt	City-states around the Aegean ally into the Delian League	Eion is taken from the Persians, securing the Chalkidikian coast for the league	An Athenian fleet prevents Naxos island from leaving the Delian League	With Eurymadon city, Athens has control of the Aegean coast of Asia Minor	Athenian civic projects invigorated under Perikles and his successors

First, Themistokles had more important building projects to complete. The Athenian-led victory at Salamis had been won by sea power, and it was the creation of a large trireme fleet that safeguarded the Greeks' continuing freedom and the colonial and quasi-imperial aspirations of the Athenian *boule*.

Lines of power

The fleet needed a base, and while the natural harbor of Peiraeus was being transformed into the largest naval base in the known world, Themistokles drew up plans for the protection of both the city and its harbor. Among the many new fortifications the most ambitious was the fortified corridor linking Athens and Peiraeus. Known as the Long Walls, this triple-wall defense guaranteed that in the event of another siege Athens would be able to maintain supply and communication links with Peiraeus, and thus the outside world.

The project was the pinnacle of Themistokles' achievements, not only because of its physical presence, but also for the political statement it made. The Long Walls symbolized Athens' transformation from a land power into a maritime empire, with mercantile and colonial connections covering the whole Mediterranean basin and beyond. Themistokles also undertook the rebuilding of the *agora* as the heart of the political, judicial, social, and commercial life of the city; a lavish theater was also built.

While Themistokles worked on the plans for the Parthenon's reconstruction, the implementation of the project was given to another Athenian civic leader, Perikles. A member of the elite Alkmaionidai family that had included Kleisthenes, Perikles had waged successful war in the East against Persia until he negotiated the peace treaty of 449. Perikles returned home, and now used the Parthenon project to help launch his political career. His ambitious schemes for civic enhancement met with the approval of the Athenian citizenry.

By the mid-fifth century Athens was well protected, and its bustling *agora* was the stage on which economic renaissance was set. In this democratic age, the city had become centered on the *agora*, while the Acropolis symbolized an older, less enlightened period of aristocratic rule. By building his new Parthenon and establishing the Acropolis as a center for political as well as religious activities, Perikles reclaimed the Acropolis for the people.

The Parthenon was dominated by an awe-inspiring giant statue of Athene (*see picture, page 30*), designed by Pheidias, which symbolically presided over the rebirth of the greatest city in the ancient world.

Below: Roman copy of the bust of Themistokles (525–460), architect of Athens' naval victory over the Persians, and inspiration behind rebuilding the ravaged city and mounting her bid for supremacy.

460	454	c.450	449	447	440	431–404	c.403
The First Peloponnesian War between Sparta and Athens begins	Delian League funds are used on Athens' civic projects, including the Parthenon	Athens is protected by the three fortified Long Walls	Athens and Persia sign a peace treaty	Athens establishes military bases around the Aegean	The Athenian navy quashes a revolt at Samos, at great expense to the treasury	The Second Peloponnesian War ends in Athens' surrender to Sparta	Military demands lead to neglect of Athens' city development program

PERIKLES AND THE GOLDEN AGE

Themistokles' successor, Perikles, symbolized the cultural and civic renaissance of Athens. The great projects of civic artwork and cultural patronage undertaken during the Periklean period were on a scale never been seen before or since in Greece.

Right: Bust of Perikles by the Athenian sculptor Kresilas, c.429. Athens' great statesman beautified the city at the expense of friendly city-states in the Delian League.

Below: The west front and south colonnade of the Parthenon—the greatest triumph of Perikles—under reconstruction.

Although the Athenian system of democratic government had been established before the Persian Wars, the city found itself divided by disputes between the old aristocratic families, and between the *aristoi* and adherents of democracy. The city's *archons* were still largely representatives of an aristocratic family, and during the war the senior military post of *strategos* had been an almost exclusively aristocratic appointment.

After the war, the *demos* began to meet more frequently than before. The military and naval victories of 480–479 had played into the hands of the citizenry rather than the *aristoi*, since it was citizens who had defended the city and

crewed the galleys.

In the two decades following the destruction of Athens, policy had been decided by Themistokles, but real power remained in the hands of the *archon* Kimon, son of the former dictator Miltiades. At some point before 471, Themistokles found himself being ostracized, an event largely engineered by several of his opponents who had themselves been earlier banished at the behest of Themistokles. After a series of scandals and reverses, Kimon was also ostracized in 460, and the democratic leader

Ephialtes passed a series of laws designed to limit the power of the aristocrats. Despite the murder of Ephialtes, this democratic transformation continued under Perikles.

Remembered for his great civic projects, Perikles was an immensely gifted politician, capable of shaping Athenian democracy and placing it on an unassailable legislative footing. Under his guidance the economy blossomed and the city's cultural patronage reached new heights. His flagship civic project was the reconstruction of the Parthenon, the first of several large-scale public endeavors that made Athens a magnet for builders, architects, masons, sculptors, and other artisans. Their works said much for the exuberance of the age—deceptively simple, elegant lines were used in architecture, mirroring a natural quality that led to an increasing level of realism in art.

Misuse of League funds

We know something about these artists, not only from their legacy, but also from the records the Athenian state kept. Builders' accounts from the construction of a temple on the Acropolis in 409 describe in detail the work of masons, painters, gilt workers, engineers, and workmen, and outline the sums paid to each. This temple was constructed after the true golden age of Perikles, which lasted for less than two decades, from 449 to 431, then continued after his death until 405. After 404 the city was in decline, since military demands prevented the expenditure of

capital on large-scale civic projects.

Under Perikles, Athens was at its peak and at its most striking. Culturally, Athens was the center of Greece, a training school for hundreds of artists and craftsmen. But these achievements were not attained without cost. Athenian wealth was based on the mercantile endeavors of her citizens, and her seaborne empire was created through the harsh repression of the city's allies and the extortion of taxes from them. This new-found Athenian imperialism helped fund Perikles' programs, but also sowed discontent that in time encouraged the Peloponnesian War.

When the funds of the Delian League were removed from Delos to Athens, the money was allocated to Perikles for building projects. Within four years a series of innovative and wide-ranging plans was developed for a centerpiece that would be the envy of the rest of Greece. And indeed, envy they engendered— the grandiose projects infuriated the Delian League and drove a wedge between the Athens and her allies that remained for the rest of the century.

The building work included the Parthenon (dedicated to Athene Parthenos; Athene the virgin), but the Delian funds were also used to build the Temple of Athene Nike (Victory) and the Erechthion. Such architecture may have impressed onlookers, but the cost was ultimately too high for Athens. The Periklean projects helped to propel the city into a war for which it was ill-prepared.

Above: Built over a number of years, the Erechthion is a complex structure of three parts, the most spectacular being the Porch of the Caryatids, said to stand above the grave of Kekrops, a mythical king of Athens. The north porch is close to the reputed grave of another mythical king, Erechtheus, after whom the temple is named.

THE APPROACHING STORM

Isolated on the margins of the Greek world, Athens' allied cities and islands felt trapped in a so-called democracy that disliked sharing power. Echoed in non-allied states, this sympathetic resentment turned on Athenian arrogance.

Below: Archaeological site of the Temple of Apollo, Naxos. For the islanders, Athenian imperialism became too much, but their rebellion failed through lack of sea power.

The Delian League was a financial godsend for Athens. With its treasury safely in Athenian hands and the seas patrolled by the overwhelming might of the Athenian navy, the city felt free to enforce its power over its friends. When Naxos rebelled against Athenian imperialism and attempted to leave the league in 470, the island was blockaded by an Athenian

control of a local gold mine. Her fleet was defeated and confiscated, and the city walls pulled down. Thasos appealed to Sparta for help, but Sparta was busy with the *helot* revolt that had been brewing for years.

With each rebellion quelled, Athens demanded tribute from the guilty *polis*. Athenian currency was made compulsory throughout the league. As we have seen, individual coinage emphasized a city-state's independence, and this further evidence of Athenian imperialism infuriated most of its allies. Liked or not, however, members of the Delian League were wedded to the Athenian star.

The defensive past against Persia—the

fleet and its citizens were forced back into line. A worse fate lay in store for Thasos in the mid-460s, when the island rebelled against Athenian

rationale behind the league—seemed to be defunct with Perikles' Greek-Persian peace treaty of 449, but the Athenian *boule* and *demos* had no intention of breaking up what had effectively become its own empire. Tribute payment to Athens in Athenian coinage was no longer for protection, but for the greater glorification of Athens.

For Athens, the mid-fifth century may have been a golden period under the guidance of Perikles; less so for the Athenian allies. The first statesman and leader of the democrats was a great orator, and from 460 he spoke eloquently of democracy, freedom, and the efficacy of open government. This, of course, was all for Athens—he was at the same time the leading advocate of imperialism. It was Perikles who first protected Athenian citizenship by introducing a series of laws designed to restrict the rights of *metics* in trade and business. He also set a foreign policy that led to the crisis that would ultimately bring disaster to Athens. Athens' alienation of its allies and neighbors reached a head after Perikles' death in 429, but the build-up had begun a decade before.

Dogged by Sparta

The Samian revolt in 440 was the most serious insurrection Athens faced from its Aegean allies, and although the navy quashed it within two years, the cost was high. Not only did it drain the treasury of over a thousand talents (roughly ten percent of the city's wealth), but it was clear that the Samians were supported by several allies and encouraged by anti-Athenian states in mainland Greece.

At the head of support for the rebels of Samos was Sparta and its Peloponnesian allies. It was becoming clear that in order to maintain the integrity of its maritime empire, Athens had to challenge Sparta to stop its rival's interference. It was feared that failure to take a stand would lead to more opposition, more revolts, and ultimately a costly struggle to maintain the vital sea links with Thrace, the Black Sea coast, and the overseas colonies in the western Mediterranean. The concern was valid: the most vital imports were grain and timber by 435, without which Attica was vulnerable.

Perikles and his fellow civic leaders recognized that a war with Sparta would be far more costly than quelling the revolt on Samos, but such a war was deemed necessary to prevent a gradual erosion of the Athenian economy. The Athenians probably felt well prepared for war.

They had the richest treasury in Greece, a fleet twice as large as the rest of the Greek states combined, and her small army could defend Athens from behind the virtually impregnable Long Walls. If the Peloponnesian League and Sparta could be humiliated, the position of Athens' maritime empire would be secure.

Once the decision was made, the drift toward war was inevitable. The greatest democratic power in the ancient world would soon find herself locked in a struggle for supremacy that would last for three long decades and shatter Athens' imperial dreams.

Above: Unlike Naxos, Samians held Athens at bay for almost two years from 440, but in the end the might of the Athenian navy told. The most important temple on Samos is the Heraion, of which this is the Sacred Way.

CHAPTER 10

RECREATION AND RELIGIOUS FESTIVALS

Below: An aerial view of the athletic stadium at Olympia, birthplace of the modern Olympic Games. To the ancient Greeks, athletics were an integral part of the religious experience.

In city-states, almost all public events entailed some aspect of religious observance. As we have seen, religion was an important part of life, and although there were no churches in the modern sense, Greeks shared a common religious belief and worshipped in a similar fashion. A shared mythology provided a basis for culture, while local gods, particular forms of regional rituals, and the tendency for cult worship enriched the religious fabric of society.

The Greeks honored gods in a variety of ways,

including sacrifices or votive offerings before marching into battle. Every city-state had its own calendar of religious observance and its own religious festivals, although gods remained the same throughout the Greek world. Failure to honor a particular god could lead to personal retribution, or worse, bring ill-fortune on the *polis*.

To the ancient warrior-Greeks, athleticism was essential to survival, so celebrating sport was a religious matter that the gods took an interest in. The first Olympian (or Olympic)

games were not a spectacle, they were religious festivals, where the athletes performed for the gods as much as for their *polis* or themselves. Athletic achievement was venerated and Olympian heroes were celebrated throughout the Greek world. In a similar way, athleticism and personal fitness was seen as a sign of spiritual as well as physical well-being, hence athletic activities were encouraged among male citizens of almost every city-state.

Religious festivals took many forms— processions, offerings, sacrifices, and even hedonistic orgies were held in honor of the gods, making Greek religion one of the most elastic, diverse, and all-encompassing faiths of the ancient world. Each god had a role, and most had cult followers, embracing the traits personified by the god and worshipping that deity above all other members of the Olympian panoply.

Religious cults held their own festivals, either in private or as part of a civic celebration. Perhaps the most interesting was the cult of Dionysos, the god of fertility and wine (*also see pages 52–53*). While many religions were an all-male preserve, the Dionysian cult was open to the faithful of both genders, and libation, sexual release, and spiritual trances formed part of the Dionysian ritual.

Drama festivals were a part of religious celebrations in which honoring the gods was combined with entertainment. For example, in the theater dedicated to Dionysos in Athens, playwrights held contests with performances of tragedies, an important element of the Athenian religious festival that honored Dionysos. While poetry, literature, and song served to eulogize the gods, it was the dramatic arts that formed a vital part of observance during religious festivals. No other society intertwined culture, sport, and religion in such a dramatic fashion.

THE ATHLETE

The ancient Greeks' great emphasis on athletic ability is reflected in their extensive artistic legacy, where sculptors captured the fascination with athleticism and male physical prowess. Athletic feats were recorded in poetry, drama, and song.

Right: The *Diskobolus* by second-century sculptor Myron only survives in Roman copies. Statues such as this masterpiece inspired Renaissance artists like Michelangelo.

Below: At the dawn of the Classical period of ancient Greek art, this Archaic relief of youths playing a ball game, c.510, has all the realism and vitality of later pieces.

Although the Greek passion for athleticism was probably rooted in civic pride, and the notion that fitness for civic responsibility was linked to mental and physical prowess, the cult of the athlete went far deeper into the ancient Greek psyche than that. It contained elements of military preparation—soldiers (or future soldiers) needed to be in prime physical condition to fight for their *polis*. The sporting arenas and gymnasia were an alternative to the barrack square, while the emphasis on physical training from childhood ensured that the majority of young males would be fit enough to fight.

By the Classical Age, this had taken a new direction. In Athens and other cities, the gymnasia became open to all young male citizens, regardless of background and parental wealth. These centers of athleticism and learning became vital social hubs for the youth of the *polis*, where they could compete against each other in sporting

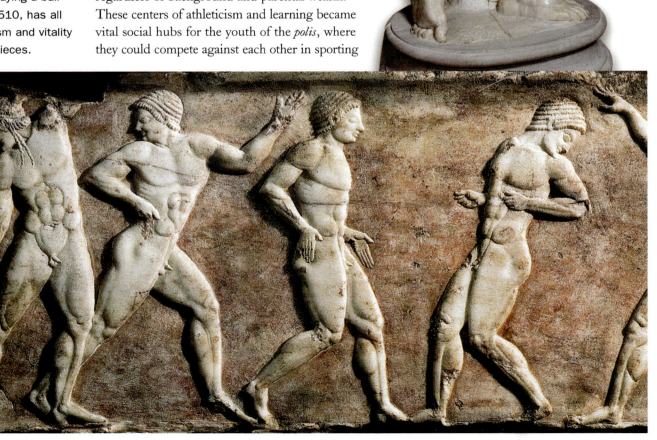

events, or simply socialize with their peers.

Athletic meetings involved an amount of ritual, both religious and practical. Since most formed part of religious festivals, similar observations became part of the athlete's daily ritual in the *gymnasion* (*see also page 95*). More practical customs included the oiling or dusting of each other's bodies with fine sand prior to an event, then communal bathing afterward, followed by a scraping of the body as a cleansing process, using a curved bronze *strigil*, or scraper. This combination of male bonding, peer competition, and pride in one's body was a major part of the athletic cult.

By the end of the Classical Age and during the early Hellenistic Age, sporting events in gymnasia had evolved into spectator events, in which people came to cheer on their favorites, but this was a subversion of the original idea of the institution. Scholastic centers that combined the training of mind and body, and encouraged physical excellence, gymnasia were designed as venues for athletes, not as entertainment for the citizens.

Admiring the male form

Another crucial element in the Greek athletic cult was the notion that the male body was inherently beautiful. Nudity was the norm in sports and—since women were excluded from most festivals—athletes were encouraged to flaunt their physiques and compare them to those of their peers.

Female nudity in Greek statuary only became fashionable during the mid-fourth century. Before that, the athletic male form was considered the personification of grace and beauty. The winners of athletic events were feted as near-gods, and like modern sportsmen solicited for endorsements. Athletes were frequently asked to pose for sculptors and artists, eager to capture the athlete at the height of his fame and physical perfection.

While sports played a frequent part in religious festivals within the city-state, the most prestigious arena for the athlete was one of the panhellenic competitions, such as the Isthmian, Pythian, or Olympian games. Of these, the latter was by far the most prestigious event, and competition for places was fierce.

The adulation afforded to the ultimate victors was immense. Olympic athletes such as Milo of Kroton, Polydamas of Skotoussa, and Melankomas of Caria became the most celebrated men in Greece, and their fame continued long after their passing. Greek writers such as Strabo, Pindar, and Pausinas wrote of their achievements for posterity, encouraging subsequent generations of athletes to strive for even greater glory.

The athletes also gained glory for their city-state and their gymnasia. Direct rewards were minimal—the ultimate prize was a simple victor's crown fashioned from olive leaves, rather than financial reward. But the wreath was cut from the sacred grove in Olympia, a physical link with the gods and the athlete's immortal achievement.

Top: When this sculpture was made in the 4th century, horse racing had become a spectacular spectator sport at the Olympic and other games.

Above: Youth exercising with stone weights. Weights were also used in jumping contests.

119

THE ATHLETIC CONTEST

The Greeks used contests to honor the gods and glorify their athletes through victory against rivals from other city-states. Although several athletic festivals took place, the most prestigious was the games held every four years at Olympia.

Right: Grooves cut into stones mark the starting line for foot-races in the Olympia *stadion* (its position can be seen to the left in the picture on page 116). These stones replaced earlier ones of the Archaic period.

Below: Competing athletes entered the Olympia *stadion* under this arch and down the passage between the seating. Cheats had their names recorded on the bases of nearby statues.

Little is known about the origins of panhellenic sporting festivals, but it seems they began during the Archaic Age in the eighth century. Designed to function as both athletic contests and religious festivals, in the eyes of contemporary writers they represented the finest notions of Greekness.

Rivalries and even warfare were set aside for the duration of an event and for an agreed period before and after, permitting sportsmen and their entourages to travel to and from the games in safety. The games were a bonding element, uniting the city-states into one coherent Greek body, even though that unity was short-lived. The games therefore encouraged the awareness that Greeks shared a common language, culture, and religion, regardless of *polis*, ethnic roots, or geography.

Since the games were essentially religious in theme, it was natural that they were often held at sites of religious importance. The Isthmian Games were held every two years in the isthmus of Corinth, a location important for its symbolism, representing the unity of the Peloponnesian Greeks with fellow Greeks to the north. The Pythian Games were held in Delphi every four years, and became the second-largest sporting event in ancient Greece.

Of greater import were the Olympian Games, held at Olympia, in the northwestern Peloponnese. Olympia was recognized as a non-political sanctuary, and the holy center was built in the midst of a sacred wood known as the Altis, beneath the Hill of Kronos, named after the father of Zeus. It was a place of mystery, myth, religion, and legend; a fitting venue for the creation of a new breed of

sporting heroes. Held every four years, the games were fielded in honor of Zeus. The Temple of Zeus at Olympia was the focal point and its temple staff the organizers.

Olympic glory

The first recorded Olympic event took place in 776, when Koroibis of Elis won the *stadion* race, a sprinting event equivalent to the modern 200 meters (actually 184 meters, 200 yards). At that stage the Olympic Games was a small, local event (Elis lies to the west of Olympia), but by the Classical Age in the fifth century it had blossomed into the major panhellenic festival of its day.

Lasting a minimum of five days, the central games were flanked by other religious festivals and diplomatic gatherings, so the celebrations lasted for almost two weeks. The itinerary of the games in 472 reveals the frantic pace of the event and the importance placed on various sports.

The first day involved an opening ceremony, involving religious celebrations and sacrifices to the gods. On the second day the *stadion* race was held, the most prestigious contest of the games. The *stadion* was an oblong arena, surrounded by tiered banks, and served as the focal point for

most of the Olympic events.

Over the next three days these events were held: discus, wrestling, boxing, long-jump, javelin, and pentathlon, which combined the two throwing events, wrestling, and long-jumping with the sprint race (known as the *stade*). The *pancration* was a combination of boxing and wrestling. This event involved a series of paired fights that continued until one of the athletes conceded, and almost anything was allowed except biting and gouging.

The final two events, horse-racing and chariot-racing, were considered the exclusive preserve of the aristocratic and wealthy. Entrants had to own their horses, and although these events became increasingly less popular as the Classical Age progressed (and democratic government became increasingly common), they attracted widespread support.

In an age of near-constant warfare between the city-states, sporting events brought out the finest qualities of the ancient Greeks and unified the Greek world, from the Black Sea to Sicily, by means of friendly rivalry and sportsmanship. It is incredible that, some 2,500 years later, the same qualities attend the modern Olympic Games.

Above: The small but perfectly shaped theater at Olympia is a reminder that in ancient Greece, sport was inextricably entwined with both religion and dramatic entertainment. The aerial photograph shows the theater after its restoration.

RELIGIOUS FESTIVALS

Religious festivals were often the only break from daily routine that most citizens enjoyed, so they were widely popular, allowing the free population of a *polis* to join together for religious devotion and civic entertainment.

Below: *Bacchanal* by the Victorian painter Lawrence Alma-Tadema portrays a cheerfully pleasing Dionysian rite (Bacchus was the Roman name for Dionysos). Since many Greek religious rituals were closely kept secrets, this whimsical vision may well be as accurate as any, and certainly accords with many similar scenes from ancient Greek vases.

Festivals were designed to please or at least appease the gods. In a civilization where gods were so numerous, religious observation was virtually a constant activity, since to omit the worship of a god was to invite divine retribution. Far more effective were city-wide festivities, where important gods and often several secondary ones could be worshipped at the same time.

To modern observers, many of these festivals appear far from religious. Festivals such as panhellenic athletic games, drama festivals, and civic processions concentrated on pleasing the participants and observers. Nonetheless, they were dedicated to the gods and held in locations that were considered to be religious centers, or had been consecrated and dedicated to one or more of the Olympian deities.

Almost all religious festivals began with a procession, where cult followers honored the deity, or other male or female citizens offered their collective civic observance. Food such as

honey, bread, and cake was offered to the gods, and sometimes livestock was slaughtered in a sacrificial ritual. Dancing and singing often featured in these celebrations, which could last for several days.

City-states such as Athens, Thebes, and Corinth held several festivals every year, while even larger events were held every two, three, or four years. Events of this kind included the great panhellenic religious and sporting events, and civic festivals, such as the Athenian Great Panathenaic procession, a week-long festival held every four years in honor of Athene. The *cella* frieze on the Parthenon depicts celebrants at a Panathenaic festival, men and women marching in procession, carrying votive offerings to the goddess. Appropriately, the Parthenon housed a giant statue of Athene, and the neighboring Erechthion temple was of particular importance during this festival.

Wisdom of the Oracle

Most festivals and cults were local affairs, but several festivals united Greece. These panhellenic festivals were often held in locations of particular religious importance, such as at Delphi (dedicated to the god Apollo) or Eleusis (cult center for Demeter). During the fifth

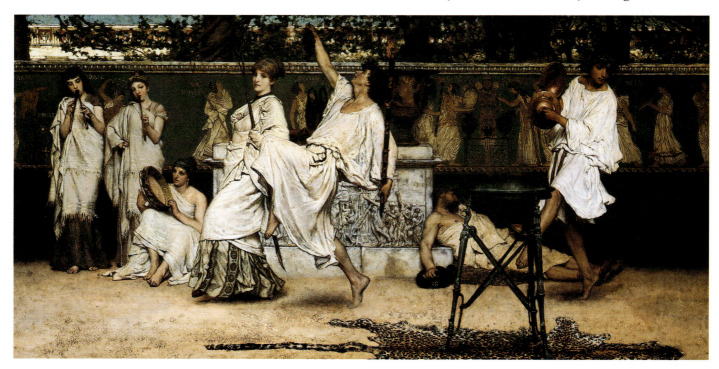

century these sites were lavishly provided with festival buildings, temples, and sporting stadiums.

Delphi was also the home of the Oracle, a location based on the premise that Apollo, known for his divination of future events, had deemed Delphi the *omphalos* (navel) of the world (*see plan on page 73*). Delegations traveled from all over Greece to seek its advice, the words of Apollo interpreted through the medium of the *pythia*, or high priest or priestess. Such consultations were accompanied by religious celebration and often took place during festivals. The site retained its neutral position throughout the wars that plagued Greece during the fifth century, so the faithful or curious who came to Delphi or Olympia were protected, regardless of where they had traveled from.

Dramatic festivals were also a form of religious celebration. Initially popular in the countryside, by the fifth century public performances were given in the *agora* of almost every city-state, with actors and orators addressing their audience from a makeshift platform, or from the back of a cart. During the sixth century some civic authorities built permanent theaters, and by the late fifth century they had become magnificent venues.

Whatever the nature of the festival, its religious overtones were never far beneath the surface. Even dramas, comedies, and tragedies could be dedicated to gods, tragedies in particular forming part of the widespread celebration of the Dionysian cult. To the ancient Greeks, celebrating the gods through festivals was an important part of religious belief, but it was also free from the constraints of later, more dogmatic approaches to religion. This made Greek festivals a unique combination of devotion, entertainment, and spectacle.

Above: The frieze that ran all the way around the Parthenon's *cella* wall of the collonade depicted the Great Panathenaic procession (*see map, page 107*). This detail is only a fragment of the north frieze, which shows Athenian *ephebes* of military age riding in the procession—the pride of Athens in all their youthful glory.

THE CELEBRATION OF DIONYSOS

Originally a Thracian deity, Dionysos was worshipped by cult followers whose devotions were sexual and hedonistic. Southern Greeks saw Dionysos purely as the god of wine, but gradually the worship of the two groups combined to form a new cult.

Right: Roman copy of a Greek sculpture of Dionysos.

The worship of Dionysos was one of the more unusual religious cults in ancient Greece. The Thracian god gained in popularity during the seventh century, combining his Thracian role as a fertility deity with his Dorian Greek incarnation of god of wine and drinking (the Roman version of Dionysos is Bacchus). Priests at the Oracle of Delphi took the initiative to combine the two Dionysian elements, creating a single godhead at the start of the sixth century.

In mythology, Dionysos was a son of Zeus—*Dios* means "of Zeus," and the root of *nysos* is Thracian—through his coupling with the mortal Thracian princess Semele. She was consumed by fire after conceiving her son, which is why Dionysos was sometimes given the appellation *pyrigenes* (born of fire). Zeus nurtured the unborn child inside his thigh until Dionysos was born. When he became a god Dionysos resurrected his mother by placing her "in the stars."

According to the Oracle of Delphi, Dionysos had prophetic abilities, making him the equal of Apollo in Greek religion. The cycle of the year in Delphi was even divided into two parts, *apollonian* and *dionysiac*. His original role was as a young god of vegetation, as well as wine and fertility, but the latter elements remained central to the Dionysian cult.

He was often portrayed as a young man or a bull (or at least a man with the head of a bull); a symbol of virility. It was this sexual connotation that came to dominate his role and played a leading part in the Dionysian cult that first appeared at the end of the sixth century.

In ancient Greece, religious "cults" meant the concentration of veneration on a particular god, at least at one particular time or in a set location. Cult ceremonies frequently involved offerings of food, drink, and even animal sacrifice. In the case of the cult of Dionysos, the Athenians celebrated in two religious festivals, known as the Great and the Small Dionysia.

For body and spirit

Elements of his Thracian origin can be seen in the mysticism associated with his worship, but the main element of the cult was a veneration of the body, of sexuality, and of fertility. Ceremonies involved orgies, trances, and even mass hysteria, where disciples acted like souls possessed, screaming and dancing themselves into a frenzy.

Of all the Greek religious cults, this was the most "pagan" and the most physical. Women were permitted to be cult followers, due to the sexual nature of the worship, and all adherents gained spiritual well-being through physical pleasure and orgiastic ritual. During these ceremonies, the faithful called on Dionysos to join them, necessitating a near-constant cacophony of chanting and shouting (*see picture on page 122*).

Civic Dionysian ceremonies involved music, the presentation of drama contests—where tragedies were judged by audiences—and street processions. Male worshippers often participated in these festivities while carrying an over-sized mock phallus in front of them, a potent symbol of the cult's sexual nature.

Of all the Greek religious movements, the cult of Dionysos was probably the most popular, yet the most mysterious. Worshipped in ivy-clad grottoes or wood glades as much as in temples, Dionysos represented the basic desires of Greek society and civic involvement in religious festivals, designed to combine civic pride with state-wide religious observation.

Greek religion had its darker sides, and although the cult of Dionysos has been criticized by conservative historians for its hedonism, it elevated social intercourse and the importance of fertility to become part of life and worship. Few other aspects of Greek religion better demonstrate the intricate mix of entertainment, devotion, and civic fulfilment that typified the majority of popular religious festivals.

Above: This marble head of a satyr was found near the remains of the Odeion of Aphrodisias, in the uplands of what is now Turkey. Alexander the Great's conquests helped spread the Dionysian cult outside Greece, and since the half-goat half-men satyrs were the god's companions, they became popular across the Hellenistic world.

Left: A fourth-century votive tablet with a relief depicting a Dionysiac ceremony. Women were allowed to join in festivities, even when celebrants became inebriated.

125

THE GREEK THEATER

During the Classical Age, theater was an increasingly important element of Greek culture, combining religious devotion with entertainment. In the fifth century new theaters were built, becoming the principal venues for recreational gatherings.

Below: Remains of the Theater of Dionysos seen from the Acropolis of Athens. The circular space is the orchestra (chorus space). The first row was reserved for the aristocracy (*see facing picture*).

Theaters in ancient Greece shared certain features. Almost all were composed of three major elements: the *orchestra* (chorus space), the *koilon* (auditorium), and the *skene* (stage, from which we derive the word "scene"). The *orchestra* was a circular, oval, or sometimes rectangular spot in front of the *skene* where religious observances took place. In the Archaic period this area was also used by actors giving performances, but as theater developed and more dramatic productions were developed, the action moved back to the *skene*. Traditionally the

orchestra housed an altar, but by the Classical Age its main function was to house the chorus leader or director (known as the *koryphaios*), standing on a *themili* in the center of the *orchestra*.

The *skene* became the main stage, although acting was concentrated on its forward edge, known as the *proskenion* (i.e. in front of the *skene*). The sides and rear of the stage were decorated with painted panels, or even permanent walls, which could screen actors standing off stage. Traditional decorations were limited to representations of temple frontages, but by the fifth century other backdrops set the scene, such as depictions of wooded glades or mountaintops.

Between the *skene* and the audience seated in the *koilon*, two walkways known as the *paradoi* allowed actors to enter the theater, and give recitations or sing as they walked. The walkways

were also used to introduce new characters in dramatic fashion, since they appeared behind the audience, then moved onto the stage.

Symbolism was important. An actor arriving on *skene* from the left side was deemed to have come from the countryside, while one arriving on the right came from the sea or from a city. Behind the *proskenion*, two symbolic doors allowed actors to enter and exit the action, moving through them from the *proskenion* to the rear of the stage, where they were deemed in the area of the action, but not directly participating in it.

The mechanics of theater

At the very back of the *skene* was a backdrop, but during the Hellenistic period a raised platform known as the *logeion* was added, allowing actors to stand over the proceedings, watching events as if from afar. The entire stage was covered with a flat roof (the *theologeion*), and the acting area lit by rushes, dipped in a sulfurous solution for steady burning, to create dramatic effect.

Stage managers' equipment included the *aiorema* (crane), which allowed actors to "fly" onto the *skene*, the *ekeclema* for presenting or removing "dead" characters, and a pair of revolving *periaktoi* (pillars), which could be turned to present a new item of scenery and remove an old one.

The *koilon* (or *theatron* in the Hellenistic period) was built as a circle or, more usually, as a half-circle. The first theaters were built of wood, but by the late fifth century the majority were of stone, with stone benches tiered up and away from the stage. The first (and lowest) row of seats, the *proedria*, were reserved for senior figures in the *polis* or for priests, usually followers of the cult that the performance was dedicated to.

Permanent theaters were built across Greece and the Aegean in the Classical Age, and this trend continued into the Hellenistic Age. They varied enormously in scale. The Theater of Dionysos Eleutheros beneath the Acropolis in Athens, founded in the fifth century, had a capacity of over 17,000. By contrast, small provincial theaters might only seat a few hundred people. The scale varied, but the basic design remained the same—the principles of theater construction were as rigidly applied as the rules governing the performances.

Principally, the Greek theater was a place of

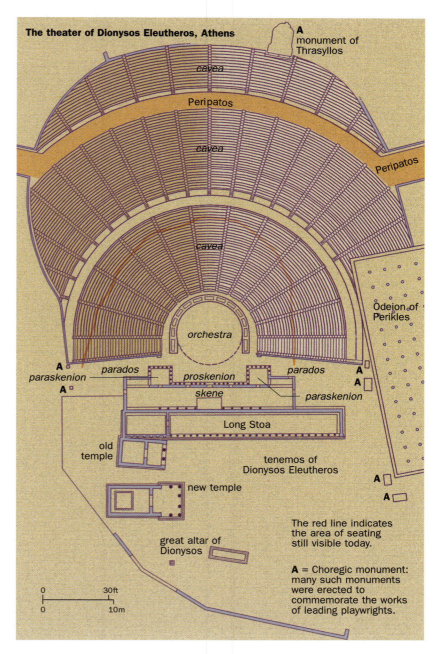

The theater of Dionysos Eleutheros, Athens

A monument of Thrasyllos

cavea

Peripatos

cavea

Peripatos

cavea

orchestra

Ödeion of Perikles

A paraskenion

parados

proskenion

A

parados

A **A**

A skene

paraskenion

Long Stoa

old temple

tenemos of Dionysos Eleutheros

A

new temple

A

The red line indicates the area of seating still visible today.

great altar of Dionysos

A = Choregic monument: many such monuments were erected to commemorate the works of leading playwrights.

0   30ft
0   10m

religious celebration. Its entertainment function was secondary for much of the period, although popular plays, and above all comedies, were also staged, and proved highly popular.

Below: Seating for Athenian dignitaries is more elaborate than for citizens behind.

CHAPTER 11
THE PELOPONNESIAN WAR

ADRIATIC SEA

Kymai
Neapolis

Taras

TYRRHENIAN SEA

MAGNA GRAECIA

415 Nikias

414 Gylippos

Lipara

Segesta
Halikyai

Himera

Messana
Rhegion

Lokroi

Selinus

Naxos

Katana

SICILY Gela

413 Syracuse

Kamarina

W ar loomed over ancient Greece. Athens had emerged as a naval power and founded the wealthy Delian League. Sparta had formed the Peloponnesian League, but it was a regional military power, lacking the financial resources of the Delian League. During the 460s, Sparta was inward-looking, preoccupied by a *helot* revolt, but when in 460 Megara withdrew from the Peloponnesian League and allied with Athens, war broke out. The First Peloponnesian War was a nine-year conflict in which Athenians dominated central Greece by fortifying Corinth and its isthmus.

However, the loss of an Athenian army in Persian-held Egypt in 454 prompted rebellion within the Athenian realm and forced Athens to the negotiating table. Athens and Sparta agreed a cease-fire in 451. And when, two years later, Persia signed a treaty with Athens, it seemed that Greece had been spared further physical conflict.

Unrest over Athens' high-handed treatment of its allies led to the withdrawal from Delian League of Boeotia and Lokris. The Spartans marched north to join in the conflict, forcing Megara to change sides and ensuring the Athenians signed another peace treaty. This time the Spartans emerged as the dominant power in central Greece. Both sides knew that the peace was only a temporary one. Athens and Sparta began preparations for a major war.

Athens enforced the loyalty of her remaining Delian allies, crushing revolts wherever they sprang up to ensure the members remained steadfast. A conflict with Corinth led the Athenians to aid the rebel Corinthian colony of Kerkyra, and in 431 they besieged Poteidaia, a Corinthian colony in Chalkidike (although a member of the Delian League and theoretically an Athenian ally as well). This was too much for Sparta, who invoked the treaty with Corinth to

declare war against Athens. The Second Peloponnesian War—a far more devastating conflict than the first—had begun.

With Sparta dominant on land and Athens at sea, it was an oddly balanced conflict in which neither side appeared capable of striking a decisive blow. This impasse forced both sides to adopt radical strategies in an effort to cripple the other. The Second Peloponnesian War is historically divided into three phases: the Archidamian War (431–21), the Sicilian Expedition or Alkibiadian phase (420–13), and the Ionian War (412–04). During these phases the war spread throughout the Greek world and resulted in a huge loss of life and revenue. In its

Peleponnesian war, 431–404

- Delian League, 431
- Athenian allies, 431
- Athenian allies in Magna Graecia
- Sparta and allied states, 431
- Spartan allies in Magna Graecia
- neutral Greek states
- Persian Empire, 404
- Macedon, 404

major offensives
→ Athenian
→ Spartan
- Athenian victory
- Spartan victory

BLACK SEA

• Apollonia

• Epidamnos

Byzantion •

Abdera • Maroneia
⊗ Amphipolis • Thasos
422 • Stageiros
Pella • • Akanthos
MACEDON • Methone CHALKIDIKE Ainos •
• Poteidaia Aigospotami ⊗
405

SEA OF MARMARA

410 ⊗ • Kyzikos

Imbros
Kynossema
411

Lemnos

EPIRUS • Larisa
THESSALY Northern
Sporades

Kerkyra
(Corfu)
Ambrakia • Skyros

AEGEAN SEA

Methymna •
Mytilene •
Lesbos • ⊗ Aginusai
406

Phokaia •

• Sardis

AETOLIA
ACARNANIA
Kephalenia PHOKIS
LOKRIS • Delphi
Zante Naupaktos BOEOTIA Chalkis
429 Thebes • • Eretria
Plataia • Dekeleia
ACHAEA Megara • ATTICA
Sikyon • • Athens
ELIS • Corinth
• Elis ARCADIA
Mantineia ⊗ • Argos
418
PELOPONNESE

Delion
424

406

411
411, 405

Chios

IONIA

Andros
Tenos

Ikaria

Ephesos •
Samos
Priene •
Miletos •

SPARTA
Pylos • • Sparta
Sphakteria
425

416

Paros

Delos Mykonos

Naxos

Halikarnassos •

Kos

411 ⊗

429
431
425
424
414 Gylippos
415 Nikias
424 Kythera

Melos •

Thera •

SEA OF CRETE

Rhodes

Carpathos

MEDITERRANEAN SEA

IONIAN SEA

CRETE

wake it would also bring disease, devastation, and famine to mainland Greece and Sicily.

Ultimately, the only winners were the states that stayed neutral in this fratricidal conflict.

The weakened Greek city-states that emerged at the end of the conflict were ill-prepared to stave off invasion by Macedon, the rising star on the northern fringes of the Greek world.

SPARTA ATTACKS

The first phase of the Second Peloponnesian War was named after the king of Sparta, Archidamos, whose policy of ravaging Attica caused untold suffering. Both sides expected the war to be relatively short and did little to prepare for a longer conflict.

The Spartan strategy devised by Archidamos was simple. Sparta's elite army would invade central Greece each year and force the weaker Athenian forces to withdraw behind the Long Walls. This was intended to leave the Spartans free to ravage Attica, deprive Athens of resources, and force the Athenians to sue for peace.

However, the strategy had a serious flaw. It either overlooked or ignored the fact that as a maritime power with the Long Walls protecting the link between itself and the sea, Athens' leaders had no difficulty in importing sufficient

food to feed the population. Further, Perikles, architect of Athenian policy, realized that the fleet could outflank the land-based Spartans to transport raiding expeditions to the Peloponnesian League's homelands.

In 431 Spartan forces invaded Attica, but as Athenians withdrew behind their walls, the Spartans returned home, leaving the Athenians free to raid into Peloponnesian territory. It was clear that this would be a longer war than anyone had anticipated, involving gradual attrition, rather than a single, dramatic battlefield victory. The Spartans returned in 430, but this time Athens was struck by a plague. The thousands of Athenians who died that summer did little to break the proud city's resolve, and the war continued with a weak Athenian campaign in Chalkidike. By this time Archidamos had realized that his Attican invasion had achieved little military advantage beyond causing famine, so in 429 he led his army northward against Poteidaia, a city allied with Athens. Poteidaia survived the subsequent siege and the Spartans returned home with little to show for their efforts.

Meanwhile, in a blow even more bitter to Spartan hopes, their only naval ally, Corinth, was put out of action by a successful Athenian sea action in the Gulf of Corinth. Athenian celebrations were marred by the plague that had set in on the heels of famine and the death of Perikles, one of its victims. The one Athenian leader who combined political genius with military common sense was gone. The war continued, and the following year the Spartans were back in front of the Long Walls.

Defeating the invincible

A revolt in Mytilene, capital of Lesbos, further threatened Athens' empire. This presented Archidamos with a new strategic option when Lesbos appealed to Sparta for help. He needed

The first part of the Peloponnesian War, 431–420

- ▨ Athens and allies, 431
- ▨ Peloponnesian League, 431
- ✖ Athenian victory
- ✖ Spartan victory
- → Athenian campaign
- → Spartan campaign

The Spartan blockade of Athens rapidly led to famine and disease in the city. One of the plague's eminent victims in 429 was Perikles.

When Lesbos seceded from the Delian League in 428, Athenian response was swift and brutal. After the island's capture, its citizens were turned into little more than paid slaves.

464	460	451	431	425	422	421	418
After an earthquake, *helot* slaves in Sparta rebel	Megara allies with Athens; the First Peloponnesian Wars begins	End of the First Peloponnesian War; Athens and Sparta sign a peace treaty	Beginning of the Second Peloponnesian War	Sparta's elite troops are defeated by Athenian warriors at Sphakteria	Though victorious, Spartan general Brassidas is killed in the Battle of Amphipolis	The Peace of Nikias ends the Archidamian War phase	The Argive League dissolves after Spartans defeat the alliance at Mantineia

a navy and began to build a fleet. However, before it was ready to sail in 428, Athens had already crushed the rebellion, and the opportunity to incite further discord within the Delian League was lost.

That same year, the Spartans captured Plataia (site of the great victory over the Persians in 479), massacring its defenders. The Greek cities were slowly coming to terms with the likelihood that they would all become embroiled in this war, as pro-democratic and pro-oligarchic elements sided with Athens and Sparta respectively. A revolt in Kerkyra on Corfu led Athenian troops to quash the pro-oligarchic faction, then the Athenians launched an ill-fated invasion of Aetolia, before defending their base at Naupaktos (seized from the Lokrians back in 459) against a joint Aetolian and Peloponnesian attack. In the ensuing battle, the Athenian commander Demosthenes defeated his Peloponnesian opponents, and inflicted the first serious Spartan setback of the war.

In 425, an Athenian expedition sailed down the western coast of the Peloponnese while the main Spartan army occupied Attica. Demosthenes established a bridgehead at Pylos to use the fortified city as a base for raids into the hinterland. Agis, the new Spartan king, raced south to Pylos, contained the Athenian base and threw troops into shore defenses on the nearby island of Sphakteria, which covers the bay of Pylos, to protect against further landings.

The Athenians held off Spartan attacks for two days before their ships returned, brushing aside the smaller Spartan fleet in the area and trapping 420 Spartan troops on Sphakteria. These men were the elite of the Spartan army; a cadre of fighters they could ill-afford to lose. Local peace talks broke down, and an Athenian amphibious attack led to a humiliating Spartan defeat, removing the aura of invincibility that for a century had given the Spartan warriors their edge in battle.

Left: Sparta was publicly humiliated by the erection of the Nike (Victory) of Paionios, which originally stood opposite the east door of the Temple of Zeus at Olympia. It was dedicated by Messenian allies of Athens in 421, who defeated a crack Spartan army at Sphakteria in 425.

415	413–04	411	411	410	406	406	404
An Athenian army and fleet are slaughtered by Syracusans in the Sicilian Expedition	Spartans strike from a fortress at Dekleleia, north of Athens	Athens' fleet is defeated by Chios, one of many cities in revolt against Athens	Athens is led by the Council of Four Hundred	Athens recaptures Kyzikos and rejects Sparta's call for peace	At Lesbos, Sparta's navy is defeated in the largest sea battle of the wars	Lysander routs Athens' fleet at Aigospotami; he then slaughters the prisoners	Besieged and starved of supplies, Athens surrenders

A FRUITLESS PEACE

A humbled Sparta was on the defensive, but Athenian over-confidence and a revitalized Spartan army, led by a shrewd young general, altered the course of the war. As the conflict spread, both sides fought increasingly brutal campaigns.

A fter their defeat at Pylos and Sphakteria, the Spartans were forced to garrison their coastline. An attempt to seize the Peloponnesian League city of Megara through treachery was foiled by Brassidas, a young Spartan general. The rising army star was then commanded to head further north to harry Athenian allies in Chalkidike and Thrace. Brassidas marched through Thessaly into Thrace, then entered Chalkidike, a reluctant Athenian ally. Athens marshalled two generals to cut Brassidas's line of communication, with Boeotia—now allied with Sparta—the key. Demosthenes based his army at Naupaktos, on the Gulf of Corinth, while Hippokrates built a fort at Delion

(Tangara), on the Boeotian-Attican border.

This division was a mistake. The larger Boeotian force easily defeated the Athenian army at Delion in 424 and killed Hippokrates. At Naupaktos, Demosthenes was too far away to affect Brassidas and feared a Spartan cross-gulf attack if he left Naupaktos weakly defended. Despite the presence of an Athenian fleet at the nearby island of Thasos, Brassidas surprised and captured the key Chalkidikian city of Amphipolis, and persuaded most of its neighbors to revolt against Athens.

Despite an attempted truce (423), the war in Chalkidike continued, and Athens sent two expeditions to reconquer it. The pro-Spartan city of Skione was besieged by Nikostratos, while a larger force, commanded by Kleon, political successor to Perikles, landed near Amphipolis. In the ensuing Battle of Amphipolis (422) Brassidas was victorious. Kleon was killed and the Athenians routed, but Brassidas was mortally wounded during the closing stages of the fight and died within hours of his enemy.

Both sides were exhausted and needed time to recover and reorganize. For Athenians, it was clear that any further campaigning in Chalkidike could jeopardize their fragile empire, while the Spartans had become disillusioned after their quick victory failed to materialize. The war was also no longer one between two city-states, but had spread to encompass rival leagues and threatened to engulf the entire Greek world. Peace talks were opened and the result was a treaty, named after Nikias, leader of the Athenian diplomatic legation.

Resumption of war

Signed in the spring of 421, the Peace of Nikias was intended to be a 50-year truce between the rival leagues. It called for the dismemberment of the Peloponnesian League, the return of all prisoners, and the restoration to the each side of all cities captured during the war. However, the Peloponnesian states of Corinth, Megara, and Boeotia refused to sign, since they felt cheated by its terms, the Spartans refused to abandon Amphipolis, and many Chalkidikian cities

The new Argive League against Sparta, 420–418

 Athens and allies, 420

 Argive League, 419

 Sparta, 419

✖ Athenian victory

✖ Spartan victory

→ Athenian campaign

→ Spartan campaign

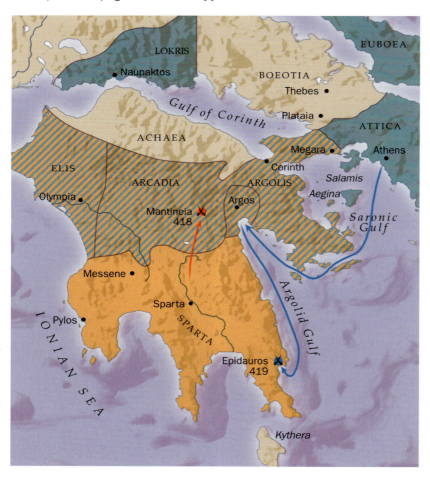

refused to realign themselves with Athens, which forced Nikias to make examples of them. When Skione fell to an Athenian army, all the men were put to the sword, and the women and children sold into slavery.

The Peace of Nikias was more of a lull in the fighting than a serious attempt at conciliation. As the Athenian historian Thucydides claimed: "The truce was never properly enforced, and each side did the other a great deal of harm, until finally they were forced to break the treaty they had made… and once more declare war openly upon each other."

This reversal began with the alliance of Corinth, Mantineia, and Elis with Argos, a new power bloc to replace the Peloponnesian League. In 419, Athens formed an alliance with Argos, which gave the city's strategists a useful bridgehead on the Peloponnese, south of the isthmus of Corinth. Clearly this was a direct threat to Sparta and a contravention of the terms of the Peace of Nikias. Alkiabiades, a young but rising Athenian aristocrat, was behind this diplomatic coup, and he promptly used Argos as a base to launch an attack on Epidauros, a Peloponnesian city within the Spartan sphere. The war had begun afresh. This time, it would spread far beyond the Greek mainland.

Below: Due to the nearby sanctuary of Asklepios, the city of Epidauros had an international medical reputation by the time of Athens' attack. The large theater was considered the most beautiful in the world. The city's temporary loss to the Spartan cause was a serious setback.

THE SICILIAN DISASTER

Faced with what amounted to open rebellion from former Peloponnesian allies, Sparta reacted swiftly against the Argive League. The resulting power shift forced Athens to rethink strategic policy.

In 418, King Agis of Sparta marched into Argos with his army and forced the Argive League into submission. As soon as the Spartans left, the Argolids abandoned the treaty and rallied their allies, a confederation that included Mantineia, Elis, and Athens. Agis returned and met the league at Mantineia in the largest land battle of the war.

Despite an initial setback, the Spartans emerged victorious. The Argive League crumbled. Argos abandoned the Athenian cause and its neighboring allies made their peace with Sparta. The volatile situation in the Peloponnese had resulted in the re-establishment of Spartan dominance. With their hinterland secured, the Spartans prepared for the next move from Athens, which was not long in coming.

However, the outflanking operation that followed in 416 was a grievous error. Athens attacked the neutral island of Melos, in the southern Aegean. The inhabitants were slaughtered or enslaved, incurring the wrath of most non-aligned Greeks. No longer able to portray herself as the rational champion of democracy, Athens was on a course to political isolation and apparent self-destruction. It was almost as if the loss of Perikles had left Athens without a strategist capable of giving the war a military and political direction—and a new direction was desperately needed.

It came in the spring of 415. Athens embarked on an expedition to capture the crucially important city of Syracuse on the eastern coast of Sicily. Originally founded by Doric Corinthians, Syracuse was naturally allied to the Dorian-Spartan cause. The intention was to extend Athenian influence over the whole island, depriving Sparta of grain, while gaining a rich and fertile addition to the empire.

Alkibiades, Athens' most gifted young commander, was originally earmarked to lead the expedition, but a scandal on the eve of his departure in 415 led to his exile and subsequent defection to the Spartan cause (*see picture caption*). Instead, the *boule* voted Nikias and Lamakkos to take joint command of the force, which comprised 134 triremes carrying 27,000 men, of which 5,000 were *hoplites*. After wintering in Katana, the generals laid siege to Syracuse, and commenced a circumvallation intended to cut off the city from the rest of the island, while the fleet blockaded the seaward approaches.

Prompted by information supplied by exiled Alkibiades, a small relief force was dispatched under the able command of the Spartan general Gylippos. He raised a willing Sicilian army and the Spartans cut their way through Athenian

Below: The scale of ancient Greek ruins in Sicily, such as the massive theater at Taormina, testifies to the wealth of the Greek city-state colonies.

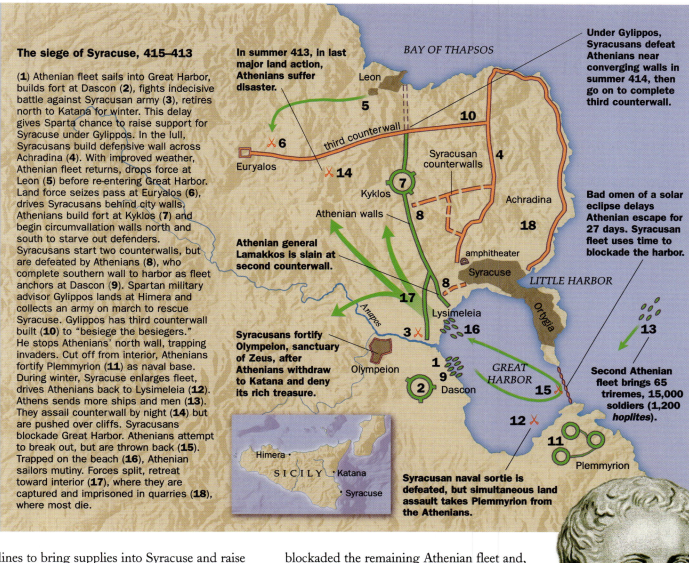

The siege of Syracuse, 415–413

(**1**) Athenian fleet sails into Great Harbor, builds fort at Dascon (**2**), fights indecisive battle against Syracusan army (**3**), retires north to Katana for winter. This delay gives Sparta chance to raise support for Syracuse under Gylippos. In the lull, Syracusans build defensive wall across Achradina (**4**). With improved weather, Athenian fleet returns, drops force at Leon (**5**) before re-entering Great Harbor. Land force seizes pass at Euryalos (**6**), drives Syracusans behind city walls. Athenians build fort at Kyklos (**7**) and begin circumvallation walls north and south to starve out defenders. Syracusans start two counterwalls, but are defeated by Athenians (**8**), who complete southern wall to harbor as fleet anchors at Dascon (**9**). Spartan military advisor Gylippos lands at Himera and collects an army on march to rescue Syracuse. Gylippos has third counterwall built (**10**) to "besiege the besiegers." He stops Athenians' north wall, trapping invaders. Cut off from interior, Athenians fortify Plemmyrion (**11**) as naval base. During winter, Syracuse enlarges fleet, drives Athenians back to Lysimeleia (**12**). Athens sends more ships and men (**13**). They assail counterwall by night (**14**) but are pushed over cliffs. Syracusans blockade Great Harbor. Athenians attempt to break out, but are thrown back (**15**). Trapped on the beach (**16**), Athenian sailors mutiny. Forces split, retreat toward interior (**17**), where they are captured and imprisoned in quarries (**18**), where most die.

In summer 413, in last major land action, Athenians suffer disaster.

Under Gylippos, Syracusans defeat Athenians near converging walls in summer 414, then go on to complete third counterwall.

Bad omen of a solar eclipse delays Athenian escape for 27 days. Syracusan fleet uses time to blockade the harbor.

Athenian general Lamakkos is slain at second counterwall.

Syracusans fortify Olympeion, sanctuary of Zeus, after Athenians withdraw to Katana and deny its rich treasure.

Second Athenian fleet brings 65 triremes, 15,000 soldiers (1,200 *hoplites*).

Syracusan naval sortie is defeated, but simultaneous land assault takes Plemmyrion from the Athenians.

BAY OF THAPSOS

Leon — 5

third counterwall — 6 — Euryalos — 14 — 10 — 7 — Kyklos — Syracusan counterwalls — 4 — Achradina — 8 — Athenian walls — 8 — 18 — amphitheater — Syracuse — LITTLE HARBOR — 17 — Lysimeleia — Ortygia — 8 — Anapos — 3 — 16 — 13 — Olympeion — 1 — 9 — 2 — Dascon — GREAT HARBOR — 15 — 12 — 11 — Plemmyrion

Himera • — S I C I L Y — • Katana — • Syracuse

---

lines to bring supplies into Syracuse and raise morale. Gylippos then had the Syracusans build their own counterwalls to prevent the city's encirclement, and cut off the Athenians from the hinterland and their supply source. In an encounter that successfully destroyed two of the counterwall, Lamakkos was slain, leaving Nikias, a general whose incompetence was matched by his bad fortune, in sole command.

Utterly and entirely defeated

Nikias appealed for reinforcements, and another 1,200 *hoplites* and 65 triremes arrived from Naupaktos under the command of energetic Demosthenes. The Athenians now assailed Gylippos's counterwall, but the assault failed. Nikias demanded the siege be abandoned, and preparations were made to evacuate Sicily. However, their leavetaking was delayed by another month after the omen of a solar eclipse heralded bad sailing.

The delay proved costly—an invigorated Syracusan fleet sortied and broke through the Athenian blockade. They then in turn blockaded the remaining Athenian fleet and, despite attempts to break out, Athens' ships were trapped in the harbor. Low moral and mutinous behavior set in. The bulk of the fleet was abandoned and the army retreated in split groups to the west. The Syracusans unleashed their cavalry and cornered the Athenian rearguard under Demosthenes, which was forced to surrender. The remainder of the army was trapped on a riverbank and many killed before Nikias surrendered (413). The two commanders were executed, and many of the imprisoned Athenians died in captivity.

Thucydides called the Sicilian expedition the "greatest action" of the war. "To the victors the most brilliant of successes, to the vanquished the most calamitous of defeats; for they were utterly and entirely defeated; their sufferings were on an enormous scale; their losses were, as they say, total; army, navy, everything was destroyed, and, out of many, only a few returned."

With the cream of its army and navy lost, Athens was on the brink of defeat.

Above: Intellectually formidable, gifted Alkibiades was the popular choice to lead the Sicilian expedition, until he was accused of drunkenly mocking religious mysteries and exiled. He fled to Sparta.

WAR WITH THE IONIAN ISLES

News of the Sicilian disaster stunned Athens. The Athenians correctly assumed that the catastrophe would encourage further revolt within the empire and economic collapse at home. Sparta was not yet winning the war, but Athens was clearly losing.

Above: Ruins of the south agora of Miletos, now flooded by the delta marshes of the River Meander. Along with most of the Ionian cities and island-states, Miletos rebelled against Athens in the latter years of the Peloponnesian War.

The destruction of the Sicilian expedition prompted a return to the war's traditional pattern. Agis led an army north in the summer of 413, the first Spartan invasion of Attica for over 12 years. This time, he had no intention of simply razing Attica and pinning the Athenians inside the Long Walls. Instead, he built a permanent fortified base at Dekeleia, north of Athens. For the next nine years, the Spartans maintained a strong permanent garrison in Dekeleia and used the base to launch constant raids on the Attican hinterland, denying its use to Athens. Dekeleia also served as a refuge for runaway slaves, and over 20,000 Athenian and Attican slaves escaped to the Spartan fortress. Worse yet, Sparta's permanent presence in Attica made it impossible to reach the silver mines at Laurion, which considerably reduced Athens' revenues.

Now the Persians sent envoys to Agis, and to Athenian horror, the old foes made a pact. Persia hoped to gain from Athens' dismemberment and Sparta gained from the Persian finance to pursue the war. Assisted by her new-found allies, the Spartans built a powerful fleet, hoping that the disaster at Syracuse would let them challenge Athenian naval supremacy and encourage Athens' Delian allies to defect.

Athens moved quickly and rebuilt sufficient ships to counter the Spartan threat by blockading it in Peloponnese waters. However, Athenian turncoat Alkibiades broke through with five galleys and reached Chios. Here, he triggered a revolt that spread throughout the Aegean. Chios, Mytilene, Miletos, and other smaller cities and islands forged a new anti-Athenian alliance, under the guidance of Tissaphernes of Chios.

Changing tides of fortune

The future of the war looked bleak for Athens, faced with a reinvigorated Sparta backed by the might of a Persian Empire still smoldering from its defeats at Athenian hands. Athens scraped together two small fleets. The first, of 46 ships, attacked Mytilene, and Lesbos soon fell. Then it sailed to Chios to confront Alkibiades and Tissaphernes. Athenian troops landed, ravaged the island and besieged the Chian capital. The second fleet, of 48 ships, blockaded Miletos. Fortune favored Athens when Alkibiades fell foul of another scandal and had to leave the Spartan cause. In 411, during a four-month oligarchic coup in Athens, Alkibiades arranged a pardon and returned, a dubious hero with revitalizing the Athenian navy his task.

But in the same year, disaster befell Athens when the Chian fleet defeated its Athenian besiegers. Rhodes now joined the revolt, and disaffection with Athens spread up the Ionian coast as far as the Hellespont. This isolated Athens from her trading links in the Black Sea—the starving city was on the brink of collapse. Spartan commander of the northern Aegean, Mindaros, smelled victory, but Athens was not finished. Alkibiades led a concentration of the fleet remnants north to meet Mindaros at Kynossema, off the Chersonesos coast. The gamble paid off, and the Spartan fleet was

scattered. A second naval victory off Abydos (411) was almost decisive, but Mindaros managed to extricate most of his galleys, which he beached and repaired over the winter.

The good news for Athens was reversed by a Spartan naval victory of Eretria in Euboea, which sparked off a Euboean revolt. In the spring of 410, fortune once again favored Athens. At the end of the winter, a joint force of Mindaros's Spartans and Persians had captured Kyzikos. The Athenian fleet pursued them, engaged, and destroyed the Spartans, recapturing the city in the process. Mindaros was slain in the battle. Now it was Sparta's turn to seek peace. In a burst of fresh hope, Athens refused. The war entered its final grim chapter.

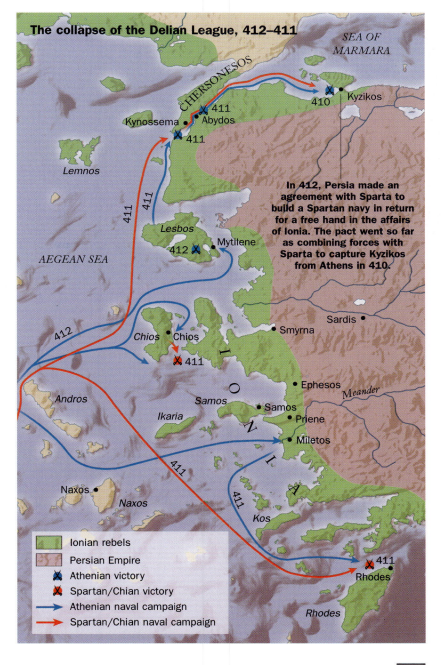

The collapse of the Delian League, 412–411

In 412, Persia made an agreement with Sparta to build a Spartan navy in return for a free hand in the affairs of Ionia. The pact went so far as combining forces with Sparta to capture Kyzikos from Athens in 410.

	Ionian rebels
	Persian Empire
✖	Athenian victory
✖	Spartan/Chian victory
→	Athenian naval campaign
→	Spartan/Chian naval campaign

The war comes to Attica, 413–404

Sparta uses Dekeleia as a permanent base to harry Attica

Spartan naval victory sparks revolt on Euboea against Athens

Sparta cuts off Athens from silver mines at Laurion

THE DEFEAT OF ATHENS

When their overtures of peace were rejected, the Spartans fought on. During the last six years of the Peloponnesian War, Athens attempted to restore its overseas empire, while Sparta sought a decisive battle that would provide the ultimate victory.

Spartan stronghold

Athenian victory

Spartan victory

→ Athenian campaign

→ Spartan campaign

In the aftermath of the Spartan and Persian collapse at Kyzikos, Athens recovered control of much of the Hellespont. Sparta's recapture of Pylos in the Peloponnese did little to offset the defeat. Alkiabiades—now, after much political maneuvering, the supreme Athenian commander and statesman—launched a major expedition in 408 to restore the *polis* and islands of the eastern Aegean to the Athenian empire. This brought Alkibiades into conflict with his old enemy and one-time unwilling colleague, the new Spartan commander Lysander, who was

based with his Persian ally Cyrus the Younger at Ephesos, on the coast of Asia Minor.

While Alkibiades besieged Phokaia to disappointing effect, Antiochos, his second-in-command, was repulsed when he attacked Ephesos. This prompted Alkibiades' recall to Athens, where he was held accountable before a furious *ekklesia*. Once again, Alkibiades was forced into exile, this time settling in Thrace, effectively leaving the picture.

A new general, Konon, replaced him and joined the Athenian navy as it refitted at Samos. He found low morale, an empty treasury, and all too soon an opponent in Lysander's deputy, Kallikratidas, who commanded a far larger force. The Athenian treasury was drained to build Konon more ships, and eventually the two naval squadrons clashed at Arginusai in 406. The Spartans were defeated and Kallikratidas was

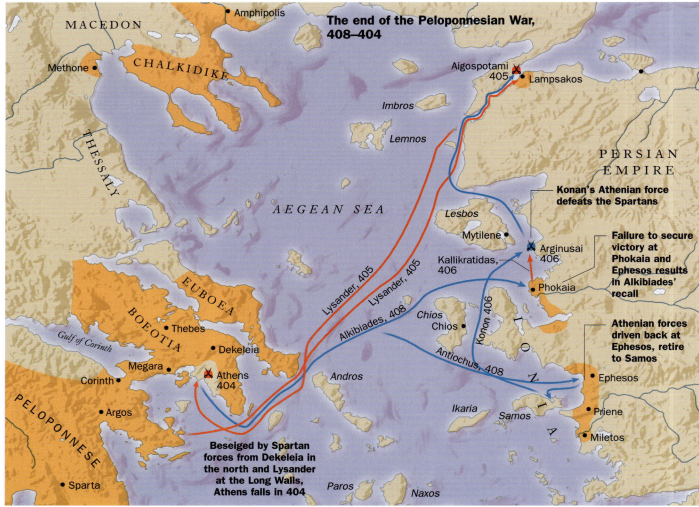

The end of the Peloponnesian War, 408–404

MACEDON

• Amphipolis

• Methone

CHALKIDIKE

THESSALY

• Aigospotami 405

• Lampsakos

Imbros

Lemnos

PERSIAN EMPIRE

AEGEAN SEA

Konan's Athenian force defeats the Spartans

Lesbos

• Mytilene

Failure to secure victory at Phokaia and Ephesos results in Alkibiades' recall

Lysander, 405

Lysander, 405

Kallikratidas, 406

✗ Arginusai 406

Konon 406

• Phokaia

EUBOEA

Alkibiades, 408

Chios
Chios •

Athenian forces driven back at Ephesos, retire to Samos

I O N I A

BOEOTIA

Gulf of Corinth

• Thebes

• Dekeleia

Antiochus, 408

Andros

• Ephesos

Megara •

Corinth •

✗ Athens 404

• Priene

Ikaria

Samos

• Miletos

PELOPONNESE

Argos

• Sparta

Beseiged by Spartan forces from Dekeleia in the north and Lysander at the Long Walls, Athens falls in 404

Paros

Naxos

killed in the largest naval battle of the war.

This victory, together with renewed mastery of the Aegean, restored Athenian confidence sufficiently to refuse a second peace offer from Sparta. But the bullishness was an illusion; the treasury lay empty and a reinforced Spartan fleet under the command of Lysander was already heading north toward the Hellespont. The Athenian fleet followed, but there was to be no repeat of Alkibiades' successes of 410.

Capturing Lampsakos on the Asian shore to use as a base, Lysander unexpectedly turned to give battle. Taken by surprise, virtually the entire Athenian fleet was trapped on the Gallipoli shore near Aigospotamoi. Lysander destroyed or captured 170 triremes. Only ten Athenian ships escaped. Lysander executed his 3,000 prisoners, removing the last military obstacle between Sparta and Athens.

A gracious victor

Athens prepared for a siege as Lysander sailed toward Attica. He arrived in the spring of 405 and besieged the Long Walls. Starved of supply from the sea, the result was inevitable. In March 404, Athens surrendered. Given the bloodshed and the longevity of the conflict, the peace terms Sparta offered were remarkably lenient. The Athenians had to dismantle their Long Walls and their fleet was to be reduced to a mere ten ships. The "empire" was broken up and Athens was required to acknowledge Spartan political supremacy over all Greece. However, the city itself remained untouched and, along with its denuded treasury, retained its Attican hinterland for domestic use.

Sparta's political dominance was based on military power, but Spartan control over the Greek world was less than total: Thebes was emerging as a powerful and troublesome *polis* in central Greece; the drain on wealth and manpower made Spartan control over the other Greek city-states hard to maintain. Worse, final victory had been won at the cost of accepting aid from Lydian Persian governors, involving them in the Aegean for the first time in 70 years. In the last phase of the war many of the Ionian cities fell into canny Persian hands again.

Democracy would re-emerge, and Athens would regain her position as the cultural center of the Greek world, but the Spartans ensured that oligarchies were the most common form of Greek government in the years preceding the Macedonian invasion. The city-states had been weakened by three decades of warfare, leaving the Greeks ill-prepared to fend off an invasion. In this respect, the Peloponnesian War marked the beginning of the end for ancient Greece.

Below: Athene, patron goddess of war and Athens, grieves over a monument to the Athenian dead of the Peloponnese War.

CHAPTER 12
THE GREEK ART OF WAR

Warfare was virtually endemic in ancient Greece. Given the division of mainland Greece and the Aegean archipelago into hundreds of small city-states and rural states, rivalries often flared into battles. Although sieges were comparatively rare until the latter stages of the Peloponnesian War, armies were capable of occupying land and razing the countryside or garrisoning it. The crowded nature of the typical *polis* meant that campaigns were often fought for control of the agricultural hinterland, since without it the population would starve.

The evolution of the *hoplite*, Greece's heavy infantryman, took place during the Archaic Age, roughly at the same time as city-states were emerging from the Dark Age. Unlike the aristocratic warlord and his bands who dominated warfare in the earlier period, the *hoplite* was a citizen soldier, fighting for his *polis*, his family, and his home. This was a highly skilled and motivated soldier, and soon battles became principally clashes between *hoplite* armies,

supported by small numbers of light troops. The *hoplite* dominated warfare until the defeat of Greek armies by Philip II of Macedon in 338.

The Greek art of war developed in time for its first real challenge, when the Persians invaded Greece in 490. The Athenians' defeat of the Persian army at Marathon provided the Greeks with a decade of peace, but also gave the Persians time to prepare for a full-scale invasion. When this came in 480, it was tough for the Greeks to contain the Persians, and only the sacrifice of the 300-man Spartan force at Thermopylai provided them with the incentive and time to organize their defenses.

Victory over the Persians at Plataia a year later ensured the freedom of Greece from invasion, and gave city-states the freedom to return to their internecine feuding. This rivalry erupted in 431 when Athens and Sparta began the Peloponnesian War. The Spartans were the acknowledged masters of mainland Greece, while the Athenians relied on their fortifications and superb fleet.

The real instrument of victory in the war against Persia was the trireme. These oared warships were the mainstay of the Grecian fleets of the Classical Age. Victory over the Persians at Salamis (480) allowed the Athenians to create their own maritime empire.

The triremes and *hoplites* were not the only elements in the Greek arsenal. Following the end of the Peloponnesian Wars, a greater emphasis was placed in the use of cavalry and lightly equipped and unarmored skirmishing troops. Greeks sought service overseas, refining their tactical skills in wars in Persia, Italy, and Sicily.

Throughout the entire period, the maintenance of a powerful army or fleet and the upkeep of city fortifications were a vital function of any city-state. In an age of near-constant warfare, the Greeks developed one of the most finely tuned military systems of the ancient world. Despite this, they were unable to stand up against the Macedonians of Philip and of Alexander the Great, or against the Romans.

SPARTA'S MILITARY MACHINE

Sparta was first and foremost a military state. Spartans' formidable reputation on the battlefield was the result of a lifetime of training. The *polis* and its hinterland were designed to support a permanent standing army; the best fighting force in Greece.

The Spartan state was a unique institution in Greece. It was ruled by two hereditary kings who could be removed from power by the army if either showed signs of weakness or became unpopular with the troops. Day-to-day government was left in the hands of five *ephors* (magistrates), elected annually. By the fifth century, *ephors* were the arbiters of Spartan policy, the kings little more than figureheads.

With almost no exceptions, every male Spartan citizen served as a soldier. Arable land was divided into numerous state-owned farms that existed purely to support a single warrior citizen and his family. These farms were run by an army of slaves, or *helots* in the Lakedaimonian tongue. Any attempt at insurrection by *helots* was brutally repressed, thus ensuring good order with only a small garrison.

Weak or handicapped babies were killed shortly after birth, since the sole reason for procreation in Sparta was to raise a new generation of citizen-soldiers. From birth, children of both genders were subjected to strict discipline and rigorous physical conditioning. When they reached the age of seven, boys were taken from their families and raised in dormitory classes, where groups learned the skills needed to become a first-class soldier.

Conditions were literally *spartan*. As a part of hardship training, food was rationed; the youths were hungry enough to steal. If caught, the child was punished severely, not for the theft,

"Superiority lies with him who is reared in the severest school"

The above quote from Thucydides referred to Spartan boys. Sparta itself has left us little in the way of literature or art; not surprising of a state brought up in a barracks. Schooling was not something Spartan boys or girls had to endure since almost everything they did was to prepare to bear either arms or become the mothers of healthy children. From the age of 12 the boys were allowed only one garment, the *chlamys*, no matter the weather. For sleeping, they gathered rushes from the banks of the Eurotas.

Fights among the boys were encouraged as tests of strength, and older youths were flogged annually as an example of fortitude to others. Even stealing was encouraged as long as the offender escaped detection (on campaign in enemy territory it would be necessary, and at home they would be stealing from *helots*, who should be expected to look after their masters' property better). There is the famous story of the boy (illustrated) who—because he was so hungry—stole a fox. Concealed under his *chlamys*, the fox began biting him. Rather than be caught with stolen goods, the boy gritted his teeth and allowed the fox to tear at his body until in the end it killed him. His fortitude was typical of the Spartan training code.

(the equivalent of a modern infantry company), led by a *lochagos*. Each *lochos* corresponded to a territorial unit within the Spartan homeland.

These were sub-divided into four *enemotia*, the smallest unit in the army, each of 36 men, commanded by an *enomotarch*. The Spartan army that fought the Persians at Thermopylai (481) had *lochos* of half the size, since it arrayed *hoplites* in eight ranks, as opposed to the 16-rank formations used during the Peloponnesian Wars.

The *enemotia* were organized into three files or lines, and in battle these men arrayed themselves in an established order, one behind the other. Four *lochos* were grouped together into a *mora* (a battalion-sized unit), commanded by a *polemarch*. Six *mora* comprised the entire Spartan army, which was commanded by one of the hereditary Spartan kings. The first *mora* was considered the elite of the army and formed the king's bodyguard. Known as the *hippeis*, it comprised men who were specially selected by representatives of the *ephors*.

The Spartan army marched into battle accompanied by *helots*, one carrying the armor and weapons of each soldier. Rations were frugal, and officers (including the king) had no special privileges. Trained from childhood to accept hardships, Spartans could travel faster, required less supplies, and could fight more efficiently than any Greek or Persian opponent they encountered.

Spartan soldiers were never expected to lose, and if they did, they were expected to die rather than retreat or surrender. To the Spartans, military honor was all-important. Spartan spear- and shield-equipped *hoplites* were considered the finest soldiers of their day, and despite their limited numbers, defeated the richest states in Greece through ability and determination.

but for being caught. Clothing was minimal, punishments severe, and academic training virtually non-existent. These boys were being trained to accept tough campaign conditions without question.

At 12, boys were introduced to military training, an education that continued until the trainee's majority at 20 years of age. Most youths were accepted into the army, while those that failed to make the grade served in military administration and formed a pool of reservists.

The finest soldiers

For the rest of his life, or at least until he reached 40, the Spartan soldier lived with his comrades in barracks, not with his wife or family. Although this may have encouraged homosexual liaisons, such encounters were partly encouraged, since they fostered camaraderie.

The army was organized differently from other Greek forces. According to the military historian Xenophon, during the fifth century the Spartan army was divided into *lochos* of 144 men

THE HOPLITE

Following the Dark Age, the emergence of the city-state was marked by the development of a new type of warrior, the *hoplite*. For centuries these heavily armed Greek infantrymen were to dominate the battlefields of the eastern Mediterranean.

The armies before the Archaic period were dominated by the aristocracy. In the former period, the bulk of armies consisted of poorly armed spearmen, while the elite of the Mycenaean army fought in chariots. In this respect the Mycenaeans were no different from other races of the late Bronze Age. It seems likely that chariot use all but died out during the Dark Age, other than as a mode of transport to and from the battlefield. Instead, Greek warfare was dominated by noble cavalrymen, the warlord, and his retinue. These elite troops were supported by spearmen; occasionally the equestrians dismounted to fight with spear and shield.

The development of the *hoplite* in the seventh century was a military revolution. Soon after the development of the *polis*, armed militiamen were raised to defend the cities. Fighting in tightly

Right: A black-figure vase of c.520 shows a *hoplite* arming himself.

Left: Iron and gold cuirass found in the tomb of King Philip II of Macedon in Vergina. The embellishments indicate that this is a ceremonial cuirass, which may have belonged to the king himself.

formed, dense formations, these increasingly well-trained spear- and shield-armed infantrymen were more than a match for cavalry, thereby marking the end of aristocratic ascendancy in Greek warfare.

Hoplites (citizen soldiers) fought in close order, with shields overlapping, to create a tight and maneuverable unit, a formation known as a *phalanx*. The men of the *phalanx* were armed with *sarise*, very long spears used for stabbing and thrusting. The increasing dependence on *hoplites* meant that city-states fielded their own troops, raised from the *polis* itself. The Dark Age reliance on noble cavalrymen and mercenaries

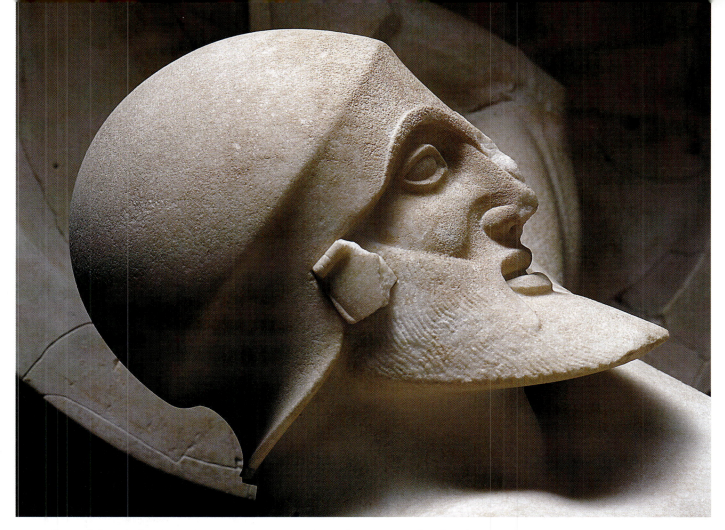

was a thing of the past by the sixth century.

Hoplites were not equipped and supplied by the state. *Hoplites* were the equivalent of "urban yeomen," having sufficient social status and wealth to buy their own arms and armor, and to purchase their provisions while in the field. This individualistic approach meant that armor type and quality varied considerably within a unit, since some were wealthier than others. Less wealthy citizens who lacked the finances to buy arms and armor were used as light infantrymen, charged with harassing the enemy, screening the *hoplites*, and driving off other light troops.

Arms and armor

Army service was an honorable aspect of civic responsibility and being a *hoplite* demonstrated a superior social status. It is not surprising, therefore, that Greek armies rarely included much in the way of light troops and cavalry. Unfortunately, this dominance of the *hoplite* lead to a stultification of tactics, since all Greek states fielded similar armies. Later, under Alexander the Great, the Greek *phalanx* of *hoplites*, when fielded with different ranges of cavalry and infantry archers, would prove irresistible in Asia Minor, but internecine battles of the

Classical Age were often fought to stalemate.

During the first decades of the fifth century, the typical *hoplite* was equipped with a large round shield, measuring approximately three feet in diameter. The convex surface was usually painted with the emblem of the *polis*—an inverted V for Sparta, a gorgon's head (among other designs) for Athens, and the club of Herakles for Thebes. Further protection was provided by a crested helmet, greaves (leg armor), and corslet designed to fit the contours of the upper body, all of bronze. He was armed with a wooden thrusting spear tipped with an iron head, approximately nine feet in length, and a straight iron sword.

By the Persian Wars, a new type of corslet made of iron scales sewn onto a leather backing was coming into fashion, since it offered greater freedom of movement. In addition, leather strips (*petruges*) formed a kilt, protecting the lower torso below the composite scale and leather corslet. During the fifth and fourth centuries, *hoplite* armor became lighter and the shield slightly smaller, but the *hoplite* himself remained a well-trained citizen soldier and the arbiter of victory on the Greek battlefield, until the Macedonian conquest of Greece in the third century.

THE ARMY IN BATTLE

Probably the best account of a Classical Age Greek army comes from Xenophon, a commander in a campaign in Persia in 401. In his *Anabasis*, he tells how a force of mixed Greeks was organized, how a campaign was conducted, and how the army fought.

Right: Although the Greek army was built around a core of citizen *hoplites*, foreign mercenaries were also relied on. The archer seen blowing a trumpet on this plate of c.500, wears typically Scythian apparel. Scythian archers were employed in Athens up until the Persian War, which cut off communications with Thrace. However, after this, Greek archers are often depicted in Scythian dress.

Right: Soldiers of the *phalanx* were armed with the long spear. These were not for throwing, but turned the *phalanx* into a spiky battering ram. On the charge, the first five ranks lowered their 9-foot spears horizontally, projecting a lethal six feet ahead of the front rank. The *phalanx* could also be formed into a formidable hollow square, defying any cavalry attacks.

When a city-state went to war, its citizens were called on to join the ranks, bringing their own equipment and provisions. Typical rations included barleycorn, cheese, wine, and salted meat and fish. Servants or slaves accompanied the Greek army, carrying weapons and provisions for their masters. The soldier's shield was strapped to his back during a march, and clothing, bedding, or provisions could be tied to it, or hung from the end of his spear.

During the expedition into Asia recounted by Xenophon (*see the account on pages 154–5*), the Greeks marched in long columns, with baggage carriers and other horse-drawn vehicles in the middle of the column. To protect against the Persian cavalry they marched in a square formation, with their baggage in the center. Camps were established each night and when a battle was considered imminent. Unlike later Roman campaign forts, these camps were rarely fortified. Troops slept in formation, surrounding their supplies, and sentries were posted to warn of attack. (Accounts of Spartan camps indicate

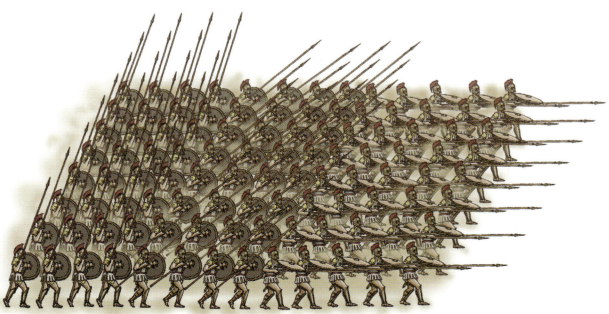

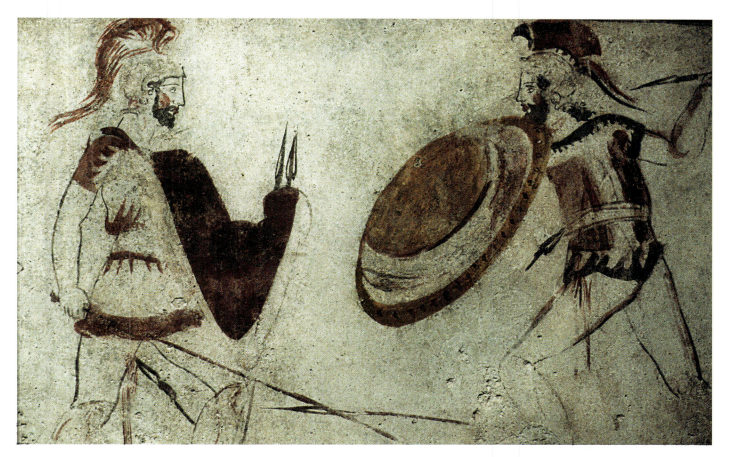

that equal effort was put into guarding their *helots*. To Spartans, a slave uprising was always a distinct possibility.)

Sacrifices and religious services were a common aspect of campaign life, as was the interpretation of events as omens of the future. If a battle was to be fought, the commanders met to discuss how and where to fight, and sacrifices of livestock were offered to the gods to ensure victory. In most cases, the army drew up for battle in a single line, with the most experienced units or, in an allied army, those of the major contingent posted on the right of the line. Where present, cavalry was either split between the two flanks or kept together as a mobile reserve and used to scatter enemy cavalry or light infantry that threatened to disrupt the line.

Motivated for victory

Hoplites were arranged in six-deep ranks, although by the time of Xenophon the 12-man-deep formation known as the *phalanx* was already coming into use. Light infantry—mainly javelin men, but also slingers and archers—were placed on the flanks, where they could harass the enemy line, or else in front of the army to screen the *hoplites* from lightly armed skirmishing troops.

Many *hoplites* hired their services abroad, usually to the Persians, who held the Greek infantry in high regard and paid well. The Greek army of the Persian campaign described by Xenophon was a mercenary force, composed of several contingents, each recruited by its own general. Mercenary *hoplites* were accompanied by a new type of soldier, the *peltast*, who operated like skirmishing light infantry but were also well armed, capable of defeating any light troops. *Peltasts* were based on the principal troops of the Thracians, who found the combination of fighting and skirmishing abilities suited the rugged terrain of their homeland.

After initial skirmishing, opposing infantry lines advanced and the battle became a vast mêlée, both armies fighting with spear and sword. Victory usually went to the *hoplite* force with the strongest will to win and the most experience in battle. In most cases this meant the Spartans, and despite several reverses during the Peloponnesian War, the Spartan army was recognized as the best fighting force in Greece.

A skillful commander understood the strengths and weaknesses of his citizen or mercenary troops and placed them where they would have the greatest effect. After that, most generals fought in the front line and victory was left in the hands of the gods. This fighting system was effective against the Persians, but less successful against better trained opponents, such as the Macedonians.

Above: Two Greek warriors from a fresco in a Lucanian tomb, Paestum. In the Classical Age, Paestum was known as Poseidonia, a Greek colony on the Italian coast south of Naples. In the fifth century it was taken over by local Lucanians, although the city remained largely Greek in character. The Lucanian Greeks are noted for their fine paintings and vigorous use of line (*see a second example on page 168*).

FORTIFICATIONS AND SIEGES

Fortified cities began to appear during the seventh century and evolved into complex defensive sites, virtually invulnerable to attack. However, the Spartans adopted Persian siege techniques in the Peloponnesian War and changed the military balance.

Below: Remains of the ancient fortifications around Athens' port of Peiraeus can still be seen (here running behind a much later church). They were a part of the complex known as the Long Walls.

The first hilltop citadels built by the Mycenaeans fell into disuse following the Dorian invasion. But the Mycenaeans' thick-walled construction and good use of natural features inspired the emerging city-states of the eighth-century when warlords began building the fortified hilltop citadel—the *acropolis*.

By the mid-seventh century extensive fortifications were built around entire cities. Mud bricks or rubble were used in the earliest city walls, but by 600 BC masons were raising walls of pre-cut rectangular or polygonal stone blocks, with mud bricks reserved for upper battlements.

During the late sixth century, walls were enhanced with projecting bastions, designed to protect gateways or weak points such as corners. Without siege equipment, attackers were forced to scale formidable walls in the face of well-armed defenders.

The most extensive use of fortifications was at Athens. Following the razing of the city twice during the Persian Wars, the defenses were extended not only to a stronger city wall but to the defensive corridor known as the Long Walls (*see page 106*). Protected by large bastions, these led to the harbor of Peiraeus, which was also surrounded by a stout wall. During the following eight decades, other Greek maritime powers built their own, smaller versions of the Long Walls, while the Athenians improved their defenses by ringing Attica with frontier forts. Across Greece and the Aegean basin, city-states and overseas colonies alike came to rely on their engineers' skills for defenses. Cities such as Syracuse had extensive fortifications, protecting

it from land and sea assault.

The Greeks did not develop siegecraft before the Peloponnesian War. Even in the Heroic Age, Mycenaean Greeks took ten years to capture Troy (according to Homer), and even then the city only fell through trickery. This was an accurate reflection of siegecraft during most of the Archaic and Classical Ages. The city-states lacked the skills and equipment to do anything other than launch a hasty assault against a city's walls, or besiege it, hoping the defenders would surrender when threatened with starvation.

Walls within and without

Athenian strategy during the Peloponnesian War centered around its impregnable Long Walls. Although the Spartans were free to occupy Attica, they had no chance of seizing Athens. The Spartans soon realized their limitations, and consequently sought help to develop siege tactics. Two sources of information were available to them. First, Greek colonies in Sicily had already come under attack from the southwest from Carthaginians who used siege engines and towers. The Spartans also hired Persian engineers, with the result that by the time they besieged the city of Plataia in 429, their tactics were heavily refined.

The Spartans built walls of circumvallation around Plataia, preventing their enemies from escaping. Next they constructed a large mound of earth raised on logs that stretched from the siege lines to the top of the city wall. This task

took over two months, but once in place the mound served as an assault ramp. The Plataians countered by raising the city wall in the threatened sector, using bricks taken from houses. They tried to undermine the mound with tunnels, with little success.

The Plataians constructed a secondary wall behind the threatened sector. This forced the Spartans to build battering rams to demolish the new structures, but the defenders bombarded the rams from the top of the walls. An attempt to set fire to the city failed. Since their assault was getting nowhere, the Spartans abandoned the attack, relying on the old and tested method of starving the defenders into capitulation. The siege continued for two years.

Siege warfare was still not an exact science, and for much of the period the advantage remained with the defender. This changed during the Hellenistic period, when engineers devised bigger and more efficient siege engines, and tactics were refined, improving the likelihood of success.

Above: The extensive fourth-century walls protecting the city of Messene in the Peloponnese were typical of the solid construction of Greek fortifications. The inspiration came from earlier *cyclopean* building technique (*see page 38*) used at Mycenae and Tyrins.

Left: The Romans were not the first to develop massive siege engines. Archimedes helped the Syracusans against Athens with many designs. This machine fired 6-foot long arrows during the siege of Syracuse.

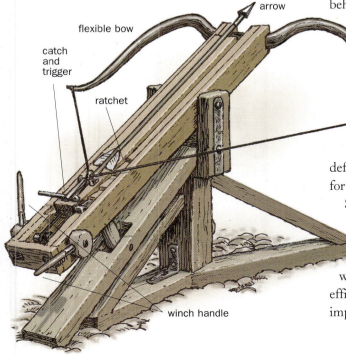

arrow

flexible bow

catch and trigger

ratchet

winch handle

THE TRIREME

At some point during the sixth century the Mycenaeans' simple biremes evolved into the trireme, the archetypal warship of the Greek world. These fast, deadly galleys were the mainstay of the Athenian and Spartan fleets during the Peloponnesian War.

The ships described by Homer in his *Iliad* and *Odyssey* were biremes. The heaviest bireme was a *pentaconter*, rowed by a hundred oarsmen, in two banks of 25 oars per side. Although fragile vessels, they were fitted with a projecting bronze (later iron) beak for ramming enemy vessels. By the mid-sixth century a third bank of rowers had been added to the typical warship, creating the trireme. By the end of that century the trireme was the standard type of war galley in the eastern Mediterranean.

Recent academic studies have led to the reconstruction of an Athenian trireme from the time of the Battle of Salamis, which has helped our understanding of how these vessels functioned. Practical reconstruction, maritime archaeology, and pictorial evidence have all proved useful.

Athenian triremes from the Salamis period were approximately 120 feet long, with a beam (width) of about 15 feet. This beam was increased by 2½ feet on each side by the addition of the outrigger framework that supported the oars. The rowers each manned a single oar, and these were arranged in three banks, one above the other. On each side of the typical galley, 27 oarsmen known as *thalamites* formed the lowest of the three tiers. These rowers placed their oars through circular rowing ports.

The next tier of 27 oarsmen, *zygites*, sat above and slightly further outboard of the *thalamites*. Above them a top tier of 31 rowers, *thranites*, sat slightly outboard of the *zygites*, resting their oars on an outrigger frame.

The rowing benches were protected by bulwarks (usually open at the upper level), but above them the deck was partially covered, providing a broad fighting platform for *hoplites*, javelin men, and archers. A pair of helmsmen steered the trireme with a large side oar at each side, but the shape of the hull

meant turning was extremely slow unless the oarsmen participated in the maneuver by backing water on one side of the vessel.

Crude tactics

Of the 200-man crew of a typical trireme, 170 were oarsmen. The remainder of the crew consisted of 12–15 sailors, who manned the sails or the steering oars, a similar number of marines (including about four archers), a flautist, whose rhythmic tones helped the rowers keep in time, and the ship's commander, known as the *trierarch*.

In ideal conditions, a trireme could travel under oars at a speed of 6–8 knots, but speeds were usually lower, due to fatigue, barnacle-encrusted hulls, and bad weather. During long passages, triremes augmented oar propulsion (or sometimes replaced it) with wind and sail. A single central mast was fitted with a simple square sail, and although its use was extremely limited when sailing close to the wind, it could propel the vessel at 4–6 knots.

On long passages the oarsmen were arranged into two or three watches so that they could mix rowing duty with periods of rest. Because it was extremely unusual for triremes to travel at night,

most ships found a sheltered bay to beach on.

Triremes lacked storage space, so their range was defined by the amount of water and provisions they could carry. Given the typical crewing number, it has been estimated that galleys would have to visit a friendly port for victuals every four days. It is easy to see, therefore, why the maintenance of friendly harbors and protected anchorages was vital in naval strategy, and why the gain or loss of Aegean islands influenced the course of campaigns. When possible, large fleets were accompanied by supply vessels to extend the range.

In battle, triremes used ramming tactics, rowing at speed into the flank of an enemy vessel to pierce its hull with the metal-tipped ram. In some instances, extra soldiers were carried, giving trireme captains the rare option to engage in boarding attacks. Otherwise, naval battles involved maneuver, searching for a weak point in an enemy formation, then attacking, ramming, and sinking the ships.

Triremes continued to be the primary warship type in Greek waters until the Hellenistic period, when larger and more powerful vessels began to appear.

Above: Detail from a late fifth-century relief showing Greek warriors rowing on a trireme. For Athenians particularly, manning the oars of a trireme was the honorable duty of all *ephebes*. The Greeks, unlike the Romans after them, never used slaves as manpower on war galleys.

Facing: The trireme was a fully developed fighting machine by the time of the Battle of Salamis in 480. This painting based on ancient sources shows the clash of Athenian and Persian ships during the battle.

CHAPTER 13

ALEXANDER THE GREAT

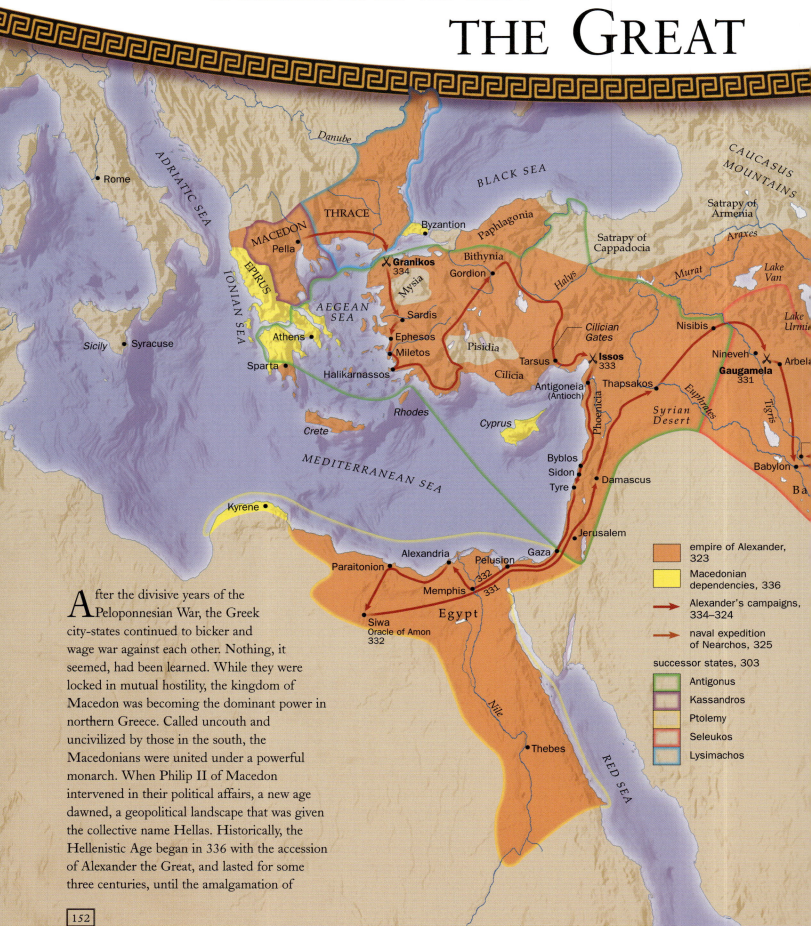

(orange)	empire of Alexander, 323
(yellow)	Macedonian dependencies, 336
(dark red arrow)	Alexander's campaigns, 334–324
(red arrow)	naval expedition of Nearchos, 325

successor states, 303

(green)	Antigonus
(purple)	Kassandros
(yellow)	Ptolemy
(red)	Seleukos
(blue)	Lysimachos

After the divisive years of the Peloponnesian War, the Greek city-states continued to bicker and wage war against each other. Nothing, it seemed, had been learned. While they were locked in mutual hostility, the kingdom of Macedon was becoming the dominant power in northern Greece. Called uncouth and uncivilized by those in the south, the Macedonians were united under a powerful monarch. When Philip II of Macedon intervened in their political affairs, a new age dawned, a geopolitical landscape that was given the collective name Hellas. Historically, the Hellenistic Age began in 336 with the accession of Alexander the Great, and lasted for some three centuries, until the amalgamation of

Alexander the Great's conquest of the Persian Empire between 334 and 324, and the structure of the successor states at 310

CASPIAN SEA

Satrapy of Atropatene

Jaxartes

328

Alexandria Eschata
(Kokand)

Kyreskhata

Marakanda
329

Sogdiana

Sogdian Rock

Oxus

Sogdia

328

Drapsaca

HINDU KUSH

Indus

Termez

Baktra

Aornus
327

328

Alexandria
(Merv)

Parthia

Zadrakarta

Hekatompylos
(Damghan)

330

Rhagai

Aria

Alexandropolis

Alexandria Areion
(Herat)

Alexandria
(Ghazni)

330

Bactria

Taxila

Hydaspes
326

Alexandria Nisaia

Kingdom of Poros

Media

Ekbatana

Darius III was murdered by his own troops near to Hekatompylos.

330

Chenab

Sutlej

ZAGROS MOUNTAINS

Dasht-Lut

Alexandria Prophthasia
(Farah)

Etymander

330

Alexandria
(Kandahar)

326

Seleukeia

The destruction of the royal palace at Persepolis brought to an end the panhellenic war against Persia, but fueled Alexander's ambition for further conquest.

Susa

330

Alexandria

The army refused to follow Alexander into the Ganges valley, finally forcing him to turn back.

330

nia

Alexandria
Susiana

Drangiana

Alexandria

Arachosia

Indus

324

Persian Gates
330

Pasagardai

At Pattala Alexander split his forces for the return to Babylon, taking one part overland while Nearchos built a fleet of 100 ships to carry the rest and explore the coastline.

Mauryan Empire after 324

Persepolis

324

Persia

Alexandria
(Gulashkird)

Pura

PERSIAN GULF

Carmania

324

Gedrosian Desert

325

Pattala

325

Gedrosia

Kokola

325

ARABIAN SEA

INDIAN OCEAN

Greece into the Roman Empire of Augustus.

In cultural terms, Hellenism represented the amalgamation of Greek and Macedonian cultures, but Alexander the Great expanded it to incorporate the Persian and Middle Eastern worlds. When Alexander the Great died in 323, his Argead empire fell apart, to be divided by his generals into smaller, Asiatic Greek kingdoms, but Greek rule was maintained and Hellenism became a cultural movement rather than a political one.

If Macedon replaced Persia as the superpower of the Greek world, it also brought an end to centuries of internecine fighting. Life as part of a superpower held greater benefits than citizenship of a war-weary city-state. The collapse of the *polis* as a political unit was not complete, but the Greeks could no longer see themselves as citizens of Athens, or Sparta, or Thebes. Philip of Macedon and Alexander the Great had made them all Greeks, perhaps their least recognized achievement, but one which was to have a profound effect on the Greek world.

CITY-STATES IN DECLINE

With the defeat of Athens in the Peloponnesian War, political leadership passed to Sparta. For the next five decades, Sparta, then Thebes dictated Greek affairs. As rival city-states fought among themselves, stronger powers began to exert an influence.

Right: Greatest of the Athenian orators of his period, Demosthenes thundered against Macedonian ambition in Greece. His speeches gave us the word "philippic," after passionate verbal attacks on Philip of Macedon. He roused Athens to rebel against Macedonian rule in 322, after Alexander's death. Macedon won, and Demosthenes committed suicide.

Athens was a spent force by 400. It remained the cultural center of Greece, but the glory days were over. The Athenians managed to overthrow the oligarchic government imposed by Sparta, but feuding between democrats and oligarchs led to widespread political killings, which in 399 included the philosopher Sokrates. Lacking political direction, Athens failed to regain its ascendancy.

Under the leadership of Agesilaos II, the Spartans continued to hold sway over the Greek mainland, while playing power games abroad. First they attempted to influence the succession to the Persian throne by supporting Cyrus the Younger, governor of Sardis and the younger son of the late King Darius II, against his brother, the newly crowned Artaxerxes II. This was the campaign recorded by Xenophon. A

scratch force of 13,000 mixed Greek mercenaries recruited by Klearchos, an exiled Spartan, joined Cyrus in Asia Minor. The combined army marched through Syria to confront the enemy near Babylon. In the ensuing Battle of Cunaxa (401) the Greeks triumphed. But it proved a hollow victory: Cyrus was killed in the battle and the

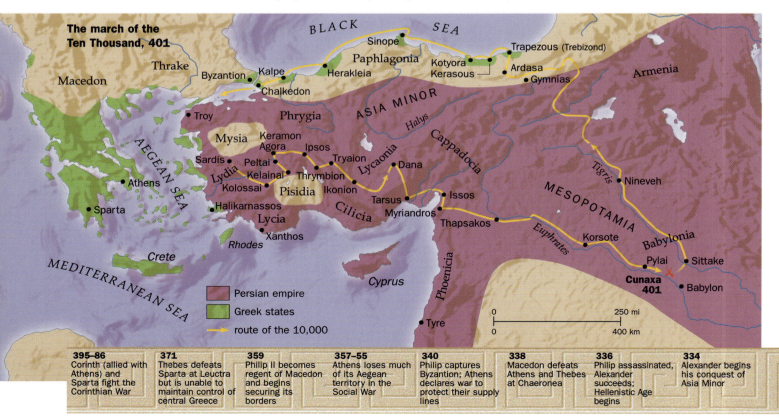

The march of the Ten Thousand, 401

Persian empire

Greek states

route of the 10,000

395–86	371	359	357–55	340	338	336	334
Corinth (allied with Athens) and Sparta fight the Corinthian War	Thebes defeats Sparta at Leuctra but is unable to maintain control of central Greece	Philip II becomes regent of Macedon and begins securing its borders	Athens loses much of its Aegean territory in the Social War	Philip captures Byzantion; Athens declares war to protect their supply lines	Macedon defeats Athens and Thebes at Chaeronea	Philip assassinated, Alexander succeeds; Hellenistic Age begins	Alexander begins his conquest of Asia Minor

undefeated Greeks found themselves isolated. The Greek commanders decided to return by the most direct route to the Black Sea and the safety of the Greek colonies there. Under cover of a peace negotiation, the mostly Spartan senior officers were treacherously murdered by the Persians, leaving the Athenian Xenophon in command. In a feat of extraordinary endurance, the remaining 10,000 retreated under constant attack from Persians and then Kurdish mountain tribes, and finally made it to safety (*see map*).

In a second overseas adventure, aid was given to the Syracusan tyrant Dionysios I, who had become effective ruler of Sicily except for territory held by Carthage. With Spartan help, he defeated the Carthaginians at Motya in 397, preventing further Carthaginian invasions for a decade. The Spartans even intervened in Egypt, virtually duplicating Athens' meddlings from before the Peloponnesian War. Because Corinth was the *metropolis* of Syracuse, tension between Corinth and Sparta over the Dionysios venture led to the Corinthian War in 395. Corinth allied with Argos, Boeotia, and Athens. Artaxerxes II brought both sides to the peace table in 386, ending the divisive conflict, but his motive was a clause that prevented further Greek intervention in Persian affairs.

Elite couplings

After 386, Thebes became Sparta's major opponent in Greece. Sparta had backed an oligarchic coup in the *polis*, but Theban *hoplites* reclaimed the city with help from Athens. The two were supported by Persian finance, which— after Cunaxa—had switched the allegiance it had given to Sparta since the Peloponnese War. The two states prevented further Spartan incursion into central Greece for the time being.

Athens resurrected the Delian League in the form of the Athenian League, an Aegean-based confederation. This time Athens was a partner, not the dominant power. At the same time, Theban military prowess increased, largely because of the Sacred Band, an elite *hoplite* division even more efficient than their Spartan opponents. It consisted of pairs of male lovers,

who were deemed more likely to fight to the death to protect their partner.

The crucial battle for mastery in central Greece was fought at Leuctra in 371, when a Theban army commanded by Epaminondas brought the once-insuperable Spartan army to its knees. Although Spartan military supremacy was at an end, Thebes was unable to enforce her dominance, despite a decade of successful campaigning in the Peloponnese against the Spartans and in Thessaly against Jason of Pherai. When Epaminondas died campaigning, no leader ascended to replace him.

Once again, Athens tried to regain the political initiative, with little success. It supported Sparta against Thebes, seeking to restore some political balance in order to concentrate on the Aegean. The Ionian leader Mausollos (who built his *mausoleum* at Halikarnassos) rebelled against further Athenian expansion. When members of the Athenian League revolted, Athens was ill prepared. During the Social War (357–5), Athens lost much of its allied territory in the Aegean, and the threat of a war with Persia prompted the Athenians to back down.

All the major city-states were exhausted after decades of strife. Their treasuries were virtually empty, their armies were war-weary, and their citizens clamored for peace. It seemed Greek political unity was an unattainable dream.

Above: The ruined base of the Mausoleum can still be seen at Halikarnassos, now Bodrum in Turkey. Mausollos, the Ionian tyrant for whom it was built, took issue with Athenian attempts to dominate the Athenian League in imitation of the city's earlier ambitions that had helped to provoke the Peloponnese War.

333	332	c.331	331	330	327	326	323
Alexander defeats Darius of Persia at Issos, securing Asia Minor	Tyre is destroyed by Alexander's army in a long siege	Alexander invades Egypt and founds Alexandria city, the first of several bearing his name	Though seriously outnumbered, Alexander's army defeats Darius's at Gaugamela	Persian Empire ends with the murder of Darius by one of his generals	After the death of Spitamenes and marriage to Roxanna, Bactria is conquered	On the brink of conquering India, Alexander's men refuse to fight on	Alexander dies, throwing his empire into disarray

PHILIP II OF MACEDON

Decades of factional fighting in the mountain state of Macedon ended after 359, when Philip II assumed control. He stabilized his country, and consolidated then expanded its borders. Soon Philip made his bid for mastery of Greece.

Above: This lifelike, expressive head from a portrait statue of Philip of Macedon was discovered in the royal tomb at Vergina. Astonishingly, the head is only 1¼ inches high.

W hen he became regent (then king) of the Argead kingdom of Macedon in 359, 24-year-old Philip governed a country split by civil war and threatened by invasions from every border. He inherited a large, well-trained army that used long pikes and deep formations, rather than the *hoplite* spears and shallow battle-lines.

After defeating an Athenian-inspired military coup, he went to war in 358 with the barbarian Illyrian tribesmen of Paionia to the north. This not only secured the frontier, but the region's rich mineral resources financed his military expansion. Next, he turned his attention to the east, invading Chalkidike. This enjoyed Athenian protection, but Athens was embroiled in the Social War and Philip was given a free hand. In 357 he captured the important city of Amphipolis, then stormed Poteidaia the following year.

For a while, Philip turned his back on Chalkidike for more interesting matters to the south. Phokis had become embroiled in a quarrel with the neighboring states over the control of Delphi. The Phokians had allegedly cultivated sacred land and were duly fined by the guardians (known collectively as the Delphic Amphictiony). When Phokis refused to pay, Thebes led the Sacred War against the state. In response the Phokians seized part of the Delphic treasury and used their opponent's money to hire a mercenary army large enough to counter the Theban threat. Next, the Phokians secured an alliance with the neighboring Thessalian city of Pherai, which forced Larisa, the other major Thessalian city, to solicit the military support of Philip.

A spectacular victory

On his way south, Philip took the city of Methone, the last Athenian ally in his path. He now took the opportunity to march through Thessaly, occupying both Larisa and Pherai, annexing the country in the process. A Phokian defense in 352 barely halted his progress, but further advance south was thwarted by an Athenian army blocking Thermopylai. Unwilling to repeat the mistakes of Xerxes, he halted.

For the next few years Philip campaigned in Chalkidike and Thrace. He became master of Chalkidike in 349, taking the immensely rich mines of Mount Pangaios. By 340 he had captured Perinthos and the Chersonesos. Faced with a bloackade of its grain supply from the Black Sea colonies, Athens formed an alliance with Thebes to oppose Macedon, and declared war. Philip raced south with his army and met

BLACK SEA

Apollonia

Hebros

Philippopolis

Capture of the Chersonesos threatens Athens' grain supplies from the Greek colonies of the Black Sea shore.

PAIONIA 358

Strymon

THRACE 341

Philippi

Abdera 347

Maroneia 346

Perinthos 341

Byzantion

SEA OF MARMARA

Pella

Vergina

Axios

Amphipolis 357

Thasos

Ainos

CHERSONESOS

Kyzikos

Methone 354

CHALKIDIKE 349

Samothrake

Imbros

EPIRUS

Olynthos 348

Poteidaia 356

Lemnos

Troy

MYSIA

THESSALY

Larisa

Pherai

Pagasai 352

AEGEAN SEA

Lesbos

Mytilene

AETOLIA

Oreos 343

EUBOEA

Thermopylai 346

PHOKIS

Delphi ✕ Chaironeia 338

Thebes

Chios

Sardis

Athens

the Greek allies at Chaironeia (338).

Both armies mustered a little over 30,000 troops, but the Macedonians were better trained and had superiority in heavy cavalry. Although the Theban Sacred Band defeated the Macedonians in front of them, the Athenian line broke and fled. Philip was free to surround the Thebans. The Sacred Band died where they stood, while the Macedonian cavalry pursued the Athenian forces and remaining Thebans from the field. In a single battle, Philip of Macedon had secured the hegemony of Greece.

Philip called a council at Corinth, attended by representatives from virtually every *polis*. There was little option but to acknowledge Philip as their leader and accept Macedonian rule. Philip established Macedonian garrisons in most major city-states, then returned to his capital at Pella to plan an even more ambitious venture: the invasion of Asia Minor with all

the might of a united Greece behind him.

Philip II never realized his dream of invading Asia. Assassinated in 337, his son Alexander succeeded him. It would be Alexander, not Philip, who would conquer Persia and thereby gain the appellation "the Great."

Left: Philip was capable of gestures toward his southern neighbors, as the ruins of this small temple he had built at Olympia proves. The king died before its completion, and Alexander finished it in his memory, calling it the Philippeion. The building held gold and ivory statues of the Macedonian royal family.

ALEXANDER THE GREAT

Alexander the Great (356–23) is one of the greatest figures in world history. A general without rival, an ambitious genius who led his Macedonian-led Greek army across the known world, he created a vast empire, stretching from Greece to India.

Born in the palace at Pella, Alexander's parents were Philip II of Macedon and his mysterious wife Olympias. Tradition insisted that Olympias could trace her ancestry back to Achilles, while legend suggested that Alexander was not the son of Philip but the child of a god, sired through a coupling between Olympias and Zeus. Alexander was raised in the palace, alongside aristocratic children of his own age, who later became his generals and companions.

To the rest of Greece, the people of Macedon were uncouth barbarians. To refute this, Philip ensured that Alexander was groomed for his future role. The finest tutors in Greece, including Aristotle, provided young Alexander with a superb education in culture and literature. Military training followed, since from the age of 16 Alexander accompanied his father on most of his campaigns. It was here that the young prince first gazed across the Hellespont toward Asia. He was schooled in the art of kingship, standing in as regent for his father.

Above: This silver *teradrachm* was minted by Alexander's general Lysimachus, who inherited Thrace after Alexander's death (r.305–281). It shows Alexander adorned with the ram's horn of the Egyptian god Amon.

Alexander took part in the battle of Chaironeia in 338 and fought with great skill at the head of his father's cavalry. His exploits prompted his father to say, "Oh my son, seek out a kingdom worthy of you, as Macedon is too small for you." The opportunity came soon. Within a year Philip was dead at the hands of unknown assassins. First, Alexander secured the Argead throne against any attempt at a coup and ensured the loyalty of the Macedonian army. Then he marched south into central Greece, ready to quash any revolt that might follow Philip's death.

By 335 Alexander was in the north, pacifying the Thebans and Illyrians. A rumor of his death in Illyria prompted the revolt he feared. The Thebans rose up, inciting other city-states to join them. Alexander raced south, defeated the Thebans, captured the city, and burned it in reprisal. This draconian lesson ensured quiet, leaving Alexander free to pursue his father's dream: the conquest of Asia Minor.

As for the young man who was soon to conquer a continent, so much has been written about him, and so much of it wrapped up in romantic legend, that historians vary considerably in their analysis. Physically, he was tall, stunningly handsome, physically perfect, and extremely intelligent. That much is agreed.

A complex leader

The problem with Alexander's recorded personality lies in its mercurial nature. He has been labeled an idealist, an adventurer, a genius, a visionary, a brutal tyrant, and even a god. What do we know about the real Alexander? His education meant that he was steeped in the heroic works of Homer—he claimed the writer appeared to him in dreams to offer advice. He also admired Xenophon's *Anabasis*, in which he saw an early attempt at conquest of the Persian Empire. He had a passion for conquest and adventure, an intuitive grasp of military affairs, and a strong personality, capable of forging ahead even in the most adverse circumstances. He could be loyal, affectionate to friends, chivalrous and compassionate. He also had moments of ruthless cruelty.

Alexander was a complex being and historians—particularly contemporary Greek and later Roman ones—were eager to highlight certain aspects of his personality, to the exclusion of less acceptable facets. Of the five surviving histories of Alexander, all were written centuries after his death and reflect the post-Hellenistic times in which they were written. The one aspect historians agree on is that Alexander the Great altered the course of world history, as one of the most amazing conquerors of all time.

Although he remains enigmatic, Alexander was certainly the most influential ruler in ancient Greece. Perhaps the best way to present Alexander the Great is to let his conquests speak for him.

INTO ASIA MINOR AND EGYPT

By invading Persia, Alexander was seeking revenge for Xerxes' invasion of Greece two centuries earlier. In a feat unmatched in history, he crossed the Hellespont, then fought his way across Asia Minor to Syria, defeating all armies sent against him.

In the spring of 334 Alexander of Macedon led 35,000 men in an invasion of Asia Minor. He launched a whirlwind campaign that was to bring the once-mighty Persian Empire to its knees. He could ill-afford to lose, since he needed revenue from Asia Minor to pay his troops—Macedonian regulars, Greek allies, and Thracian and Cretan irregulars.

The main strike force consisted of 5,000

Alexander's first test came in the summer, when his way south was blocked by a Persian army formed behind the River Granikos. It was commanded by a trio of Persian *satraps*, who in turn were advised by skilled Greek mercenary commander Memnon of Rhodes. Alexander broke the Persian army with a headlong cavalry charge across the river, supported by a steady advance from the infantry. Despite a counterattack designed to kill or capture Alexander, the Persians broke under the assault.

Western Asia Minor lay open, and Alexander advanced south and east, liberating the cities along the Ionian coast, including the Persian regional capital of Sardis. He captured Miletos by assault, denying the Persian navy its main

Above: A Roman mosaic depicts the Battle of Issos, with Alexander on horseback at the left chasing after a fleeing Darius in his great chariot at the center. The likeness of Alexander is believed to be reasonable.

superbly trained cavalry, including Alexander's elite bodyguard (the Companions), heavy Macedonian cavalry, and mercenary light horsemen. If this was the hammer of his force, the Macedonian heavy infantry *phalanx* was his anvil—a wall of *sarise* (pikes) made these troops superior to enemy spearmen and cavalry. The elite of this infantry division were the 3,000 *hypaspists* and *phalangites* of the royal household. Back in Macedon, Alexander left Antipater, his father's old trusted general, to maintain order in Greece.

Aegean base. Although Memnon held the important coastal city of Halikarnassos, Alexander captured the city after a brief siege, then handed it over to his new ally and "adoptive mother" Ada, wife of the late Carian *satrap* (who probably died during the Battle of Granikos).

With the Ionian and Carian coast secure, Alexander set off east and north to conquer central Asia Minor. The winter of 334–3 was spent subduing the hill peoples of Phrygia and Lycia, notably the Phrygian city of Gordion.

According to legend, a chariot in its temple was bound by the city's founder, King Gordios, using a knot so complex no one could untie it. Whoever loosened the knot would become ruler of Asia. After a failed attempt, Alexander drew his sword and cut through the knot.

Sharp solutions

The Greeks continued through the Cicilian Gates in eastern Asia Minor and entered Syria. While he was recuperating from a fever at Tarsus in autumn 333, Alexander learned that the King Darius III had maneuvered to Issos behind him, blocking the Greek line of communication. Alexander retraced his steps, and despite being heavily outnumbered, threw his army into the attack. Although the Persians held the Macedonian charge, Darius and his army took flight. Alexander even captured the king's wife, baggage, concubines, and immense treasury. Seeing this wealth, Alexander supposedly commented, "So this is what it means to be a king."

Alexander's greatest concern had been the presence of the Persian fleet in the Mediterranean. Nearchos, his naval commander, had largely neutralized the Persians by countering with Athenian ships, but now, with Asia Minor secure and all the coastal cities in Alexander's hands, the Persians were denied a port and their fleet eventually dispersed.

Alexander now led his army south along the fertile and wealthy Phoenician coast of the Mediterranean to the bustling merchant city of Tyre. Unlike the coastal plain cities that—with significant populations of Greeks—had welcomed Alexander, the mostly Phoenician citizens of strongly fortified Tyre shut their gates against him. The main city stood on an island, so to reach the walls Alexander's engineers built a causeway, while under ferocious attack. After the first was destroyed, Alexander ordered a second, larger structure. The port's citizens held out for months, but eventually paid for their temerity. At the conclusion of the long and violent siege in 332, Alexander had Tyre razed.

Another bloody assault at Gaza (332) opened the way to Egypt—a nation already used to the incursions of Greek adventurers. Alexander marched across the Sinai to the banks of the Nile at Memphis. The Egyptians accepted Macedonian rule after Alexander made a private desert pilgrimage to the Oasis of Siwa, site of a sacred oracle associated with Dionysos and the Egyptian gods. Alexander was welcomed by Siwa's priests as the "son of Ammn" (God), the traditional salutation for a pharaoh. Intrigued, Alexander consulted the oracle himself, which affirmed he was the son of Zeus-Amon; Amon and Zeus. Alexander was no longer a conquering general and king. He had become a god.

Above: The ruins of ancient Siwa overlook the modern town. The temple of Amon, where Alexander was convinced by the oracle that he had become a god, has long since toppled. Coins have been found as far away as Thrace showing Alexander wearing horns, which identify him with the ram-horned god Amon, whom the Greeks associated with Zeus.

TO THE EDGE OF THE GANGES

With the shores of the eastern Mediterranean secured, Alexander led his army north for a final battle with the Persian Empire, where he displayed the full extent of his military prowess. Next he would lead the Greeks east, beyond the fringes of the known world.

Below: The ruins of the royal palace of the Achaemenids at Persepolis. After the death of Darius III, the complex was destroyed.

The Egyptians had welcomed Alexander as a liberator and a god. He reformed Egypt's political administration and founded his own city, Alexandria, to provide a commercial and political link between Greece and Egypt. With the Persian fleet neutralized and his army's logistical and fiscal demands catered for, he went north in search of the Persian king in spring 331. He established a governor in Syria and reached Thapsakos, on the banks of the Euphrates, by early summer.

Some 300 miles to the east, Darius was gathering the largest army the ancient world had ever seen. Modern historians believe it numbered almost 250,000 men, including 40,000 cavalry and 200 scythed chariots. Even with reinforcements from Greece and Macedon, Alexander commanded little more than 35,000. Persian victory appeared a foregone conclusion.

The two sides met in October 331 at the battlefield chosen by Darius's advisors—Gaugamela, a village between Arbela and Babylon. The battle opened with a massed chariot charge, but Alexander's men opened their ranks to let them through, then attacked from behind. Alexander commanded the right wing, and after a furious cavalry battle, his Companions scattered their Persian opponents. The Macedonian *phalangites* advanced on the Persian center, which broke and ran. Darius III left the field, as he had at Issos, and his force crumpled. Now nothing stood in Alexander's way.

Darius fled to Media, while Alexander's victorious army captured Babylon, Susa, and Persepolis, capital of the Persian Empire. News arrived that Bessus, commander of the Persian left wing at Gaugamela, had captured Darius III. Alexander set off in pursuit, but found the king abandoned by his captors and dying. It was written that Alexander was furious at this perfidy and he ordered a state funeral to be held in 330—a tribute from one great king to another. After his capture, Bessus was handed to Darius's brother for execution. With the focal point of Persian resistance gone, Alexander laid undisputed claim to the title of Great King—or Lord of Asia, as his contemporaries called him.

He now did the only completely barbarous act of his career: the ancient royal palace of the Achaemenid dynasty at Persepolis was burned and its stones toppled. The sacking may have been committed by his hot-headed companions hoping to please their commander, but whoever ordered the destruction, Alexander was said to have been appalled by the result.

Defeated from within

Alexander established Macedonian governors in every captured province, but now the army found itself south of the Caspian Sea, with Greek and even most Persian civilization left behind. In front, to the east, lay deserts and mountains, homeland to Persia's barbarian allies, the Bactrians. It was necessary for Greeks and Persians to combine and Alexander advocated a cultural merger through interracial marriage. He even executed senior officers who demurred, which caused unrest among many, especially the Macedonian contingent. However, the majority of the army still supported him, even when he led them further east, into Bactria.

For the next two years the army marched south, east, then north, reaching the capital of Bactria in late 329. Several new Alexandrias were founded during a campaign that proved to be far from easy. After capturing Marakanda (now Samarkand), Alexander fought Spitamenes, a skilled Bactrian guerrilla who caused more casualties than the battles against Persia. Peace only came through the murder of Spitamenes by his Scythian allies. Alexander secured his hold over the region by marrying Roxanna, a local princess, in 327.

After hearing of the splendors of India Alexander led his army in the following year over the Hindu Kush (in modern Afghanistan). An Indian army was defeated on the banks of the Hydaspes and the way into the Ganges valley lay open. Alexander was on the verge of conquering the Indian sub-continent. Instead he was defeated, not by the enemy, but by his own men. Weary after eight years of conquest and 3,000 miles from home, they refused to follow him any further.

Forced to retire, he led his army down the Indus to the sea, fighting all the way. In the winter of 325 the much-reduced army returned to Persepolis and Babylon, having crossed some of the most inhospitable desert in the world.

Alexander had to content himself with consolidating his empire. For the next year he was occupied with administration, punitive expeditions, and the integration of Asians with Greeks. Suddenly, in the summer of 323, he was taken ill and died, probably from malaria, although poison has not been ruled out. The Alexandrian dream was over, and it was left to his companions and generals to save what they could from the sprawling empire they had helped to create.

Above: Set in a river valley near Dasht-e Qala in the south of Afghanistan, the remains of a town built by Alexander can be seen because of the numerous holes dug by local people seeking ancient artifacts to sell.

CHAPTER 14

ART AND ARCHITECTURE

More than 2,000 years after the collapse of the Hellenistic world, Greek art and architecture is still regarded as the epitome of elegance, grace, and composition. Its influences can be seen around us, from the Greek frontage of buildings such as the Capitol in Washington D.C. and the British Museum in London, to the realism and sense of movement found in many forms of modern art. The Greek influence is almost incalculable, since it formed the basis

incredible colored statuary and artwork that
once adorned its inner sanctum.

Painting was considered one of the most
advanced forms of Greek art, yet few examples
survive, save the decoration on a handful of
ceramic or metal objects, and the faded remains
of once vibrant frescoes. Even the body of
information we can glean from sculpture is
limited. Many pieces no longer exist in their
original form, and our knowledge of them is
limited to surviving Roman copies. Like most
copies, they are rarely a completely accurate
reflection of the originals, and we have to assume
that these were at least, if not more impressive.

Despite the relatively limited first-hand
examples of Greek art and architecture, the
pieces that survive provide a priceless insight
into a past civilization. Art historians have
categorized, analyzed, and delineated this
collection of art into neat categories, such as
Helladic, Archaic, Classical, and Hellenistic.
There was no division to the Greeks, since their
art and architecture developed continuously
from the renaissance of the eighth century until
the end of the Hellenistic Age and beyond.
This movement spanned over seven centuries,
making it one of the longest-lasting examples
of uninterrupted artistic development of any
civilization, one which exerted an influence long
after the collapse of ancient Greek culture.

The divisions imposed by modern art
historians highlight the salient points in this
lengthy evolution, although trying to define it
too rigidly does the Greeks a disservice. Its
evolution from symbolism and abstraction to
more lifelike forms, and its transition from
geometric forms to *symmettria* and then to
proportion and realism, is a fascinating journey
that established the principles on which later
artistic efforts were based. A study of art and
architecture not only provides a greater
understanding of the Greeks, but also helps us
understand the cultural roots of our own age.

for almost all art that came after it.

Even more incredible is that our knowledge
of Greek art and architecture is based on a
relatively small sample of extant examples. Over
the centuries, cities, temples, and civic buildings
have been destroyed, statues lost, and decorative
pieces broken. Most surviving examples are far
from pristine—the Parthenon is just a shell,
with no roof, little decoration, and none of the

165

PRE-CLASSICAL ART

The emergence from the Dark Age represented a fresh start, a cultural as well as a political renaissance. The ensuing Archaic Age established the pattern for Greek artistic development, and the emergence of the *polis* created new demands for art and architecture.

Above: This ceramic 7th-century statue of a horse and rider has the simple form and color banding typical of the transition between the geometric period and more realistic later styles.

Center: The *kouros* from Melos dates from c.550, a little later than the *kore*, **right**, of a priestess holding a pomegranate.

Examples of Helladic Greek art exist, but demand was limited after the fall of the Mycenaean civilization, since most people were simply trying to survive. Pockets of artistic productivity survived during the Dark Age, and finds from the Ionian settlement of Lefkandi on Euboea suggest a continuity with Mycenaean cultural traditions not taken up elsewhere.

From the mid-11th century, Ionian potters in Athens and some of the Aegean islands produced ceramics decorated with concentric circles or other, more abstract geometric patterns, a style that existed in the later Mycenaean period. By 900, this style had given birth to what art historians have dubbed the Geometric period, which lasted approximately two centuries. The theory that Attica remained an Ionian (and post-Mycenaean) enclave during and after the Dorian invasions is largely supported by links between geometric artistry of the region and earlier Mycenaean art.

At first, vases of the Geometric period were covered in plain linear motifs, but later examples included spirals, diamonds, squares, swastikas, and cross-hatched decoration (*see illustration in map on page 59*). Decoration was limited to the creation of a pattern on the pottery, and had not yet emerged as a form of natural representation.

By around 800 trading links had been re-established between the Greek world and the East, leading to a cultural exchange. This first manifested in the adoption of a variant of the Phoenician language, and then in the use of human and animal forms in ceramic decoration from around 700.

Statues were also produced during this phase, which was dubbed the Orientalizing period, a century of transition from simple linear art to more complex forms. These crude statues were created in clay and even bronze, presumably designed as votive offerings for religious observances.

Displaying the male form

When figures first appeared on pottery around 800, they were portrayed in an abstract form, with rectangles for limbs, triangles for torsos, and circles for heads, almost exclusively standing squarely to the front or side. Realism was not a consideration. This changed as the Oriental influence spread, and during the eighth century the human figure was executed with a greater degree of realism. Animals and mythical creatures also made an appearance, often forming part of a decorative scroll intertwined with vegetation, such as leaves or abstract plant

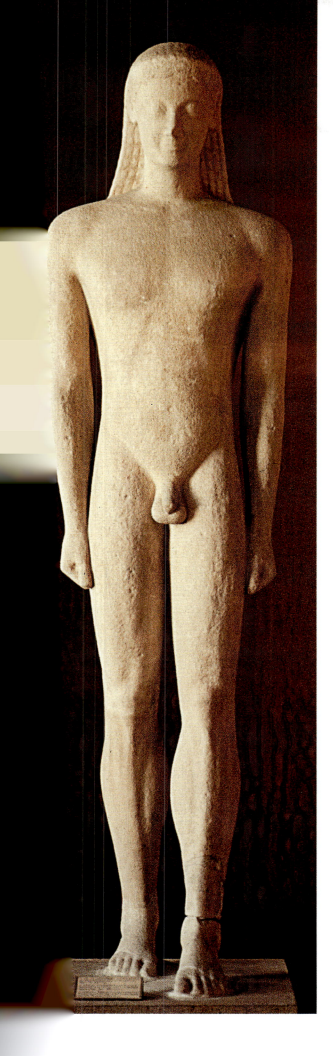

forms. Horizontal banding was still the norm, but representation on them was increasingly realistic.

The seventh century was a watershed in Greek civilization, since it marked the emergence of the city-state and the resumption of extensive trading links. Public art in the form of civic and religious buildings was constructed in this Archaic Age (600–480). Increasingly, the subject matter of decoration was man (and to a lesser extent, woman).

To the Greeks, the nude male body was an object of pride, and this was reflected in Archaic Greek statuary. In contrast, women remained covered, a practice also represented in art. Male statues (*kouros, kouroi* in the plural) represented gods, athletes, and warriors, while the female equivalent (*kore, korai*) was limited to religious subjects.

Both forms of statue were shown in rigid poses, often with a thin "archaic" smile. Still designed as votive statues or grave markers, these works gradually adopted a more relaxed appearance. By the sixth century *kouroi* such as the extant examples from Keos and Anavissos showed their subjects in a form that followed the physique of the body, but still retained an abstraction of anatomical detail. Marble became the most common sculpting medium, and there is evidence that surfaces were often painted.

During the later Archaic Age figures also appeared on vases, depicting scenes from mythology. Eventually, large scenes filling the whole circumference of the vessel were common, displaying a degree of action and realism that suggested a new phase in artistic representation.

THE CLASSICAL STYLE

The Persian Wars marked the beginning of a phase in art when the representation of the human form became far more realistic, and staid symmetry gave way to energy of pose and remarkable depictions of the human body in motion.

During the Classical Age (480–323) the major city-states became political and cultural centers, none more so than Athens. As Greece's economy boomed, so did state and private patronage of the arts. Temples

Above: From nearly the only example of early Classical fresco painting, this diving boy in a tomb from Paestum (c.480) displays a new vitality, realism, and sense of relaxed enjoyment of form for its own sake.

and public areas in the city-states were decorated with increasingly grandiose statues, and architectural embellishments were sculptural works in their own right.

The Greek artists' perception of man had evolved from the geometric and abstract to a more plausible image during the later Archaic period. Although these trends were seen in vase-painting and other decorative arts, the leading form of the age (as it is seen by art historians)

was sculpture. Sculptors realized the symmetry of the human form and ascertained the correct proportions of its anatomy. From the fifth century this developed into comprehensive understanding of how the body functioned when it moved or weight was shifted from one part of it to another.

As an example of this new realism, the *kouros* known as the Kritios Boy (*see picture, right*) depicts a well-realized naked youth, with limbs that are rounded and in proportion. He wears a contemplative expression, while his facial features and build reflect the beauty and easy grace of youth. More important, he is not posed symmetrically. Instead, the youth rests his bodyweight on the left leg, leaving the right leg slightly bent at the knee. The unknown artist had observed, then captured a realistic and wholly natural stance.

True to life

Realism developed even further over the next few decades, prompting the artist Polyklitos to record his views on the ideal proportions of the male figure in or around 440. To demonstrate his principles, Polyklitos produced the figure known as the Doryphoros (spearman or spear-bearer), which was regarded as the ideal representation of man. Like the Kritios Boy, the weight of the figure rests on one side, while the torso is twisted to reflect the natural position of a man carrying a spear.

The Discobolus (discus-thrower) by Myron of Eleutherai, produced around the same time, is a masterpiece of captured energy. The athlete is shown bending, about to throw a discus from his right hand, with his tensed musculature emphasizing the subject's motion. Not all statues were so realistic—gods were often depicted in dramatic attitudes, which abandoned realism for imposing grandeur.

During the high classical period of the late fifth century, stele sculptures (decorative panels containing figures) were increasingly used to

decorate tombs, temples, and public buildings. The stele *metopes* (panels) on the Parthenon are perfect examples of this artform, many depicting scenes from mythology, civic ceremony, and battles between good and evil, humans and mythical beasts, or Greeks and barbarians. The common theme was the triumph of Greek civilization over barbarism.

While the first of these works were bas-relief sculptures, by the end of the fifth century they had developed into more three-dimensional representations, such as deities observing the birth of Athene, mounted on the eastern pediment of the Parthenon. A new breed of sculptors, including Lysippos and Praxiteles, experimented with the "canon of proportions" in an ongoing struggle to produce even greater realism. The trend introduced the first female nude figures and the use of comic relief.

In decorative arts, the emphasis on realism encouraged the depiction of scenes from everyday life, a body of ceramic art that provides a priceless insight into Greek life and how Greek society perceived itself. The violence of combat, the exuberance of the stage, and the artistry of craftsmen were suitable subjects for decorative artists, a field that was no longer reserved for the devotional and mundane. Greek art had come to reflect life in all its aspects.

Left: The early Classical Age statue known as Kritios Boy shows significant development of the *kouros* from that of the earlier Melos youth shown on page 167.

Below: Mastery over three-dimensional realism is almost complete by the fourth century, exemplified by these masterful renditions of horses by Lysippos. The sculptor's fame was such that he was one of only a select few that Alexander the Great would allow to represent him, although none of these famous sculptures survives.

HELLENISTIC AND GRAECO-ROMAN ART

The Hellenistic period witnessed a late, great flowering of Greek art. This was the era of the Seven Wonders of the World and the export of Greek civilization halfway around the known world. In its final centuries, Greek art came of age in dramatic and exuberant use of mediums, subjects, and styles.

Facing: The fighting Gaul—essentially a dramatic development of the *kouroi* as seen on the previous two spreads—represents the vibrant, emotive aspect of Hellenistic sculpture, while the Venus de Milo belongs to the neo-classical stream. Both forms became a persuasive influence on Roman sculptors.

Right: At Petra, capital of the ancient kingdom of Nabataea, in present-day southern Jordan, the Hellenistic baroque style achieved its most extravagant point. Perhaps most impressive of the temples and tombs cut into the sandstone cliff faces is the Khazneh (treasury). Its large scale—the frontage is over 130 feet high—suggests it may have been a tomb for a Nabataean king.

Some art historians disagree with the view that ancient Greek works continued to excel, claiming that the styles and subjects seen in the Hellenistic Age, from the pompous to the insipid, were too diverse, lacking direction. Despite this, it provided the Romans with the foundation of their own styles, and even its most vociferous critics are unable to deny that some of the greatest examples of Greek art were created during the period. These include the Winged Victory of Samothrace, the Venus de Milo, the Dying Gaul, and the decorative friezes from the Temple of Pergamon.

One reason for the reticence is the confusing nature of this artistic period. Sculpture diverged into two distinct forms: a drive toward experimentation with increasingly theatrical images, and the apparent return to classical themes, albeit ones interpreted in a new and more realistic way. Of the artistic works described above, the Venus de Milo, sculpted in the second century, represents the neo-classical stream, while the Pergamon friezes (*see picture, page 176*) and the Dying Gaul are splendid

examples of more experimental sculpture (*see picture, page 180*). Increasingly, the more conservative form was reserved for private patronage, while the dynamic experimental style was used for civic embellishment.

The drive toward experimentation led to a more imaginative use of space and juxtaposition of characters to create a dramatic and energetic sculpture. Friezes ceased to be carved in bas-relief, and instead became increasingly three-dimensional, containing masses of twisting, cavorting figures, such as the representation of the battle between gods and giants at Pergamon. This early second century masterpiece is

particularly indicative of the new realism found in Hellenistic art, due to the range of emotions displayed on the combatants' faces.

Commercial art

The German art historian Gerhard Krahmer suggested that Hellenistic sculpture be divided into three phases: an initial "closed" form, a high form, which was popular from 240 to 150, and a late form. The first was defined by the closure of composition, where the eye of the observer is drawn toward a central point. The second phase saw the establishment of several focal points. Sculpture of this period was known for its grandeur and emphasis on pathos. The final style represented a return to classic forms, albeit with more open composition.

Krahmer's typology has been questioned in recent years due to its reliance on a limited number of dated sculptures. It is now considered possible that while his two earlier forms represent

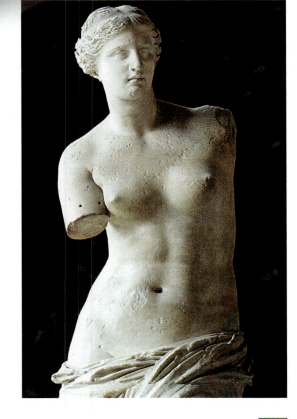

a linear progression, his latter neo-classical form developed concurrently, aimed at a different (non-civic) audience.

This emphasis on theatrical composition, grandeur, and experimentation was also apparent in the decorative arts. Ceramic ware was often decorated in painted relief, and the affluence of the period was reflected in the increasing demand for highly decorated pottery, silverware, painted friezes, and mosaics.

A gradual transition from pure Hellenistic art to the Graeco-Roman form was largely a reflection of a new Roman market for art, one which Hellenistic artists were ready to supply. Although this commercialization was characterized by trivialization, it simply reflected the trend toward large-scale private patronage that had existed since the Classical Age. Above all, this created a demand for Greek art that led directly to its influence in Roman and hence Western civilization. The Hellenistic period therefore represents an artistic apotheosis, rather than a decline.

ARCHITECTURAL CONVENTIONS

The development of the city-state brought a demand for civic and religious architecture. A distinctive style evolved, exemplified by some of the finest and most influential extant buildings from the Greek world.

During the Archaic Age the first examples of a new form of architecture emerged, a visible symbol of the renaissance that had lifted Greece from the Dark Age. Few of these buildings survive, other than as badly dilapidated ruins, but through their study, archaeological discoveries, and diligent archival research, a pattern has emerged.

Most domestic buildings from 600 to 480 were relatively simple structures, while by contrast temples and civic buildings became grandiose affairs, symbols of the pride of the *polis*. Similarity to the phase of cathedral building in medieval Europe has been proposed, where religious buildings towered over secular hovels occupied by the townspeople. The big difference in Greece was that the townspeople themselves were the driving force behind the grand constructions.

Architecture was the most important of the Greek arts, since it provided a statement that everyone could see. Sculpture, painting, and other artistic forms embellished these public buildings, rather than compete with them for artistic primacy. Most of the important commissions during this period were for the decoration of public buildings—not the austere ruins we see today, but vibrant, elaborate edifices designed to reflect glory on the gods and the city-state.

Through trading links, Greeks had come into contact with Egyptians and studied their impressive temples. The Greeks built in a similar style, using columns and beams. There was little scope for architectural ingenuity, such as the introduction of arches, vaults, and other features associated with medieval cathedrals. Instead, architects were required to produce buildings that evoked the spirit of the age, concentrating on subtlety of design, symmetry, and above all, elegant beauty.

Elaborating simplicity

Typically, an Archaic temple consisted of a rectangular walled building (the *cella* or *naos*), surrounded by a pillared colonnade, or peristyle. The columns surrounding the structure supported the pediment and roof, despite the scale of the building (some had double or even triple colonnades). Small variants on this basic structure followed, but they were largely stylistic, not structural.

New conventions developed regarding the dressing of columns, which evolved into the three distinctive systems (orders) of temple architecture: Doric, Ionic, and Corinthian. Each had their own system of proportion, and varied through detailing. The Doric order appeared in

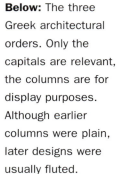

Below: The three Greek architectural orders. Only the capitals are relevant, the columns are for display purposes. Although earlier columns were plain, later designs were usually fluted.
A) Doric—severe and plain; **B)** Ionian with volutes; **C–E)** Corinthian, showing the increasing complexity of decoration, with acanthus leaves as the common form of adornment.

A   B   C   D   E

the seventh century on the Greek mainland, then spread through southern Italy and Sicily. A plain capital, or top, capped a sturdy column, and gave Doric structures a severe but elegant simplicity.

A century later the Ionic order developed on the Ionian coast of Asia Minor and spread through the Aegean islands. Ionic columns were thinner and their capitals were decorated with a scroll-like design (a *volute*). The Corinthian style developed soon after the beginning of the Classical Age, but its use was limited until its widespread adoption by the Romans. Corinthian columns were elaborate, heavily fluted, and typically adorned with decoration on the capital.

These styles continued in tandem, although the Doric style (as used on the Parthenon in Athens) became less common as the Classical Age continued. By the fourth century the Tholos plan (*see picture above*) used the Doric order to produce elaborate, circular structures, and combined them with Corinthian embellishments. These late Greek architectural designs may have resulted in buildings such as

the Mausoleum at Halikarnassos (one of the Seven Wonders of the World), but they represented a stylistic amalgam of the old orders, trading elegance for what would become Hellenistic pomposity. Greek architecture had lost its way. The simple grace and proportion that typified traditional Greek architecture was gone, replaced by ostentation and glitter.

Above: The Tholos (a round temple) which stands outside the sanctuary of Delphi is a fourth-century monument with a circular peristyle surrounded by 20 Doric columns, plan left. Much damaged by earthquakes, it has been substantially restored.

THE PARTHENON

Many art historians argue that the temple of Athene Parthenos, on the Acropolis, is the epitome of ancient Greek cultural achievement. This architectural masterpiece combines order, reason, and elegance in a way that typifies the spirit of the age.

Above: the columns were not straight. To avoid the thinning illusion that tall, straight sides give, the columns bulged outward about an inch one-third up, and were narrower at the top than at the base (the effect has been exaggerated here). Each column was made from 11 drums, with the fluting carved after erection.

From 449, Perikles had embarked on a wide-ranging program of civic improvement, rebuilding Athens in a style that better reflected its imperial status (*see pages 110–113*). The pinnacle of his program was the transformation of the Acropolis. Once the symbol of oligarchic or aristocratic power, in Perikles' hands it became a dramatic symbol of the new democratic city-state.

The highest point in Athens, the easily fortified rock outcrop of the Acropolis had been the site of several temples and palaces in previous centuries. Its near-level summit was covered with the ruins of these structures, but Perikles elected to transform it through the creation of a giant temple to the goddess Athene, the city's principal deity. This building was to be the Athene Parthenos, a building of classical symmetry, the climax of four centuries of Greek temple architecture.

A public board examined models and proposals before the Athenians settled on one design. Its implementation was left in the hands of the master-architect and sculptor Pheidias, supported by two builders, Iktinos and Kallikrates. Their design was a Doric temple, with some Ionic features to emphasize Athens' panhellenic aspirations.

There are eight Doric columns at each end and 15 along the sides. These stood on the *stylobate* (platform) and formed the support for the pediment. The high *cella* is rectangular, with a *procella* (porch) of six internal pillars and an additional set of two-story Doric columns running around its inside. An *ospisthodomos* (rear inner sanctum) was located behind the *cella*, supported by four Ionic columns. This small space was a treasury for votive offerings presented to the goddess (including the seized funds of the Delian League).

A stunning spectacle

In the center of the *cella* a wide interior aisle ran the length of the building, leading to the 35-foot statue of Athene that dominated the temple's interior. Designed by Pheidias, the appearance of the awe-inspiring ivory and gold statue is only known to us through written records and the survival of miniature replicas. The whole structure was decorated with Ionic friezes around the outer walls, Doric bas-relief *metopes* around the pediment, and high-relief sculptures adorned each end of the marble-tiled roof. When it was built, these decorations would have been painted in bright colors.

The effect on the temple visitor must have been incredible. With no windows, the only source of natural light came from the large double doors, which would have shone sunlight

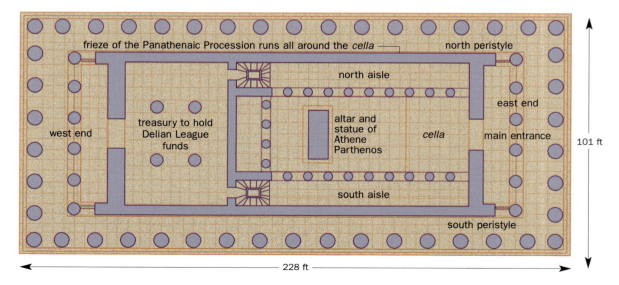

Left: Viewed through the gateway of the Propylaia, the entrance to the Acropolis, the west end of the Parthenon glows in Athens' evening sun. This is the first view of the great temple celebrants would have after climbing the ramp from the Panathenaic Way.

down the length of the *cella* toward the statue. The effect of incense, the reflection of light from the golden statue, and the atmosphere of humble reverence can only be imagined by visitors to today's sun-bleached ruins of the Parthenon.

As well as building the Parthenon, Pheidias and his successors filled the top of the Acropolis with smaller religious structures and statues, creating a landscape of complexity, color, and grandeur. Of these, the most important was the Erechthion, a temple sanctuary dedicated

to Athene Polis, Erechtheus, and Poseidon.

While impressive, these secondary structures did not reduce the dramatic architectural statement made by the Parthenon. Despite extensive damage over the intervening centuries, the masterpiece of Perikles and Pheidias is a stunning visual lesson in order, beauty, balance, and harmony, the four cornerstones of Greek art and architecture.

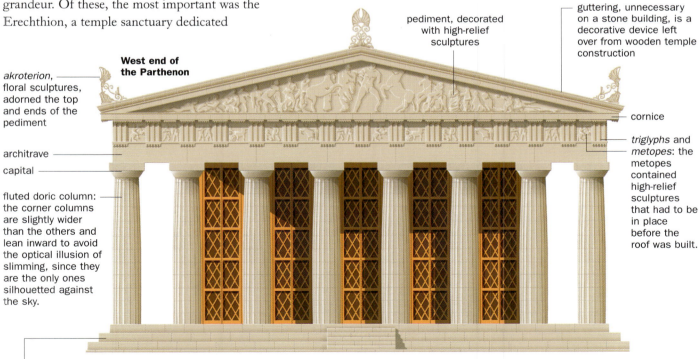

pediment, decorated with high-relief sculptures

guttering, unnecessary on a stone building, is a decorative device left over from wooden temple construction

West end of the Parthenon

akroterion, floral sculptures, adorned the top and ends of the pediment

architrave

capital

fluted doric column: the corner columns are slightly wider than the others and lean inward to avoid the optical illusion of slimming, since they are the only ones silhouetted against the sky.

cornice

triglyphs and *metopes*: the metopes contained high-relief sculptures that had to be in place before the roof was built.

stylobate: consists of the traditional three steps all around. The *stylobate* is not flat; like the columns, the architects used tricks to avoid the illusion that long, straight platforms appear to sink in the middle, so each curves upward as it nears its center. The long sides are

4$^{1}/_{3}$ inches higher and the east and west ends 2$^{1}/_{3}$ inches higher. This west end of the temple, seen also in the picture above, is not the entrance, which was at the east end. The room behind the doors seen here guarded the treasury of the Delian League.

The *triglyphs, metopes,* pediment and *cella* friezes were all brightly painted; traces of color can still be seen.

CHAPTER 15
THE WORLD OF HELLAS

In its simplest form, Hellenism represents the fusion of Greek culture with that of others. Despite the political turbulence of the late Classical Age, the Greeks united under a political banner for the first time in their long history. Although many view this period as one of decline, it can be argued that Greek political and cultural influence was spreading across the known world. The words "Hellenic" and "Hellenistic" derive from Hellas (Greece) or Hellene (Greeks), which—if taken literally—means "The Greek Age."

Although Macedonian sovereignty had led to the collapse of the city-state as a political unit, the benefits accrued from the creation of a Hellenistic empire outweighed the loss of political freedom. In Greece, Macedon, Asia Minor, Syria, Palestine, Egypt, Persia, Iran, Bactria, and beyond, Alexander the Great created a ruling culture that integrated with the existing civilizations it encountered. In so doing, it changed the nature of Greek civilization and moved its focal point from central Greece to the Middle East.

Alexander's death caused upheaval as his powerful Macedonian generals fought each other for the so-called successor states. The eastern Greek world became dominated by two great powers, the Seleukid empire in Asia, and the Egyptian kingdom of Ptolemy and his successors. As these two large empires flourished, so too did smaller states. These included Greek states, such as the maritime league centered on Rhodes, and the independent kingdom of Pergamon in western Asia Minor, but other non-Greek states also emerged and survived, such as Pontus and Cappadocia.

It was almost as if the political unit created by Alexander

the Great was too large for any single ruler to govern, and eventually only the culture and commercial bonds he helped create remained in place to bind the Hellenistic world together. As the Greeks themselves were well aware, shared cultural and linguistic bonds were no real substitute for political unity. In this, the successor states—like the city-states before them—failed. Their squabbles reduced their ability to resist outside pressure from the Romans to the west, and the Parthians to the east. One by one, the successor states fell and Greek political identity was extinguished. Only Greek culture survived. The Romans assumed it and, even through the guise of the Roman Republic, Greek forms of democratic government. This Hellenistic export influenced civilizations and religions that followed, those of the Romans, Jews, Christians, and Muslims and educated a new world on the splendors and civilization of a vanquished people.

The fate of the successor states from 303–63

- Antigonid territory
- Seleukid territory
- Ptolemaic territory
- Roman empire
- Parthian empire
- independent kingdom

Below: Detail from north frieze of the Great Altar of Pergamon (c.156), one of the most splendid examples of late Hellenistic art.

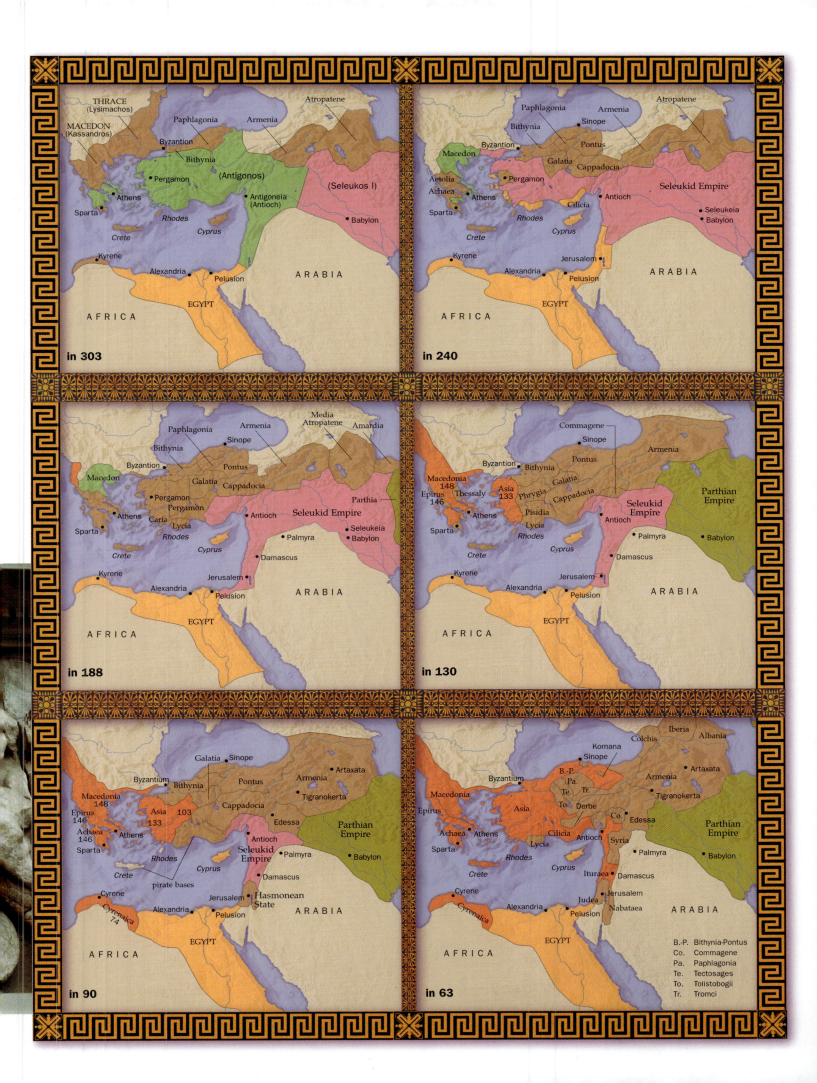

THE SUCCESSOR STATES

The death of Alexander the Great prompted a power struggle between his companions and generals. From Greece and Egypt to Bactria, the kingdoms collectively known as the successor states arose from the ashes of the Argead dream.

Below: This head of Ptolemy III Eurgetes (r.246–222) still shows a strong affinity for Hellenistic style. Eurgetes oversaw three wars with the Seleukids in Syria and expanded Egyptian influence over the kingdom of Axum to the south in Ethiopia.

Alexander had created the Argead empire in name only. Political stability was ensured by the presence of his army, but the vast scale of his conquest made it impossible to maintain control of the whole. Stretching from Greece to India, Alexander's empire was linked by language and culture, but little else. His dream of a *cosmopolis*—a *polis* encompassing the known world—became a battleground fought over by his successors.

When Alexander died suddenly in 323, his Asiatic wife Roxanna was pregnant with his son, Alexander IV, but in practical terms the child was of little consequence; nor was Alexander the Great's retarded step-brother Arrhidaios. Alexander's opportunistic, hard-bitten generals agreed that the empire should be ruled jointly by the infant prince and Arrhidaios. In fact real power lay between Antipater—Philip's last surviving general, left behind by Alexander to govern Hellas—and Perdikkas, who was the most able of Alexander's generals. Perdikkas was in Asia, and therefore held Alexander's son.

Other generals became local lords of the governorships granted to them by Alexander: Seleukos in Babylonia, Antigonos "the one-eyed" in Asia Minor, called Phrygia, Ptolemy in Egypt, and Lysimachos in Thrace. The Macedonian generals swore loyalty to the joint successors of Alexander and waited for the opportunity to make their bids for greater power. The wait was not long. Perdikkas was the first to be crushed, assassinated by his own soldiers while trying to invade Ptolemy's Egypt in 321. Antipater died in 319, to be succeeded in the regency by his son, Kassandros. Antipater and Antigonos, however, formed a new power bloc and seized Syria on behalf of the regency, returning Alexander's son to Macedon. Kassandros now established his power base through the virtual imprisonment of Alexander's mother Olympias, his step-brother Arrhidaios, and the prince. In 315, Kassandros formed an alliance with Lysimachos and Ptolemy, linking Hellas with Thrace and Egypt against Antigonos in Asia Minor.

Antigonos and his son Demetrios offered the Greek city-states their freedom (an unfulfilled promise) in return for aid, and they became active in Greece between 307–3. The struggle for power spread throughout the *cosmopolis*, with neither side gaining any significant advantage. In 311, war-weariness forced the generals to negotiate, and they divided the empire between them. Lysimachos retained Thrace and Ptolemy Egypt (with the gain of Cyprus). Antigonos controlled Phrygia and Persia, while Seleukos ruled in the east. Kassandros retained Hellas in the name of the young prince. The peace was short-lived.

Kassandros murdered Arrhidaios, Olympias, and the 13-year-old prince Alexander in 308.

Their deaths prompted a new round of campaigns. In 301 Antigonos was killed in a battle against an alliance of his opponents, who divided his kingdom, despite the continued resistance of Demetrios. Kassandros died in 297, leaving Seleukos and Lysimachos vying for control of Hellas. Lysimachos was killed during the Battle of Corupedium in 281.

The longest survivors

The aged Seleukos appeared to have emerged as the ruler of Alexander's empire, but within a year he was assassinated by his own army, leaving Macedon, Thrace, Asia Minor, and Greece in a political vacuum. Antiochus I (r.281–61) succeeded Seleukos and struggled to hold his father's kingdom together. Its fluctuating borders were only defined during the reign of the energetic Antiochus III (r.223–187). The Seleukid dynasty, with its old but efficient Persian administration, was governed by Macedonian regional *satraps*. To cope with the kingdom's huge scale two administrative centers were established, one in the east at Seleukia on the Euphrates, and the other to the west, at Sardis, although the real seat of power was Antioch, at the top of the eastern Mediterranean.

Despite a tolerance of local customs, the Macedonians were unable to prevent a large revolt in Judea, and after two decades the province was granted its independence. Similarly, the eastern provinces of Parthia and Sogdia revolted, followed by Bactria in 240, which evolved into its own Greek successor state.

The wars of succession also led to an erosion of Seleukid control over Asia Minor, allowing Greek cities such as Pergamon to break away from the kingdom, followed by the non-Greek states of Galatia, Cappadochia, and Pontus. Beset by the Parthians on their eastern borders and rebels in Asia Minor and Palestine, the Seleukids were barely able to retain control. Under Antiochus III and Antiochus IV (r.175–64) the kingdom underwent two brief periods of revival. But by the time the Romans arrived in the Middle East at the start of the first century, the Seleukid state had contracted to northern Syria and eastern Asia Minor. Defeated by the Romans, it collapsed in 64 and was integrated into the Roman province of Syria.

In Egypt, Ptolemy and his descendants ruled

for two centuries. Egypt's natural resources made it the richest successor state. Unlike his rivals, Ptolemy enjoyed a secure geographical base and control of the seas, and within a century of its foundation, Alexandria was the busiest port in the known world. At first, the administration was exclusively Greek, but by the reign of Ptolemy II (r.283–46), integration began and Egyptians were permitted to hold high office. The process continued during the reign of subsequent Ptolemaic monarchs until Egypt had become an integrated Egypto-Hellenistic state.

Ptolemaic Egypt retained its independence for three decades after the collapse of the Seleukids, and a century after the defeat of Macedon at the hands of the Romans. In the end, Egyptian involvement in the Roman civil war that followed the assassination of Julius Caesar led to the country's conquest, the last of the kingdoms of Hellas to survive. Egypt fell in 30, completing Rome's conquest of the Greek world.

Above: In comparison, by the time of Ptolemy VIII (r.170–116), the integration into ancient pharaonic tradition is clear. His rule proved intolerable to many Egyptians, however, and there was continual unrest. After he had himself proclaimed pharaoh at the ancient Egyptian capital of Memphis, he secured all the Alexandrian trouble-makers and had them expelled.

HELLAS

The Hellenistic period is often associated with decline and the loss of independence among the Greek states. The once-proud cities had become little more than pawns in a political game, and Hellas a battleground fought over by a succession of Macedonian rulers.

When news of Alexander's death reached Greece, there was insurrection among the city-states against the yoke of Macedonian rule, fueled by that Athenian democrat and orator of freedom, Demosthenes. Early success on the Greek side resulted in Antipater being besieged in Lamia (323). But he broke out and defeated the Athenian-led Greeks at Krannon in central Thessaly in 322. In the aftermath of the Lamian War, the city-states were stripped of many of their political powers and the last semblance of democracy.

Polyperchon, Antipater's immediate successor after his death in 319, made the mistake of promising greater independence for the Greeks. This prompted further civil unrest in Athens with the execution of pro-Macedonian supporters.

In 311, Antipater's son Kassandros became regent and, under his authoritarian rule, the Greeks were given no opportunity to rebel.

His death in 297 sparked another upheaval, as Demetrios, Seleukos, and Lysimachos descended on Greece. Demetrios was the first of the contenders to go, captured by Lysimachos and Seleukos and dying in prison (283). Lysimachos died in 281. The death of Seleukos in 280 at the hands of Macedonian troops loyal to Lysimachos was probably a plot, engineered by a son of Ptolemy, Ptolemy Ceraunus.

This political vacuum resulted in two things. It permitted the establishment of a new Macedonian ruling dynasty, founded by Antigonis Domates, son of Demetrios, with the support of Antiochus I, son of Seleukos. Secondly, it encouraged Celtic tribes north of Thrace under the command of Brennus to invade Macedon and Greece in 279. They were

defeated by Demetrios and Antiochus, and a degree of stability was restored. However, further incursions of Gaulish Celts crossed the Hellespont and invaded Pergamon, whose king turned back the invasion. Then, using diplomacy rather than force, he arranged for the Gauls to settle in the center of Asia Minor, an area later referred to as Galatia.

Inevitable in-fighting

Fifty years of fratricidal warfare had damaged both Greek and Macedonian economies, and the remnants of the old ruling Argead dynasty of Philip and Alexander had been wiped out by Kassandros, son of Antipater. Despite this political upheaval, the city-states functioned with little change, save loss of political determination. Some cities, including Athens, Syracuse, and Ephesos, prospered during the early Hellenistic period, while the establishment of Macedonian overlordship ensured that the old ways of settling disputes by warfare had been replaced with a system of arbitration and discussion, under the guidance of the Macedonian king.

In Macedon itself, Pella emerged as a leading cultural center, and the royal court established by Antigonis provided patronage to some of the finest Hellenistic artists. Antigonis II Gonatas (r.277–239) brought stability back to Hellas, although his grandson, Antigonis III Doson, tried to encroach on the city-states' limited

powers, prompting them to band together into defensive alliances—the mutually hostile Achaean and Aetolian Leagues.

The former confederation linked ten cities in the northern Peloponnese, which ejected Macedonian-imposed tyrants from the region. Under the guidance of Aratos of Sikyon, Corinth joined the alliance, as did Athens and Aigina. The Macedonians, weakened by their fratricidal wars, were unable to prevent the creation of the Achaean League. North of Corinth the rural Aetolian tribes formed their own league, which extended its control to encompass Boeotia, Phokis, and Lokris.

To the south, Sparta had maintained its independence throughout the period of Macedonian rule through its isolationist policy. However, after the accession of Kleomenes in 240, the Spartans resumed their political interference in the affairs of the Peloponnese, bringing them into conflict with the Achaean League. Sparta was a shadow of its former self, and the city fell to the Achaeans in 221, ending a fascinating chapter in Greek political history.

True to form, the Achaean and Aetolian Leagues became increasingly hostile to each other and the Greeks resumed their centuries-old tradition of fighting among themselves. By that time, the Macedonians had bigger problems to contend with, since the Romans had begun to take an interest in Greek affairs.

Facing: The king of Pergamon celebrated his defeat of the Celts by commissioning numerous statues to fill the city, like this one of a dying gaul. It heralded a new style in Greek art, one that combined a high level of finish with horrific realism.

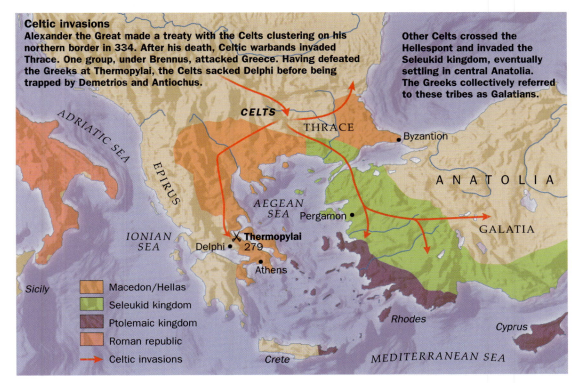

Celtic invasions
Alexander the Great made a treaty with the Celts clustering on his northern border in 334. After his death, Celtic warbands invaded Thrace. One group, under Brennus, attacked Greece. Having defeated the Greeks at Thermopylai, the Celts sacked Delphi before being trapped by Demetrios and Antiochus.

Other Celts crossed the Hellespont and invaded the Seleukid kingdom, eventually settling in central Anatolia. The Greeks collectively referred to these tribes as Galatians.

ADRIATIC SEA

CELTS

THRACE

Byzantion

EPIRUS

ANATOLIA

AEGEAN SEA Pergamon

GALATIA

IONIAN SEA   Delphi • 279 Thermopylai

Athens

Sicily

Macedon/Hellas

Seleukid kingdom

Ptolemaic kingdom

Roman republic

Celtic invasions

Rhodes

Cyprus

Crete   MEDITERRANEAN SEA

HELLAS AND ROME

The decline of the Macedonian kingdoms was mirrored by the rise of Rome. Confrontation seemed inevitable, especially after Greek interference in Italy. When it came, the Roman invasion altered the political landscape and replaced the Hellenistic kingdoms of Greece with the mastery of Rome.

Below: Centralized discipline and sheer organized energy of the Roman legions ensured that the dysfunctional Greek governments would rapidly fall under Roman sway.

Rome's involvement in Greek affairs came about largely as a result of typical Greek squabbling. The earliest conflicts were the Italian campaigns of Pyrrhos of Epirus from 280–275. He had already failed in an attempt to conquer Macedon to his east in 287, after which he was thrown out, only to regain his throne in 281 on the death of Lysimachos. The Antigonids were, therefore, happy to see Phyrros turn his attentions across the Adriatic. Despite Roman inability to defeat him, his powerful army was largely destroyed, giving rise to the derogatory term "pyrrhic victory." His setback also left the Greek colonies in southern Italy and Sicily vulnerable and no longer assured of Greek support against the Romans and Carthaginians.

Rome was happy to adopt the southern Italian Greeks' long-running war with Carthage, which resulted in the two Punic Wars. It was during the second (218–207), that Hannibal invaded Italy. To protect his supply lines from North Africa, Hannibal made an alliance with Philip V of Macedon, thus earning Rome's enmity. Rome showed it by supporting Philip's Greek enemies during the First Macedonian War (214–205).

This conflict came about through friction between the older Aetolian League and the newly reformed Achaean League, and both leagues' antipathy to Macedon. There had been frequent conflicts between the neighboring Aetolian League and Macedon, but Philip quickly came to regard the Achaeans as a bigger threat and launched a military campaign to restore Macedonian order in central Greece. The Achaeans appealed to Rome for protection, which was granted in revenge for Macedon's alliance with Hannibal. Although Roman aid was limited, the pattern of Roman involvement had been established.

Roman interference increased during the Second Macedonian War (200–196), when Roman contingents openly trained the Achaeans, and Roman warships patrolled the Aegean. At the same time, Rome succeeded in conquering Illyria, pushing the boundaries of the Roman sphere as far as Macedon's borders. A confrontation was inevitable, and both sides prepared for a war to decide the future of Hellas.

Reduced to a province

When the Roman Republic declared war in 171, it sent its best troops and commanders to the region. The campaign that ensued pitted the older Macedonian style of warfare against the Roman method. At the Battle of Pydna (168),

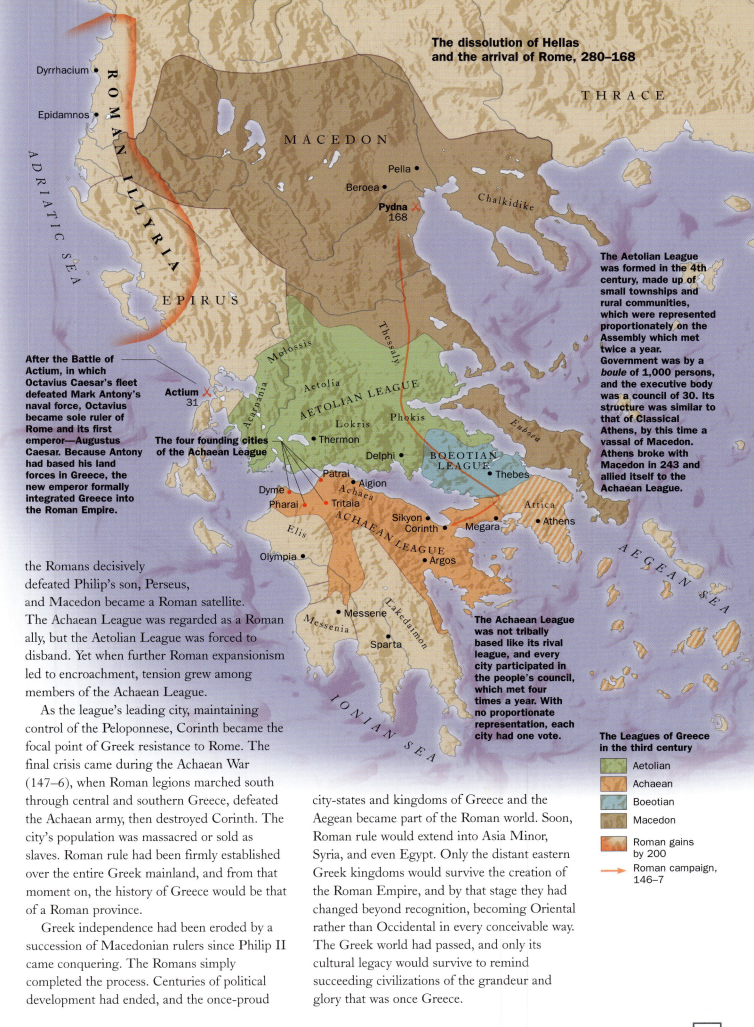

The dissolution of Hellas
and the arrival of Rome, 280–168

THRACE

ROMAN ILLYRIA

Dyrrhacium

Epidamnos

MACEDON

Pella

Beroea

Chalkidike

Pydna
168

ADRIATIC SEA

EPIRUS

The Aetolian League
was formed in the 4th
century, made up of
small townships and
rural communities,
which were represented
proportionately on the
Assembly which met
twice a year.
Government was by a
boule of 1,000 persons,
and the executive body
was a council of 30. Its
structure was similar to
that of Classical
Athens, by this time a
vassal of Macedon.
Athens broke with
Macedon in 243 and
allied itself to the
Achaean League.

After the Battle of
Actium, in which
Octavius Caesar's fleet
defeated Mark Antony's
naval force, Octavius
became sole ruler of
Rome and its first
emperor—Augustus
Caesar. Because Antony
had based his land
forces in Greece, the
new emperor formally
integrated Greece into
the Roman Empire.

Molossis

Acarnania

Aetolia

Thessaly

AETOLIAN LEAGUE

Actium
31

The four founding cities
of the Achaean League

Thermon

Lokris

Phokis

Euboea

Delphi

BOEOTIAN
LEAGUE

Thebes

Patrai

Aigion

Achaea

Dyme

Tritaia

Pharai

ACHAEAN LEAGUE

Elis

Sikyon

Corinth

Megara

Attica

Athens

Olympia

Argos

AEGEAN SEA

The Achaean League
was not tribally
based like its rival
league, and every
city participated in
the people's council,
which met four
times a year. With
no proportionate
representation, each
city had one vote.

Messene

Lakedaimon

Messenia

Sparta

IONIAN SEA

The Leagues of Greece
in the third century

Aetolian

Achaean

Boeotian

Macedon

Roman gains
by 200

Roman campaign,
146–7

the Romans decisively
defeated Philip's son, Perseus,
and Macedon became a Roman satellite.
The Achaean League was regarded as a Roman
ally, but the Aetolian League was forced to
disband. Yet when further Roman expansionism
led to encroachment, tension grew among
members of the Achaean League.

As the league's leading city, maintaining
control of the Peloponnese, Corinth became the
focal point of Greek resistance to Rome. The
final crisis came during the Achaean War
(147–6), when Roman legions marched south
through central and southern Greece, defeated
the Achaean army, then destroyed Corinth. The
city's population was massacred or sold as
slaves. Roman rule had been firmly established
over the entire Greek mainland, and from that
moment on, the history of Greece would be that
of a Roman province.

Greek independence had been eroded by a
succession of Macedonian rulers since Philip II
came conquering. The Romans simply
completed the process. Centuries of political
development had ended, and the once-proud

city-states and kingdoms of Greece and the
Aegean became part of the Roman world. Soon,
Roman rule would extend into Asia Minor,
Syria, and even Egypt. Only the distant eastern
Greek kingdoms would survive the creation of
the Roman Empire, and by that stage they had
changed beyond recognition, becoming Oriental
rather than Occidental in every conceivable way.
The Greek world had passed, and only its
cultural legacy would survive to remind
succeeding civilizations of the grandeur and
glory that was once Greece.

THE SEVEN WONDERS OF THE WORLD

Few elements of the Hellenistic world have captured the imagination of later generations more than the Seven Wonders of the World. These edifices exemplified the final flowering of Greek achievement in the Mediterranean.

The Seven Wonders of the World were incredible examples of human enterprise and engineering skills. Although the first mention of seven wonders may be found in Herodotos's fifth-century *History*, this refers to an old tradition of the Seven Sages, a semi-legendary group of the "wisest men of Greece," of whom Periander (*see page 71*) was said to be one. But at some time in the second century a list of the Sages appeared linked to a list of seven "wonders," and within a decade the first list of Seven Wonders of the World was published. Kalimachos of Kyrene (305–240), chief librarian of the Alexandria Mouseion, produced a work entitled *A Collection of the Wonders of the World*, but it was lost in the great library's destruction. Several lists were compiled, but the final Hellenistic colophon of wonders was produced well after the collapse of the ancient Greek world.

Traditionally, the Seven Wonders of the World comprise the Hanging Gardens of Babylon, the pyramids at Giza, the statue of Zeus at Olympia, the Mausoleum of Halikarnassos in Asia Minor (*see picture, page 155*), the Temple of Artemis in Ephesos, the Pharos of Alexandria, and the Colossos of Rhodes. While two were not Greek, their inclusion implied that the list was not simply a piece of Hellenistic propaganda, but that in the span of thousands of years of cultural development, the most dynamic civilization was Greece. Other Greek candidates were put forward as replacements for the Babylonian and Egyptian wonders, such as the Mouseion (Library) of Alexandria, but rejected.

Lost to time and disaster

The Temple of Zeus in Olympia was graced by Zeus's statue from about 450. Pheidias, designer of the Parthenon and sculptor of its Athene statue, was commissioned to create the huge, 40-foot statue. The historian Strabo recorded, "He has shown Zeus seated, but with the head almost touching the ceiling, so that we have the impression that if Zeus moved to stand up, he would unroof the temple." After the temple fell into disuse during the later years of the Roman Empire, the statue was transported to Constantinople (formerly

"I have lying over me a gigantic monument such as no other dead person has, adorned in the finest way with statues of horses and men carved most realistically from the best quality marble."
—**King Mausollos** in Lucian's *Dialogues of the Dead*

Byzantion), where it was destroyed by fire in AD 462. We have no clear impression of what it looked like.

By contrast the Mausoleum at Halikarnassos (now Bodrum) was designed to house the body of the local tyrant, Mausollos of Caria. Completed in 350, three years after the king's death, the building was a large rectangle, its outer walls filled with statues. The burial chamber sat on a pillared podium, topped by a pyramidal roof. On its summit, a marble statue of a chariot pulled by four horses dominated the structure. Archaeological evidence has given us a good idea of the shape and size of the mausoleum, although its statuary has long since been plundered.

The Pharos of Alexandria in Egypt and the Colossos of Rhodes were both constructed to dominate their respective harbors, both apparently begun around 300 and completed 12–20 years later. The Colossos stood in place for 56 years (282–26) before an earthquake toppled it into the harbor. Contrary to popular legend, it did not straddle the entrance to the harbor, but was placed behind it or to one side. Constructed from bronze sheets, the remains of the fallen statue were probably looted, since no traces remain.

The Pharos (lighthouse) was a different matter, since it remained in service through much of the Ptolemaic period, a practical addition to the port, until it too was destroyed in a natural calamity, 80 years after its completion. The Temple of Artemis at Ephesos was the largest religious shrine in the ancient world, boasting 117 columns, each over 50 feet high.

The two foreign inclusions were the Great Pyramids at Giza and the Hanging Gardens of Babylon. Greeks admired the pyramids as an example of architectural ambition. These mammoth structures served both as tombs and monuments to the Egyptian rulers buried inside them. The Hanging Gardens were built across massive tiers, making the Babylonian royal palace a haven of tranquillity and fertility. Although—pyramids aside, and ironically the oldest—these wonders were lost centuries ago, they still remind us of the vitality of the civilizations that created them.

Above: Little enough remains to remind us today of the Temple of Artemis at Ephesos, but at the time, one Wonder compiler had this to say of it: "But when I saw the sacred house of Artemis that towers to the clouds, the [other Wonders] were placed in the shade, for the Sun himself has never looked upon its equal outside Olympos."

Left: Of all the wonders, only one still exists to awe the modern visitor, the Great Pyramids of Giza. As an old Arab proverb says: "Man fears Time, yet Time fears the Pyramids."

THE LEGACY OF ANCIENT GREECE

Although the Greek world ended with the conquest of the Hellenistic kingdoms and the occupation or destruction of the city-states, Greek civilization survived. Ironically, it was the Romans who encouraged this, adopting many aspects of the culture they had all but destroyed.

The Romans became masters of Hellas during the mid-second century, extending their rule to encompass the entire Mediterranean Sea over the course of the next century. While Rome became the political and military center of a vast empire, the Greek city-states and new cities of the successor states became provincial backwaters, midway between Rome and the profitable lands of the Middle East. Roman political directives arrived from the west, but increasingly, elements of Greek culture were encouraged to spread from the east, permeating Roman society. Even Roman politics came to incorporate aspects first applied to the *polis*. This cultural flow was so pronounced that the Roman writer Horace declared: "Greece, though conquered, conquered its wild conqueror."

Greek literature had a significant influence on Latin literature, and Roman writers, artists, poets, historians, and architects found inspiration in the visual and scholastic archive left by the ancient Greeks. The result was a stronger, more cultured form of Roman civilization, a culture that served as a guide for later Latin scholars, who preserved the Greek achievement through the European Middle Ages into the Renaissance of the late 15th century AD.

Right: Sunset over the Temple of Poseidon in Sounion, Attica.

A golden inheritance

Although Roman culture now dominated, Greek painters and sculptors still produced masterpieces of Graeco-Roman art for ever-eager patrons in Rome or the provinces. Following the division of the Roman Empire into east and west, the importance of Greek culture increased, since it served to underpin the supremacy of Byzantion (Byzantium in Latinized Greek) during the collapse of the Western Roman Empire to the barbarians.

When Europe finally shook itself free of the Middle Ages, many of the great works of Greek literature, philosophy, science, and drama preserved by Byzantine, Muslim, and Christian clerics formed the body of work that scholars of the Renaissance turned to for inspiration. They also studied extant statues and ruins of Greek temples. The cultural spirit of ancient Greeks lives on in our modern world largely through the efforts of Renaissance scholars.

Government, political structures, legal

systems, the ordering of a society, and the apparatus of the state have their roots in the cultural achievements of the Greeks. The modern world is beholden to ancient Greece for the basic tenets of civic life and the role played by the individual in society. The Athenian experiment in democracy stemmed from oligarchic government and ended in the establishment of government by kingship, but its principles remained, to be refined centuries later.

Intellectuals of the Scottish and French enlightenment of the early and mid-18th century AD drew on the political systems of the Greeks for a model of good government, philosophy, and the ordered composition of rational argument. These men included David Hume and Adam Smith, the thinkers behind the key assumptions that underlie modern politics, economics, morals, and culture.

Without the Greeks, there may have been no French Revolution, no American Revolution, and no widespread acceptance of democracy as the ideal form of government. The tenets that bind our modern world were first imagined in ancient Greece, and the political and social rights we enjoy today were established as components of citizenship. In this respect, we owe the ancient Greeks our freedom, our society, and our civilization—an astonishing legacy from an incredible people.

GLOSSARY

acropolis: *Akropolis*, the strongest point of a community, usually sited on top of a rise or defensible hill, from the Greek *akro* meaning top of, or point, and *polis*. The word citadel is also used.

agora: originally an open market space in a town, but which later developed into a political meeting place. The modern word agoraphobia (fear of open spaces) is derived from the Greek.

akroterion: Ornament on the pinnacle or edge of the roof of a building.

amphora: Two-handled pot for carrying liquids such as wine or oil strapped to a donkey or mule and usually with a pointed end for standing either in soft sand or in a special support.

Anabasis: The account written by Xenophon of the heroic retreat of the Ten Thousand, a mercenary army of Greeks, after winning the Battle of Cunaxa (401) in support of Cyrus the Younger against his brother. The *Anabasis* was a favorite read of Alexander the Great.

archon: Chief magistrate of Athens (the title was later adopted by some other city-states, usually allied with Athens).

aristoi: Literally "the best people," from which we derive the word aristocrat.

basileios: Literally "kingly," a warlord of Dark Age Greece.

basilica: The hall of a king or warlord, although in later periods, the word came to signify a large rectangular hall such as Romans used for conducting business. Later still it was adapted to

describe the nave of a long Christian church.

bireme: Twin-decked war galley rowed by oars (*see* trireme).

black-figure: Pottery decorated with black figures on a reddish-colored background (*see* red-figure).

boule: Governing council; in Athens, this consisted of 500 men, 50 from each of the ten Attican *phyle* (tribes).

bouleuterion: Meeting house of the *boule*.

cavea: The auditorium of semi-circular stone benches to seat the audience in an ancient open-air theater.

cella: Inner room of a temple housing the god's statue.

centaur: Mythical creature with the upper torso of a man and the lower body and legs of a horse. Traditionally, centaurs were wise beings.

chiton: Short tunic for boys and men.

Chthonians: Earth gods; the gods of Bronze Age Greece before the Dorian invasions of the Dark Age (*see* Olympian gods).

clepsydra: A large public clock operated by the flow of water.

Cyclopes: Mythical giants possessed of only a single eye in the center of the forehead. Members of the Titans, they were the sons of the incestuous marriage of Uranos with his mother Gaia. Greeks of the Archaic Age thought the massive walls of ancient cities like Mycenae were built by Cyclopes, since the stone blocks were too heavy for mortal men to lift.

demarchos: Head of a deme; mayor.

deme: A community, village, or small town in Attica.

demos: literally, the people; but those with citizenship, and therefore in Athens also a vote.

diolkos: A paved slipway for portage, most famously at Corinth, where it was used to transport ships across the isthmus (*see* olkos).

Dioskouri: The twin-brothers Kastor the athlete and Polydeukes the boxer (the Roman Castor and Pollux), semi-divine sons of Zeus worshipped especially in Sparta.

ekklesia: The assembly of the *demos* of Athens.

enemotia: Smallest unit of the Spartan army, consisting of 36 men. Four *enemotia* made up a *lochos*.

enomotarch: Commander of a Spartan *enemotia*.

ephebe: Male youth, young adult.

ephor: Spartan magistrate; five were elected annually.

frieze: A length of relief sculpture decorating the upper walls of a temple.

gerousia: The council of Spartan elders.

gymnasion: Complex of facilities including a *palaistra*, baths, and teaching arcades.

gymnos: Naked.

helot: *Heilot*; slave or the lowest class

of serf in Sparta, probably derived from the town of Helos, whose inhabitants were enslaved by the invading Spartans in the Dark Age.

herm: A tall block of stone with the head of a god on top and an erect *phallus* on one side. Herms usually marked significant points in a city, such as crossroads. It was the destruction of the herms of Athens that Alkibiades was accused of, the scandal that drove him into traitorous exile in Sparta.

hetairos, hetaira: Male companion, female companion.

himation: A cloak.

hoplite: The heavily armed foot soldier of ancient Greece; initially drawn from the growing middle class of the Archaic Age. The *hoplite* had to pay for his own arms and armor, which proved his usefulness to the *polis*.

kalyx: Mixing bowl shaped like a deep cup.

kleroteria: A form of random selection used in Athens to pick trial juries.

koilon: Auditorium of an ancient open-air theater; also *theatron*.

kore: Female equivalent of a *kouros*, although almost always fully clothed.

kouros: Statue of a male nude youth, of a formal archaic shape.

krater: A bowl for mixing wine with water; at a *symposium*, the wine was usually heavily diluted… at least at first.

kyrios: Head of a household (father, husband, or other male relative).

Linear A: The earlier of the two Bronze Age Greek scripts, as yet undecoded although similar to Linear B.

Linear B: Script of Mycenaean Greece in the Bronze Age. This has been decoded, and is an early form of the Greek language. Linear B is syllabic, not alphabetical.

lochargos: Commander of a Spartan *lochos*.

lochos: Spartan military division of 144 infantry men (*see* enemotia).

logeion: A raised area at the rear of the stage in a Hellenistic Age theater for actors to stand above the proceedings.

megaron: The throne room of a Bronze Age or Archaic king.

metic: A foreigner or other Greek outsider in Athens; as legal aliens, *metics* were welcomed and undertook many functions, principally mercantile, but were not allowed citizenship and therefore could not vote.

metope: A slab of relief sculpture used in series between plainer slabs of vertical lines (*see* triglyph) around a temple, below its pediment or roof.

metropolis: literally "mother city," the Greek mainland city which originally supplied the resources to found an overseas colony and to which that colony owed allegiance.

mora: A battalion-sized unit of the Spartan army, consisting of four *lochos*. Six *mora* comprised the entire Spartan army, which was commanded by one of the hereditary Spartan kings. The first *mora* formed the king's bodyguard, called the *hippeis* (*see* polemarch).

odeion: A theater with a roof covering.

oikos: Family unit.

oligarch: A government in which the ruling power is in the hands of a few people, usually members of the *aristoi*.

olkos: Wheeled vehicle for the transport of large, heavy objects (*see* diolkos).

Olympian gods: Sky gods; the gods of the Doric people who invaded Greece during the Dark Age and merged with the indigenous Chthonian gods. Home of the Olympian gods is Mount Olympos, which stands in the north, on the edge of Macedon.

orchestra: Area between the stage and the audience in an ancient open-air theater for dancing and the chorus.

ostracism: System developed by Kleisthenes in Athens to take the heat out of political debate by allowing the people to vote a single person per year into exile.

paidogogos: Household servant or slave whose function was to accompany a young boy to his schooling and ensure he paid attention to his teacher.

paidotribes: The man at a *gymnasion* or *palaistra* who taught youths gymnastics and physical exercises.

palaistra: An open-air sports ground surrounded by a colonnade for the physical education of young male Greeks and the continued exercising of adult men.

parados: Actors' entrance in an ancient open-air theater.

peltast: Mercenary skirmishing light infantry based on the principal troops of Thrace.

pentaconter: Heaviest version of a bireme, rowed by 100 oarsmen in two banks of 25 on each side.

peplos: Long flowing robe for women.

periaktoi: A pair of revolving pillars used to present new items of scenery and remove old ones in an ancient theater.

perioeci: Serfs in Sparta; the indigenous people of Lakedaimon reduced to serfdom by the invading Dorian Spartans in the Dark Age.

peristyle: Row of pillars surrounding a temple, forming a colonnade along its sides.

petruges: Leather strips that formed a kilt to protect the lower torso of a *hoplite*.

phalanx: Military formation in close, deep ranks with shields overlapping and spears (*sarise*) extended.

phallus: Representation of the male reproductive organ, worshipped as a symbol of generative power, especially at Dionysiac festivals; also found on the side of a *herm*.

phoros: Religious donation. The largest single donation made in ancient Greece was by the Delian League when its treasury was removed from Delos to Athens to help pay for the building of the Parthenon and other temples on the Acropolis.

phratry: A local social group for men (*phrater* is the ancient Greek for brother), from which the word fraternity (brotherhood) is derived.

phyle: A tribal grouping in Attica.

polemarch: Spartan commander of a *mora*.

polis: City-state; in ancient Greece a city-state may have been little more than a rural community or as much as a city like Athens, which considered the whole of Attica as part of its *polis*.

proedria: The first row of seats in an ancient theater reserved for magistrates

and the priests celebrating the specific god's festival that the play honored.

propylaion, *pl.* **propylaia:** Literally, "before the gate," in ancient Greek architecture, a vestibule or grand entrance, usually to a sacred site or a palace.

proskenion: Literally, "before the *skene*," the forward edge of the stage where the acting was most concentrated.

prytanaion: Meeting room for a *prytani*.

prytani: A political block of 50 men representing an Attican *phyle* (tribe) in the *boule* of Athens.

red-figure: Pottery decorated with reddish-colored figures on a black background (*see* black-figure).

sarise: The 9-foot long pike used by *hoplites* in a *phalanx*.

satrap: Persian regional governor.

satyr: Half-human, half-animal (commonly a goat) being with divine powers, associated with a powerful sex drive; associates of Dionysos.

skene: The stage of an ancient open-air theater, from which we derive the word scene (*see* proskenion).

stoa: In the Archaic Age a portico with a wall one side and pillars on the other. By the Classical Age, a *stoa* might be large, with rooms behind the walled side used for commercial purposes. Some were two-storied.

strategeion: Headquarters of the *strategos*, the building in which military strategy was planned.

strategos: Chief military general of a *polis*, charged with the strategy for the entire war effort.

strigil: A curved instrument of bone or metal used for cleansing by scraping the skin while taking a bath at the *gymnasion*.

stylobate: The platform, usually of three steps, on which a temple or public building was built.

symposium: A congenial gathering of men for dinner or for drinking, usually accompanied by poetry readings, music, and *hetaira*.

tenemos: Enclosed holy ground belonging to the god of a sanctuary.

thalamites: Oarsmen on the lowest of the three tiers of a trireme. The rowers placed their oars through circular rowing ports (*see* zygites and thranites).

theatron: Auditorium of an ancient open-air theater; also *koilon*.

theologeion: A flat roof that covered the entire stage of Hellenistic theaters.

thetes: Lowest social class.

thranites: Top tier of oarsmen on a trireme (*see* zygites and thalamites).

triglyph: A slab of stone carved with vertical lines representing the open grain of roof joists used in ancient wooden temples. *Triglyphs* alternated with *metopes*.

trireme: Triple-decked war galley rowed by 170 oars (*see* bireme).

tyrannos: A sole ruler appointed by popular acclaim; the first tyrants were elected to check the power of the oligarchs.

zygites: Middle tier of oarsmen on a trireme (*see* thalamites and thranites).

INDEX